THE EARLY YEARS OF
Alec Waugh

Alec Waugh has also written among other books

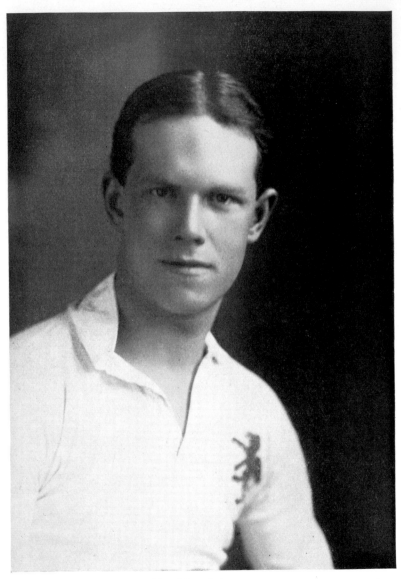

Alec Waugh in 1919

THE EARLY YEARS OF
Alec Waugh

CASSELL · LONDON

CASSELL & COMPANY LTD
35 Red Lion Square · London WC1
and at
MELBOURNE · SYDNEY · TORONTO · CAPE TOWN
JOHANNESBURG · AUCKLAND

———

© *Alec Waugh 1962*
First published 1962

Printed in Great Britain by
Cox & Wyman, Ltd., London, Fakenham and Reading
F. 662

To the memory of my father
ARTHUR WAUGH
with a love that the
years have deepened

Contents

CONTENTS

PART 5 — *'His Honour Rooted in Dishonour Stood'*

Illustrations

Acknowledgements

The author is indebted to Mrs. George Bambridge and Messrs. Macmillan & Co. Ltd., for their permission to quote lines from 'A School Song' by Rudyard Kipling; and to Messrs. Secker and Warburg Ltd., for permission to quote lines from 'The Dying Patriot' by James E. Flecker.

Foreword

Ralph Straus was the first professional author to become my friend. I met him in the spring of 1917 when I was a cadet at Sandhurst with my first novel in the press. Straus was then nearly forty. He gave me this advice: 'Never choose a novelist for your hero.' He developed his theme, avuncularly. In the 1930s, when as chief fiction reviewer on the *Sunday Times*, he was a man of influence, he was known affectionately as 'Uncle Ralph'.

Certain axioms, he asserted, are laid down in the manual of the craft of fiction. One of them concerns the hero. He must be positive. He must stand for something, strive for something. It is not until he has been shown in terms of his ambition that the reader is prepared to be interested in his domestic trials. If not actually heroic he must show resolution in a crisis. A board-room can be as ruthless as a battlefield, the floating of a company as hazardous as the launching of a frigate, a group of directors in lounge-suits watching the ticking of the tape-machine can be shown as the twentieth-century equivalent of the last Spartans at Thermopylae.

The novelist's life, so the homily continued, provided no such drama. Flaubert's picture of himself seated at a window in a dressing-gown watching the Seine flow past, waiting for the inevitable word, is a caricature of the average author, but it bears a recognizable resemblance. No career could be less dramatic than the novelist's. His problems are worked out in privacy; they involve no personal relationships; there are no directors to be conciliated, exposed or shouldered out of office; no refractory cabinets to be cajoled or overridden. His interviews with publishers and editors are of a social nature. His battles are fought out in his own mind.

The novelist is a favoured person. He can work where he likes, when he likes, under conditions of his own choosing; no one bosses him around; he carries his office with him; the circumference of his world is drawn by the radius of his interests. But the very nature and extent of that good fortune make him an unsuitable hero for a novel. Many thousands of words have been written about 'the agonies of composition', but is there, Straus concluded, a single novel about a novelist in which the hero does not seem a playboy?

I reminded him of that advice a few months before his death in 1950. He smiled. 'It's time I was giving you a second warning. Don't write an autobiography.'

I saw his point. An autobiography is a novel of which the narrator is the hero, and when that narrator is a novelist, the book suffers from the same intrinsic weakness as a novel that has a novelist as its hero.

At the same time there is no escape from subjects that assert and impose themselves, and most men when they turn into the straight and, in terms of their career, see the white tape ahead, feel a need to relive the past on paper. But I am not, as I write these opening sentences, forgetful of my old friend's advice, and I hope to avoid some of the dangers against which he warned me, by making this book the story not of a novelist's ups and downs during nearly half a century in the literary arena but of how I became a certain kind of novelist. It will be in fact only a partial autobiography.

I hope that this will prove to be in its favour. A novelist does not necessarily take his hero from the cradle to the grave. He can halt his story at any appropriate watershed, and I have usually found that the early chapters of an autobiography are more interesting than the later ones. Partly because it is easier to be outspoken about things that are distant than about things that are close (I do not, for instance, see how the father of children can tell the truth about the marriage that produced them), but chiefly because an ambitious man, once he has made up his mind about himself and taken stock of his capacities and limitations, advances towards his goal in blinkers. He may in the second half of his life be the witness and sometimes the creator of big events, but he is less likely to be as interesting in himself as he was in the days of uncertainty before he had acquired a sense of self-direction. During his period of potentiality, a man is the prey of chance and circumstance. His talent may develop along any one of half a dozen lines; the eventual line may be chosen for him by a casual meeting, a missed train, a telephone call that he does not bother to answer.

That is what happened to me. I wrote my first novel when I was seventeen. Published eighteen months later, it was, in England, an immediate success. It has never been out of print. I have no illusions about the quality of my work. I know myself to be a very minor writer. But it was apparent from that novel that I had been endowed at birth with the one essential gift that is possessed equally by the worst novelists and the best, without which nothing can be achieved in fiction; the knack of narrative, the capacity to make a reader turn the page to see what is on the other side. You have to be born with that. You cannot acquire it in a college course of creative writing. Yet even so, as the early chapters of this book will show, it was only through an unusual sequence of circumstances that that book, *The Loom of Youth*, was written. I might never have realized that I had that knack.

And even after the book had been written, after I was established as a professional story-teller, it was chance—a cablegram that reached Tahiti on a Wednesday evening instead of on a Thursday morning—that made me the kind of novelist that I am, a restless, perchless traveller, avid of change and of the sun, searching for his plots and characters between Capricorn and Cancer.

That is the story that I have to tell here. It will end in the summer of 1930, when I was at the close of my thirty-second year.

PART 1

*Childhood
and
Boyhood*

My Father—Arthur Waugh

In 1931 my father, Arthur Waugh, published his autobiography *One Man's Road*. Much of his story is my story too. He was then in his sixty-sixth year and had recently retired from the managing directorship of Chapman & Hall—Dickens's original publishers—a post that he had held for twenty-seven years. The book shows very clearly why he was one of the most loved and honoured figures in the literary London of his day. As a critic, he held it to be his duty to interpret an author to the public. A man of wide reading, sound judgment, generous powers of appreciation, with a fine sense of language—he had won the Newdigate Prize Poem at Oxford—he reviewed as far as possible only the books that he respected. Where he could not praise he preferred to remain silent.

As a publisher he considered it a privilege to introduce to the public, work that he admired. Publishing was for him a calling not a trade.

'Of all forms of merchandise,' he wrote in his centenary history of Chapman & Hall, 'books are surely the most human and the most companionable; and the authors of books, take them for all in all, the veritable salt of the earth. As dusk falls in the publisher's room and the titles on the rows of volumes fade into the grey, the man of business stirs his fire once more, as Edward Chapman stirred it upon the retreating form of Trollope, and the firelight is filled with memories, visions and dreams, and almost all of them are happy. Here, in the company of so many shining witessnes to the triumph of man's indomitable imagination, here at least is a citadel of pleasantness and peace and a refuge from the noise without.'

The final photograph in *One Man's Road* carries the caption 'Myself today'. It was taken when he was sixty-three. He was stout then, rubicund, white-haired, clean-shaven, genial and beaming. Ralph Straus dedicated his *Dickens—The Man* 'to Arthur Waugh, an old friend and colleague who without resembling Mr. Pickwick in personal appearance so closely as some of his admirers choose to think, shares all that great man's most lovable characteristics', and there was indeed a Pickwickian air about the warmth with which he welcomed visitors to the office in Henrietta Street on whose mantelpiece stood a bust of Dickens.

Many writers have testified to the help, advice, encouragement he gave them in his twin capacities of publisher and critic. Authorship is a soil in which envy, jealousy and malice take root easily, but no writer suffered injustice or even unkindness from my father's pen.

§

The early chapters of *One Man's Road* describe its author's boyhood as the son of a West Country doctor—he was the eldest of a family of five, three sisters who never married and a sailor brother who died young—and I have read few books that give as charming and intimate a picture of family life in Victorian England.

He was born in 1866 in Midsomer Norton, a small village in north Somerset on the edge of the mining district. In days when there were no cinemas or radio, children relied on their own ingenuity for entertainment. In the summer the young Waughs arranged picnics and cricket matches, in the winter they organized theatricals, writing their own plays, painting their own scenery, and each Christmas they produced a family magazine, with original poems, stories and illustrations. When the last of my aunts died a number of these programmes and albums came into my possession. As I turned the pages and thought of all the happy nursery hours that had been devoted to their composition, I could not help feeling that my father's family had led a fuller life than do the children of this generation; certainly they have left for their descendants a fuller record of their childhood.

4

For me that childhood is very real. The links between Midsomer Norton and my various homes were close. As a schoolboy I went there every summer holiday. My grandfather's house was not a large one, but it had rambling outhouses, stables, greenhouses, a chicken run, a garden upon different levels. For me, living in a London street, it was the country. For me it had also the fascination of being the house where my father's boyhood had been spent. It gave me a sense of continuity. The groom who had taught my father to ride was now my grandfather's coachman. My aunts were frequent visitors to us in London. I heard so much talk of their nursery days that their nurse, Budge, whom I never saw, is now in retrospect an actual character. My aunts spent their whole lives in the house where they were born. The years were few when I did not visit them.

Most of us today are, emotionally, displaced persons. Death duties, easier divorce, the lack of servants, the conveniences of the service flat, wartime evacuations, and the long separations involved by service overseas have made it rare for anyone to inherit the house in which he was born, and few can be bothered to wonder what their great-grandparents were like when they do not see their portraits on the walls, when they are not surrounded by visible reminders of their existence—the cushions they embroidered, the water-colours that they painted, the rose-garden they planted, the lawn they laid down for tennis. It is easier for a modern couple entering upon matrimony to see themselves as a unit in the social structure, than as the mingling of two family trees, and I am very glad that by the long series of visits to Norton and the many hours I have spent talking with my aunts I should have come to see myself as a link in a long chain of relatives.

They were none of them persons of high eminence, but they were not without distinction; the majority of them were clergymen. Originally farmers in South Lanarkshire, our branch of the family came south in the middle of the eighteenth century, and Dr. Alexander Waugh's biography, published in 1830, gives an intimidating picture of the dour, rigorous Bible-reading life that his grandparents had led.

Dr. Alexander Waugh, my father's great-grandfather, one of the chief Nonconformist preachers of his day, helped to found the London Missionary Society and Mill Hill School; and my own great-grandfather was for many years rector of Corsley. Nowadays men of fifty diet themselves, do morning exercises, behave and try to look as though they are twenty-five. A hundred years ago they anticipated the authority of age, grew long beards and talked of the 'Summoning Finger' as though they were in hourly expectation of it. When he was still in his forties, the rector of Corsley used to approach the peroration of his Sunday-evening sermon with the phrase, 'When this quivering voice is still and this shaking hand no longer leads you.'

§

My grandfather died when I was eight, my grandmother eighteen months later. I have clear memories of them both; my grandmother grey and gentle, with lace about her throat, teaching me to paint; my grandfather bluff and hearty, a keen sportsman, showing me how he shot a bird and cast a fly. He would return late from his rounds, after we had finished lunch, and I would sit with him during his meal of cold meat, cheese and salad. He had a glass-bottomed tankard, which I would watch him drain, waiting with fascination till I could see his features, distorted through the beaded cider. An excellent doctor and a surgeon—he had been a gold medallist—his love of sport had made him prefer a country practice to the possibilities of advancement in a city. He was a popular figure in the neighbourhood. Generous and open-handed, he kept a good table, and was never happier than when he had his friends gathered round him. Every Christmas he sent us a hamper; the unpacking of his ham, crystallized fruit, pies, galantine of chicken and individual presents was for me as big an event as our Christmas tree.

In the reconstruction of one's childhood it is hard to dissociate what one actually remembers from the things that are remembered for one, and my picture of my grandfather is largely composed of things I have been told about him. When I was five years old, he came to London to pay us a four days' visit. I was an indulged child. When he left he said to my father, 'I think, my dear boy, that you have a very happy home but a week of your son and your dog would render me insane.'

My father was born on August 24 and my grandmother during the previous weeks was terrified lest her confinement should interfere with her husband's first day of partridge shooting. I see the man very clearly in those two incidents.

The later incident is symptomatic of my grandmother. She was infinitely apprehensive and her imagination pictured dangers everywhere. If I was walking across the nursery with a sharpened pencil, she would say, 'Oh do be careful, dear, you may fall down and the pencil will go through your eye into your brain.' My mother, a most unnervous person, after a couple of days in her mother-in-law's company, herself began to fuss.

Sometimes my grandmother's qualms would be surprisingly justified by subsequent events.

During my father's engagement, his future parents-in-law invited him to join them on a tour of a local coal-mine. His mother begged him not to go. She assured him it was dangerous. He reminded her that the miners went down into the pits every day of their lives and overbore her objections. An early start was to be made and she agreed to call him at six o'clock. When he woke, it was eight o'clock. She told him that at the last moment she could not run the risk of letting him go down the mine. He was indignant, but two hours later he was to learn that his future father-in-law had been seriously injured. A heavy rock of coal had fallen from the roof and stunned him. Had my father been on the expedition the rock would have hit him, since the victim had been immediately behind my mother. As a small boy I would look with fascination at the blue scar on my grandfather's temple. It seemed the fingerprint of fate.

My father inherited his mother's nervousness. Psychiatry did not exist in the 1870s, and my grandfather had little patience with what he considered imaginary maladies. When he heard that his children were proving troublesome and would not go to sleep—they had become terrified of the dark through listening to servants' whisperings about mysterious murders— he decided to cure them of this fear of shadows. Every evening before his dinner he went into their nursery to teach them wisdom; he put them upon the rocking-horse and made it rear

7

upon its back rockers; he sat them on the narrow mantelpiece; he sent them down into the smoking-room to kiss his gun-case in the dark. He took my father with him on his rounds, making him hold the reins while he was visiting his patients. The mare would stretch herself and amble across the road in search of grass. My father had been strictly ordered not to let her feed. When the reins were pulled, she began to back and the dash would grind against the garden wall. Each wait was a torture to my father. As he sat there holding the reins, he would imagine every calamity that might befall him.

Such treatment only accentuated his natural nervousness and all his life he worried over possible calamities. If my mother returned half an hour late from a visit in the country, he would endure agonies of apprehension, picturing a pony trap over-turned in a country lane or a car skidding on to the pavement. She always, when she went away, telegraphed or telephoned her safe arrival. He could not eat, he could not sleep unless he knew exactly where she was. His imagination worked upon his anxiety.

Yet physically he was extremely brave. A dislike of losing consciousness made him refuse anaesthetics. As a young man, having had his adenoids removed in London, he caught a train to Somerset half an hour later and endured a three-hour journey standing in a crowded corridor on a hot August day. In the later 'fifties, before novocaine was invented, he had his teeth removed, four at a time, without any deadening of the nerves. He went to each appointment as unconcernedly as he went to have his hair cut. In 1940 he was unmoved by the London bombing; though the house was shaking, he slept in his own bed every night, refusing to be disturbed. And during the Munich crisis, when Londoners were waiting in queues to collect their gas-masks, he declined to join them. He would wait, he said, till the rush was over. Even when the carrying of a mask was obligatory, he left his at home.

This hereditary nervousness had its effect upon his health. Two photographs in his autobiography, headed 'Myself at six and ten years old' carry the caption, 'I was a pale, peaky sort of child.' Asthma is now recognized as a nervous complaint, and he was a slave to asthma all his life. It was a cruel handicap.

8

At school he was allowed neither to play football nor to swim: and at more than one turning-point of his life fear of asthma was to act as a deciding factor. He refused both the editorship of the *Morning Post* and the post of dramatic critic to the *Daily Telegraph* because he did not think his chest could withstand the constant attack of the damp night air. The visitors to Henrietta Street, who were welcomed by the benign reincarnation of Mr. Pickwick as genially as though they were week-end guests, had little idea of the strain to which their host was all the time exposed. Beneath his hearty, healthy, red-faced exterior, he was the 'pale, peaky child' of those first photographs. Every night at home he burnt Himrod's Asthma Cure.

§

In my father's day the preparatory school as we know it did not exist, and one of the best chapters in *One Man's Road* describes the dame school at Bath to which he was sent at the age of ten. Among the papers that came to me when the family home in Norton was broken up, was the letter he wrote his mother on the first Sunday there.

'Dear Muz'—it finished—'I will try to be a dutiful son and put cold cream on my lips at night.'

The use of the word 'dutiful' is pathetically typical of the Victorian era.

From this dame school he went to Sherborne, which in the course of a generation had emerged from the status it had held for three hundred years as a small grammar school for some thirty pupils, the majority of them day boys, into the full stature of a public school with three hundred names upon its rolls. It presented a disconcerting change of atmosphere from that of a private day-school, and for his first few terms my father dreaded the end of the holidays, but his last years there were happy.

He edited the school magazine, and inside the copy of a book he presented to the school library he was to write—

Do you remember your son in the study that looked on the
    cloister,
Twenty-five years is it back covering reams in the shade,
Dreaming his pen was a sword that would open the world
    like an oyster. . . .

9

It had been hoped for him, naturally, that he would inherit the family practice, but it was soon apparent that he had no aptitude for medicine and that he was essentially a bookman whose livelihood must be somehow earned from books. His father was not a literary man; he would sob over *The Song of a Shirt* and the death of Little Nell, but he never read the kind of book that his son hoped to write. If a son of his had to earn a living by his pen, he would have preferred that pen to indite 'good slashing articles on the Home Rule Bill', but he was very un-Victorian in his refusal to oppose what he recognized as his son's instinct, and when my father won the Newdigate at Oxford he agreed that he should be allowed to try his luck as a free-lance in London and promised him a yearly allowance of £150 until he was on his feet.

To many, at the time, it must have seemed an improvident adventure. My father had no financial prospects, no eventual inheritance awaited him. He knew nothing of London, and nothing of the literary market. His plans were vague. He hoped to contribute critical aticles to the Press, but his most definite ambition was a half-time job as reader for a publisher. He was in no sense a bohemian, he never ran up bills, he liked to know when his next cheque was due. The bachelor's life did not attract him. Half engaged to my mother, he was anxious for a home of his own. Walking back at night to his Bloomsbury lodgings after a day spent in the British Museum reading-room, he would look enviously at the lighted windows with their framed interiors of family life. He had the constant handicap of asthma, but he had youth, great powers of concentration, a deep love of literature, a need for self-expression, a natural sense of language, courage and the resolution to succeed. He had in addition one asset that was of greater value to him than a private income—a blood relationship with Edmund Gosse.

Gosse, then in his middle forties, was one of the most prominent figures in the London literary scene. As official translator to the Board of Trade, he had a good deal of spare time during office hours for his own work—one of Max Beerbohm's early cartoons shows Joseph Chamberlain surprising Gosse and Austin Dobson at work upon a ballade—but on most nights of the week, after an early supper, he would spend a further three hours at his desk.

On Sunday afternoon, however, he kept open house, and his drawing-room in Delamere Terrace was crowded with the poets and critics of the day. As six o'clock approached, he began to move among his guests asking this and that one to stay on to supper. My father soon became one of those who stayed behind, and very often when the party dispersed he would linger for a final talk. Gosse would then throw himself back into an arm-chair with a gesture of mock exhaustion. 'My dear Arthur, when you have made yourself a walking epigram for seven hours, it is a great relief to relax with one of your own flesh and blood.'

At the start my father owed everything to Gosse. It was at Gosse's Sunday afternoons that he was introduced to his con-temporaries and seniors; through Gosse that he met Wolcott Balestier, Kipling's brother-in-law, from whom he received his first office job; on Gosse's recommendation that he was com-missioned by Heinemann to write a life of Tennyson; he was lunching with Gosse at the National Club when Henry Harland and John Lane burst in on them with their plans to launch the *Yellow Book*, and it was his contribution to the first number of the *Yellow Book*, 'Reticence in Literature', that established him as a critic of consequence. In 1889 he came up to London an unknown Oxford graduate. By October 1893 he was in a position to undertake the responsibilities of marriage.

My mother's name was Catherine Raban. Her father, who died when she was a few months old, had been an Indian Civil Servant. Her mother was a Cockburn and my great-great-grandfather was the Lord Cockburn who wrote *Memorials of My Time* and whose face appears, or appeared, on the Com-mercial Bank of Scotland currency.

My father's marriage was a very happy one. They were always a team, he and my mother. He was lost without her.

II

Childhood

I was the first son, born in London, in West Hampstead at No.
11 Hillfield Road in July 1898. London today with its bombed-
out areas, its barrack-like blocks of flats and offices, its widened
thoroughfares—the legacies respectively of the 'forties, the
'thirties and the 'twenties—typifies architecturally in every
street and square the changes since the First World War. Yet
curiously enough the London that I knew in childhood is
scarcely altered. For a stretch of some half a mile, Hillfield
Road runs due east and west south of the Finchley Road. It is
lined on either side by a stretch of gabled red-brick late Victorian houses with bow windows, behind which run narrow
strips of garden. It is one of the least known streets in London.
A reservoir has made it a cul-de-sac. Fifty yards to the south,
Mill Lane, curving west to Kilburn, serves as a traffic artery.
No vehicle would enter Hillfield Road unless it was visiting
a house there. I doubt if one London clubman in a hundred
would have heard of it. The other day when I went back to see
it, I was astonished at its emptiness and quiet.

It was not, socially, a good address; it catered for middle-class
families with incomes of £500 to £700 a year. But propinquity
of residence does not in a big city constitute an introduction
and my father was the last person to place store on writing-
paper. He had no money except what he earned. His
yearly income then was about £600. He wanted a house with a
garden; he wanted to live in Hampstead, both because he was
asthmatic and its air was good and because two of his best
friends, Ernest Rhys, the editor of the Everyman Library and
Sydney Pawling, Heinemann's partner, lived there. At his

club—the National—he could lunch daily with Edmund Gosse and Austin Dobson; he was within easy distance of the Heath for walks. No. 11 Hillfield Road satisfied his requirements.

He did not choose unwisely. The garden was very narrow, the bare width of the house, less than twenty feet, but it was long enough to be divided into a lawn and kitchen garden. It had an apple tree and a willow that was tall enough for climbing. Looking from the upper windows with trees to left and right, you had a sense of being in the country; there were owls at night. The bow-window of my nursery faced due south. I had a clear view across South London to the Surrey Hills. I could see the dome of the Crystal Palace and the Great Wheel of the Earl's Court Exhibition. It was a bright warm room, large enough for indoor cricket. I would throw a tennis ball against the wall and play it on the rebound. The chairs were arranged as fieldsmen and if the ball landed on a chair first bounce I marked myself down as 'caught'. I was also adjudged out when a ball, first bounce or not, landed on my brother's cot. I played this game for hours.

A modern sociologist taking stock of Hillfield Road, of its unpretentious houses and the small string of shops in Mill Lane that supplied their needs, might well assume that a boy born there at the end of the century must have contrasted with his own position both the affluence that lay a few miles to the west and south in Mayfair and Belgravia and the poverty and destitution that were to be found only a few yards away in Kilburn. West Hampstead was a half-way house. Surely, he would argue, the boy who could look on both sides of the picture would be spurred towards achievement by envy of the rich and dread of being poor. But that is a modern point of view. For people like myself there was then no sense of insecurity.

That is, I believe, the main difference between the England to which I was born and the England that my sons are now inheriting. It would be easy to draw up a list of the changes that science has made in domestic living conditions. In Hillfield Road we had no telephone. There was no electric light. There was gas on the stairs and in the hall. The larger rooms were lit with lamps. Candles were in use on mantelpieces. Buses were horse-drawn. When we came back from our summer holidays, a bare-footed man would follow our cab all the way out from Paddington to earn a shilling by carrying down our luggage. But the essential difference between 'then' and 'now' does not lie in a catalogue of details, but in the general atmosphere of confidence and security with which the past was reverenced, the present accepted and the future awaited.

Above the mantelpiece in every school in England hung a map a sixth of whose surface was painted red. That was the British Empire on which the sun never set. Its history was presented as a success story. Mistakes had been made and there had been reverses; bad Kings, corrupt ministers, base generals had stained the record; Henry VI had been flung out of France; Calais was engraved on Mary's heart; Boston Harbour had been black with discarded tea. But the novel in which no misfortunes befell the hero would be unreadable. The great thing was the ending. And what else was the nineteenth century but the triumphant climax to the long series of struggles that had been English history from 1066 to the Battle of Waterloo? For ninety years Britain had fought no major war. She had enlarged her frontiers, loaded her exchequer, increased her influence. 'Wider still and wider shall thy bounds be set, God who made thee mighty, make thee mightier yet.' That at any rate is how the story showed itself to the average English schoolboy of the middle and upper middle classes in the first years of the twentieth century.

Certainly I myself never had any sense of insecurity, nor did I feel any sense of envy. I never wished my parents had more money. I never felt that I was prevented from doing or possessing anything I wanted from lack of money. The fires were well banked, my clothes were not shabby, there was plenty to eat. My father set off for his office in a silk hat. We were waited on at table by a maid in a cap and apron. A nurse in uniform took me for my walks. There was no cinema in those days, but I was taken to the theatre reasonably often. I watched cricket, either at Lord's or on the Hampstead Cricket Ground. In the summer I went to stay with my grandparents in Somerset.

My father was a wonderful companion. When I look back on my first years—the years which the Jesuit father described as being all that mattered—I find that every memory I have is connected with him. My nurses are shadowy figures, my mother did not become distinct until a much later day. I remember my father reading to me, my father taking me for walks, my father playing cricket with me.

I had a small book in which every evening on his return from work he would draw a picture. They depicted battle, violence and sudden death. Sometimes they represented scenes from history, from Shakespeare and Arthurian romance; more often they dealt with potential calamities befalling our own household, in which were involved not only my parents and my relatives but our black poodle. They were concerned also with a race of humans called 'Hurrah Boys', who wore cockaded hats and carried spears. I had seen in an illustrated Christmas magazine a picture of revellers thus attired under which had run the caption 'Hurrah Boys, Hurrah!' and I had formed the impression that Hurrah Boys were a special kind of human.

To begin with my father drew me a picture every night. Then the pictures became more elaborate. Towards the end of the book they required, each of them, three or four nights to finish. Finally they became so elaborate that our interest in them waned. At that point, my father, on the recommendation of W. L. Courtney, who had been his tutor at New College and was now literary editor of the *Daily Telegraph*, was appointed managing director of Chapman & Hall as a co-director of Courtney's. He now did not leave his office until half-past five, and there was no time for pictures. But though there was no time for drawing, there was still time for reading. It was always poetry that he read me: Shakespeare, the *Idylls of the King*, the *Lays of Ancient Rome*. I loved the sound of verse long before I could understand it. 'Noble words,' I would say. 'Noble words.' At the age of six I was writing verse and I was acting Hamlet.

My father also taught me to love cricket and we used to play single-wicket matches in the garden. We must have begun these matches at the latest during my fifth summer, because when my brother Evelyn was born in October 1903, my first remark was, 'Splendid. Now we shall have a wicket keeper.'

That winter, P. F. Warner captained the M.C.C. team in

Australia. I followed every Test match. I learnt arithmetic and writing so that I could make my nursery cricket realistic. I wrote down the names of the heroes I was supposed to represent—Duff and Trumper, Lilley, Braund and Hayward and entered their scores run by run. . . . '*O, my Hornby and my Barlow long ago—*'

III

Schooldays—Fernden

In December 1906 my father's father died. The legacy my father received from his estate was small, but it decided him to move into a more gracious neighbourhood, and in the summer of 1907 we moved into a newly built house in North End, Hampstead, below the Bull and Bush, which he christened Underhill.

It all looks very different there today. In the spring of that year North End was a village, Golders Green did not exist and buses stopped at Child's Hill, but in July the Hampstead and Highgate tube was opened and very soon villas were running out to Hendon and shops were clustering at the crossroads. Soon the houses in North End Road were numbered and Underhill became 145; eventually the postal address became Golders Green, N.W.11.

No one passing Underhill today would be able to guess at the kind of family life that we enjoyed there. A subsequent owner has installed a petrol station in the garden; there is a perpetual roar of traffic; there is no sense of privacy. It was a very different place in 1910 with its lawns and greenhouses and rose-beds behind the shelter of high hedges.

My father was very happy there; he appreciated the pride of ownership; and he enjoyed being able to improve his property, with the purchase of an extra piece of land, with an oak floor laid down in the library, a balcony built out from the nursery. Each year saw a new addition.

Everything conspired to make him concentrate upon his home. Fear of asthma and the damp night air made him reluctant to go out to dinner. Moreover, as a subaltern in the

17

volunteers, he had caught a cold through sleeping on a damp pillow and he was a little deaf in his left ear. In consequence he disliked big parties. He could not keep track of the various conversations. He enjoyed small groups of people. In the formal sense he did not entertain. There were no elaborate dinners with place cards and even numbers. But there was a constant coming and going. There were relatives from the country. There were friends looking in to tea and being urged to stay on for dinner. There was always a welcome for them. In later years when I had a life of my own I would rarely pay an unexpected visit to my father's house and not find some visitor.

In the same year that we moved to Underhill I went at the age of nine to a boarding-school. This change did not in any way break the close links between my father and myself. On the contrary it strengthened them.

Many Americans feel that the influence of the home is disturbed by the English habit of sending boys to boarding-schools so young. In some cases this may happen, but not in the majority. On the contrary a home means more when it is seen as the reward of a term's work. Holidays do not mean merely a getting up later in the morning and a not starting off after breakfast with a satchel. A home becomes something special. It is not taken for granted. It is very easy not to see people at all when you are seeing them all the time. You need to come fresh to them. Many husbands and wives in wartime rediscover each other when they meet only at week-ends. There is, moreover, in the schoolboy's case a disturbing atmosphere in a small household in the early evening when he is settling down to his homework at the very moment when his father is returning at the end of his day's work.

My own separations from home were made the easier by my father's letters. He was the best letter writer that I have known, and he always hoped that one day a collection of his letters would be published. Much of his best writing went into them. But the very qualities that made him a good letter writer have made such a project difficult. In his letters he adjusted himself to his correspondent, referring to matters that would only be of concern and interest to that one person. Often when reading the letters of famous men one suspects that they were written with an eye to posthumous publication. My father's letters were not like that. They were his means of keeping in touch with his friends. Many of his letters have been preserved by their recipients, to be re-read often, but they are not of general interest.

While I was at school he wrote to me two or three times a week. When I was in the army he wrote to me every day. We were in the closest touch. At the start of each holidays I picked up the threads where they had been dropped. The days had passed when he drew 'Hurrah Boys'; but when he returned from Henrietta Street in the evening with the green *Westminster Gazette* under his arm, he would change out of his office suit into a grey one and we would take an hour's walk over the Heath. I confided in him all my ambitions, all my problems. I have never since been so completely myself with anyone.

Most evenings he read me poetry. His study—he called it the book-room—was charming in the winter. It had an oak floor and oak bookshelves; a fine mahogany bookcase, and many of the shelves were faced with glass. There were two small red reading-lamps, one on my father's desk, one on a shoulder-high bookcase by the fire. The top light was turned off and my father read from the light by his desk. When he died, more than one letter of condolence referred to 'these red lamps in the book-room'. He read very well, giving the lines their accented rhythms, following the sense, not stopping at the end of a line if the meaning ran on into the next line; but he made it very clear that it was poetry not prose that he was reading. In my Fernden days he generally read me Kipling, Shakespeare, Tennyson; later he turned to Browning, Shelley, Swinburne. When I was sixteen he introduced me to the silver poets, Dowson, Housman, Rosetti. When I re-read now the poems he read to me, I can hear the intonation of his voice. What treasures he was laying up for me. I was not able to do the same for my children. There was always the more powerful attraction of the radio. I am glad that there was no radio when I was young.

§

I have a suspicion that several of my father's friends shared my grandfather's views about his home, in regard to his elder son. I was a very spoilt child, and I had to pay for it later. At my preparatory school I was subjected to a discipline that has made everything else in life seem tame.

Fernden School, Haslemere, has now well over a hundred pupils and both my sons appear in its Old Boys' list. When I went there in September 1907 it was in the third term of its existence and I was its seventh pupil. I left in 1911, one of forty.

There are many disadvantages about going to so small a school. There is no competition, no sense of working up the school, form by form, and there are not enough boys at the start for organized games; but there are advantages. You get more individual attention, you are closely identified with the headmaster's ambition, you are his first exhibition blooms. He stands or falls by you. You have also a strong feeling of *esprit de corps*. You are building a tradition. It is a great day when you win your first match against another school. The advantages and disadvantages even out.

Fernden is now run by Charles, the son of its first headmaster, Norman G. Brownrigg. Over the mantelpiece in the library hangs a portrait of its founder. It shows a firm, lined, stern face, blue-eyed, clean-shaven, with short-cut white hair parted in the centre. N.G.B. had the strength, qualities and characteristics of a New England Puritan. He did not drink or smoke. His morality was of a rigid order. He dressed simply, but his clothes were of good material, there was never a grease-spot on them though his elbows might be patched with leather. He looked as though he had washed five minutes before. His face shone with soap. He was punctilious about hygiene. He gave us lengthy lectures on physiology. We were taught how our bodies worked. We had no false modesty about our physical functions and we bathed naked. Fernden is set on a hill, in lovely country. It is built on sandy soil. We were well fed. The standard of health was high.

As regards manners, particularly table manners, N.G.B. was

a rigid martinet. 'Don't rest your wrists on the table.' 'Don't talk with your mouth full.' 'Don't bite out a piece of bread, cut it in small sections.' 'Don't pile your fork with vegetables.' 'Don't pick and choose, take the first cake offered you.' 'Finish up your porridge.' It was there that I paid the penalty for my indulged childhood. At home I had only eaten what I liked eating, and my table manners had been neglected. I was the particular butt of N.G.B.'s disapproval. 'If you must eat like a hog, Wuffy, you must eat somewhere else. Take your plate to the boot-hole and finish your pudding there.' How often was not that shouted at me during my first year.

On my first Sunday I wrote home that I had 'great difficulty in eating the food provided by Mrs. Brownrigg'. The food was excellent and wholesome, but the platter had to be scraped clean. Fat and gristle, hard lumps of porridge, the blackened crust of a rice pudding, they all had to be consumed. Some kind of a milk pudding was served every day as an accompaniment to an apple tart or a plum duff. Once when it was served with strawberries, I ate the pudding first; as I was preparing to enjoy the strawberries, N.G.B. caught sight of my plate. 'Bring your plate up here, Wuffy.' He poured a ladle of rice pudding over the strawberries. 'That'll teach you to pick and choose.'

Sago pudding was the one which I faced with most misgiving. Once as I swallowed the last mouthful, nausea overcame me and I vomited into my plate. N.G.B. looked down the table. 'Finish up your pudding, Wuffy.'

Since I left Fernden, I have never eaten a milk pudding.

N.G.B. would often say to us in his addresses, 'If you don't learn to behave here, you'll get short shrift at your public schools.' The austerities of our public school life were as menacingly presented as the threat of hell-fire to the New England pioneers. But how tame Sherborne seemed after Fernden. It was not a question of physical discipline—at Sherborne I received forty-one strokes of the cane, at Fernden two—it was that voice harrying me from dawn to dusk, shouting at me down the table, shouting at me across the playing-fields. 'Who is that boy paddling in the stream? Ah, Wuffy again. I thought it would be somebody from Golders Green.'

I still dream of him sometimes. It is always the same dream.

I remind myself that I am now an adult. 'You cannot treat me like this,' I say. I raise my voice. I begin to shout. But suddenly the power of speech deserts me. My jaw moves, but no sound emerges. I try to scream and as I try, I wake.

I will not say that I was unhappy at Fernden, because it was not until I went to Sherborne that I realized how happy it was possible for me to be at school. I have a natural zest for living; as long as something is happening I can enjoy myself. Eventlessness is the one thing I dread. I did not dislike N.G.B. Boys respect a disciplinarian and he was just; he had no favourites. One expected and received a fair deal at his hands. After I had left, we became good friends. He was loyal to his old boys, he always gave them a warm welcome. Every summer he organized cricket matches in which he invited me to play.

§

The function of the preparatory school is to remove and iron out the idiosyncracies acquired in the home so that a standardized product may be presented to the public school. The nine-year-old boy has many of the primitive instincts of the jungle and what is popularly supposed to be the public school code of honour is rigidly enforced. There is no stricter moralist than the reformed rake, and 'owning up' becomes a fetish.

The fear of being thought a coward will make the preparatory schoolboy confess to sins that he has never committed, and it is usually the ones who are most often in trouble who find themselves in this position. After all, if you are always getting into scrapes, are always engaged in some misdemeanour, it is very hard to tell whether, on a particular occasion, you are innocent or not. The headmaster comes into a classroom in the afternoon.

'Now look here, you fellows, you know I've told you that I won't have you running down that steep path to the football field. You are bound to fall down; and you must walk. I've told you that a hundred times. Now the matron tells me that she saw one of you running down there this morning. I want that boy's name.'

What is Jones mi. to do? He has run down that path so often. Whether or not he did so that morning he cannot remember.

He has had so much to think about since then. Yet, suppose he did run down the hill, and suppose someone saw him. If he does not own up, he will be called a coward. Far better 'own up', and receive some small punishment. Indeed, it may be said that the Jones mi.'s of the world form a rule for themselves, that they own up to every offence of which they are not dead certain that they are innocent.

It is equally difficult to acknowledge innocence in the midst of crime. At Fernden there was an excellent rule that for half an hour after lunch we should sit in our classrooms and read quietly. One afternoon this peaceful period was disturbed by a loud, fierce and general discussion of the superiority of York-shire cricket over that of Lancashire. The particular classroom unfortunately happened to be situated beneath the nursery and the angry voices of the disputants roused from her slumbers a recent addition to the family. The complaints of an indignant nurse disturbed N.G.B.'s siesta. On this occasion the usual formula was reversed. He did not ask the names of the boys who had been talking, he asked for the names of the boys who had not been talking. Now, as it happened, I had taken no part in the argument. I am a Middlesex supporter, I had just received as a birthday present a bound volume of *Chums*, I was also, at the time, in popular disfavour. So I had seated myself in a far corner of the room and read steadily, with my fingers pressed into my ears. But I did not dare to say so. I should never have been forgiven. It would have been the action of a conscientious objector. No one would have believed me. I realized how hope-lessly out of things I should feel while the rest of the school were receiving their punishment. Suppose a half-holiday was stopped—what on earth should I do with a half-holiday all to myself? I should be much happier working out theorems in a classroom. And it was also possible that I might have said something that someone had overheard; at any rate, I was not going to risk it. I sat silent at my desk and accepted meekly the common lot.

§

In retrospect one Fernden year merges with another. My four summers there stand out in detail, because of the cricket and my individual scores; but the winter terms are indistinguishable. It always seemed to be raining. My most vivid winter picture of Fernden is of the rain sweeping in waves across the valley against the dark background of the pines. We were always, because the ground was too wet for football, being sent for runs, or being employed on what N.G.B. called 'odd jobs'.

These odd jobs were mainly concerned with the levelling and enlarging of the cricket ground. In 1907, cricket was played on a large tennis court, at the foot of a hill; flanked by a stream and consequently damp. By the time I left, the tennis court had been lengthened, broadened and drained into a field capable of accommodating two games simultaneously. This enlargement was mainly the work of Fernden's first pupils. We shovelled earth, we carried turves, we pulled up brambles. I liked none of it, but the turves were the special focus of my hate. The actual preparing of them fascinated me. The digging down along a line of string with a sharp, short-bladed spade; then the cutting under the soil with a bent, long-handled shovel. That I would have loved to do, but that was a master's task. I was the slave who carried the turf after it had been rolled up, to the other side of the field. It was heavy and the earth was cold. I had to carry it away from my body, so that the damp earth did not rub against and befoul my jersey; this was very difficult as I was pot-bellied. My frozen fingers would lose their grip; the turf would unroll, split and fall apart. A voice would thunder from the back, 'Wuffy, you wretched creature, here am I giving up my afternoon, cutting turves, so that you can enjoy your cricket and there you are wasting my work with your infernal carelessness.'

When one of the school passed into Osborne, we asked if we might have a half-holiday in his honour. N.G.B. reflected. 'I'll tell you what I'll do. I'll drive a bargain with you chaps. If you'll help me with odd jobs, you can have your holiday.' My spirits sank. I would have much preferred to spend the afternoon writing Greek iambics.

The lent term was odd-job term, the football matches against other schools being played during the autumn. It was also chilblain term. Neither of my sons had chilblains, and I have been told that they have been largely exorcised by modern, balanced diets. But for most of us they were February's bane. They attacked the lowest section of the finger; they would itch, they would swell, then they would burst and have to be wrapped in bandages. One February, during the chilblain season, N.G.B. opened a campaign against nail-biting. All those who bit their nails had their fingers dipped in brown bitter liquid. I was one of them. My hands with brown finger-tips and several of the lower joints wrapped in ink-stained bandages looked like a carrion crow's claws.

§

I stand deep in N.G.B.'s debt on many counts, most of all for the feeling he gave me for France and for the French. He taught French as a spoken and live language not a dead one. At lunch there was a table where only French was spoken. Every Easter he took a group of us to Boulogne for a fortnight. At that time most English schoolboys tended to despise foreigners, dismissing them as 'froggies'. No Fernden boy made that mistake twice. 'They are different from us, but they are admirable in their own way,' N.G.B. would say. Later that day his voice would ring down the table. 'Look at the way Wuffy shoves food into his face. He calls the Frenchmen froggies. I wonder what a well-bred Frenchman would call him.'

He had French friends in Boulogne and on our Easter visits we were taken to Sunday lunch at their house. It was an ordeal. We sat down at twelve and did not rise till three. But it was an experience. Many of my best times since have been due to an ability to mix with the French on easy terms. I owe that entirely to N.G.B.

I have wondered since why N.G.B. should have had so strong a feeling for the French and France. He did not care for the things that endear France to most of us. He was not a man of letters. He cannot have appreciated her literature or painting. He was a teetotaller. He was indifferent to the pleasures of the table. French morals must have shocked him. I should have expected him to have been more in tune by temperament with the marshalled and Spartan Prussians. But though he taught German, he had no feeling for Germany or the Germans.

What bred in him this love of France? Sometimes I have wondered whether as a student he did not fall in love with a Frenchwoman, with whom he cannot have visualized a career in marriage. Perhaps, through loving her, he fell in love with France, seeing France as her background, realizing that no other country could have produced her, loving her country because of her.

§

I was very far from being one of his best French pupils. He disliked my accent—*Vache Espagnole*, he would say—and I doubt if it is any better now. I have a limited vocabulary; or rather, a vocabulary that is limited by my interests. I can describe a landscape, discuss a poet, dilate upon the pleasures of the table and the bed, but I am unmechanical and unscientific. During the Second War I was for a while a liaison officer with the Free French forces. Many of the conferences I attended were concerned with the transport of stores and the repair of damaged vehicles. My Major after setting out the problem would turn to me. 'Now, Captain Waugh, will you explain the situation to our French colleagues?' I was forced to reply that I did not know what the situation was in English, let alone in French. It soon became apparent that General Spears would have to find as staff captain to his mission an officer with a less specialized knowledge of the language. Yet I must quote in my defence the tribute paid by a French colonel to the speech I gave at my farewell dinner in Beirut. Never, he said, had he heard an Englishman speak French so fast.

It is possible that this early saturation in the French tradition has had in my case results of which N.G.B. would not have approved. I have devoted a good deal of time to the hazards of what is called in America 'extra-curricular romance'. Its pursuit has brought me a variety of emotions—rapture and despair, pride and humiliation, boredom and a supreme consciousness of heightened living; but never has it been attended by a sense of guilt. My attitude has been Latin, not Anglo-Saxon. I cannot see why two adults should not make love together if they want to, nor why a proposal of marriage should be the only honourable sequel to an irregular week-end. I have inherited no puritan streak from my Scottish ancestors. Is this, I have sometimes wondered, because the first novels that I read were French and I absorbed the practical French point of view?

§

One of the features of Fernden in my time, possibly in consequence of our being a small school, with ourselves the first generation of senior boys, was a complete sexual innocence. N.G.B. lectured us on the functions of our bodies, but no reference was made to sex. When Mrs. Brownrigg at the end of my second year had her second baby, we learnt something of the facts of maternity, but nothing about paternity. We were not only incurious, but did not know there was a secret in connexion with it. When N.G.B. shortly before I left gave me a talk about the dangers that awaited me at a public school—'How can you ask some pure woman to be your wife, if you have been a filthy little beast at school?'—I had no idea what he was talking about.

One curious aspect of sexual development did, however, manifest itself, though we did not recognize it as such—how could we have since we did not know that such a thing existed? During my last year we indulged in a form of flagellation, belabouring our bared posteriors on bath nights with knotted boot laces and hairbrushes. This was partly due to a pleasure in inflicting pain, partly due to a desire to show courage under pain—and as such it showed a kinship with the initiation ceremonies of the Red Indian braves—but it had a very definite sexual basis. Once when we were discussing our experiences, in the changing-room, a boy pointing to a rampant display of masculinity remarked that it was funny he 'always got like this' when we discussed beatings.

I presume that this was a normal development, since we evolved the practice for ourselves and it was not put into our heads by older boys. I fancy that small boys take a morbid interest in the subject. In school stories, written for boys, which are usually read by preparatory not public school boys, beatings are often described in detail and with relish. At Sherborne I saw no similar sign of interest in the subject.

IV

Schooldays—Sherborne

I went to Sherborne in September 1911. Nearly all boys enjoy their last terms at a public school but I had a good time from the start. I enjoyed every aspect of its life. I was excited by the atmosphere of competition of which I had been deprived at Fernden, where from the start I had been the best classic, the best bowler and one of the two best batsmen—one year my only rival would head the averages and the next I would. Though I had never liked soccer and was never any good at it, I had played in every first-XI match.

I have always been ambitious and now, at Sherborne, I was in the arena. Fernden had been in every sense preparatory. There was no public record of its victories and failures. No one in the big world knew at what preparatory school a man had been. With the exception of the schools in the neighbourhood, I did not know the names of half a dozen other schools. But I knew which public schools had produced my heroes of the cricket field. P. F. Warner from Rugby, R. E. Foster from Malvern, J. N. Crawford from Repton, K. L. Hutchings from Tonbridge. A. W. Carr, the captain of the School House during my first term, had been given his Notts cap the previous summer. I saw myself in the distant future going in to bat at Lord's for Middlesex and reading in the next day's paper that 'the old Shirburnian was at his characteristic best'. On my first evening I looked up at the raised sixth-form table, wondering how long it must be before I sat there.

The road was marked out for me in clear-cut stages; colts cap, colts badge, house cap, seconds, firsts. Every term offered its own prize for winning. A promotion in form, a cap upon the

28

field. My ambition was fanned by my father's absorption in my career. He was not only reliving his youth in me, he was doing through me the things he had not done himself. He would have given anything to be an athlete but his weak chest would not allow him to play football and at cricket defective eyesight prevented him from focusing a moving object. He was delighted when I won the English Verse prize but that was something that he had done himself. It was an altogether different matter when he saw me wearing the blue and gold blazer of the XI. A large part of the pleasure that I took in my school achievements was the knowledge of how much excitement the telegram announcing them would cause at home.

The life of a public school is essentially dramatic: there are the rivalries of individual boys and of the various houses. The drama is concentrated within a short space of time, four to five years is the average span. Only a few months have passed before the fag has become a prefect, and the drama of each success and each reverse is heightened by the fact that in a small self-contained community you are under constant supervision.

When the list of the first XV to play against Tonbridge is posted on the notice-board and everyone crowds round to see who has been dropped and who has been included, you are within half an hour, inside the circumference of your own small world, the object of congratulation or of sympathy. It is not like that in adult life, except for those very few who live under the high-pressured arc-light of publicity. Writers have their ups and downs. My 'ups' have come to me nearly always when I was far from home, and I could share my good luck with no one. In March 1930 I learnt as I was disembarking at Mombasa that my travel book *Hot Countries* was a Literary Guild choice. The cablegram announcing it was for me a door opening upon new horizons. But there was no one on that ship, no one in Mombasa, to whom that cable could mean anything. I was to them the same person that I had been five minutes before. Yet to myself, and to a minute section of the world that lay outside that ship, I had become a different person.

It is the same in moments of adversity. My fortunes struck their lowest point during 1951–3, when I lost the knack of writing magazine short stories. For twenty-five years this knack had been my chief support. It left me suddenly, inexplicably—in the same way that for some the desire to write poetry goes. I suppose that I was passing through an interim phase, on my way to writing novels on big canvases. But I did not know that at the time. I felt I was washed up. I came up to New York from the West Indies in February 1953. I had been working on short stories for eighteen months. Not one of them was any good. Carl Brandt went over them with me. Carl Brandt was not only the kindest man in the world and the wisest agent, he also had a great editorial sense. Innumerable times he was able to give an author a new slant on a story. (There is a portrait of him in John Marquand's *Wychford Point*.) He tried to see if there was not some way in which he could 'fix' at least one of mine. But the talk petered out. We both knew that it was hopeless. 'I feel like an executioner,' he said. 'Peters may be able to do something with these in England. But I can't here.'

Where do I go from here? I thought. I walked out into Park Avenue, as I had how many dozen times in the last quarter of a century. It was all unchanged, on a bright February morning; the gilded tower of the Grand Central station glinting in the sunlight, the spire of the Chrysler Building silver sharp against the pale blue sky; taxicabs were sweeping over the elevated bridge, pedestrians were hurrying by upon their duties, exactly as they had done on mornings when I had walked down that street, jubilant in spirit with a one-shot sold to *Red Book*. No one had guessed then the reason of my jubilance. No one knew now that I was debating the advantages of that phial of barbituric tablets. The anonymity of adulthood protected me.[1]

It is very different at school for the batsman who drags his feet back to the pavilion after his third single-figure innings in succession, knowing he will never again read his name on the school board; just as it is very different for the three-quarter back who twice in an afternoon rounds the defence and plants the ball between the posts, knowing that a tasselled cap is his.

The crowd is silent or applauds. Every incident is dramatized, and there is so much that is dramatic in school life. The weekly

[1] Three weeks later to everyone's astonishment, Twentieth Century Fox bought a short story of mine that had appeared in *Esquire*. This gave me the breather that I needed. The film, starring Suzy Parker, was shown in 1961 under the title *Circle of Deception*.

orders in form; the prize-givings on the last day of term; the anxieties and rewards of the struggle for a place in the house or school XI. It was the practice at Sherborne for colours to be given after a match, with the captain coming round in person to congratulate you. He usually came round in second hall, the period after prayers before the bell went for bed, a period given up to the brewing of cocoa in the studies. How well I remember the anxious waiting after a match in which one tried to persuade oneself that one had done well enough to get one's colours, the listening for each footfall in the passage.

I remember, in particular, an evening in the late July of 1914. The XI were just back from a two-day match against Radley. I had made 15 in the first innings. We were led by over 100 runs, but in the evening I had squared the balance with a hard hit 65. It rained the whole of the second day. I had already been given my seconds, I did not see how I could fail to get my firsts. I waited confidently in the School House games study, with three or four others, over an evening supper. There was a tap on the door. The captain was standing on the threshold. My heart bounded; I was ready to jump up to meet the extended hand. But it was not for me that the captain had paid his call, but to give a junior member of the side his seconds.

§

The caps and cups of the playing-fields, and the terminal race for promotion in the classroom are the most obvious aspects of the drama of school life; but there is also the invisible, intangible drama of a constantly widening horizon, and I was growing up mentally as well as physically. At Fernden and during my first years at Sherborne, I had been acquiring facts; now I was grasping at the meaning of those facts.

I had not the scholarship cast of mind, and when I reached the sixth, I specialized in history. But from the days when I had acted Hamlet in the nursery, 'noble words' had held their magic for me; I was learning now every term how rich was the heritage of English literature, and it was extremely lucky for me that there should have been at Sherborne then three masters particularly fitted to develop a growing literary sense.

Schoolmasters, for the most part, work within the narrow

circle of their cloistered world and are known only to their pupils. It was of such men that Kipling wrote:

> 'Let us now praise famous men'
> Men of little showing
> For their work continueth,
> And their work continueth,
> Broad and deep continueth,
> Greater than their knowing.

Usually there is no point in writing of them except as characters in a novel, because their names will convey nothing to the general reader, and I have already written of these three masters in *The Loom of Youth* as Claremont, Ferrers and the Chief. But in fact these three men have reputations that are not limited to Sherborne.

In Cecil Day Lewis, Sherborne is proud to honour as its own, one of the finest poets of our day. He was Claremont's son-in-law. In his autobiography *The Buried Day*, he has paid tribute to what he owes to Claremont. In every biographical study of Day Lewis and as far as we can be certain of anything it is that the literary history of the future will contain many, there will be a reference to his father-in-law, Henry Robinson King.

When I reached Sherborne, King who had been a master in my father's time was a venerable figure; grey-haired, with a shaggy white moustache, and in holy orders. He loved poetry with a passion that I have not seen equalled. He had memorized some 50,000 lines and one of Sherborne's most familiar sights was that of him bicycling out into the country in the afternoon to recite selected passages as soon as he reached solitude; he would lean over a gate, and the cows of the field would slowly gather round as he declaimed, staring at him with bland, mute eyes. His form was privileged to hear such recitations far oftener than the limits of the curriculum recorded. In a memorial paper Cecil Day Lewis wrote, 'He did not waste time "explaining" what poems meant; he just read them to us—read them with golden tones and a quiet inner conviction of the supreme importance of poetry to the human spirit and we listened or half listened or dozed off. But for some of us at least, imperceptibly it sank in, just as the beauty of Sherborne itself was sinking in, not through our eyes and ears as much as through the pores of our being and the course of our life was changed thereby because its meaning was insensibly enlarged.'

§

'Ferrers' was a very different character. As S. P. B. Mais, he is well known as a novelist, the author of travel books, and a broadcaster. He started as a schoolmaster. After two years at Rossall he arrived at Sherborne in September 1913. He was then in his late twenties. He has changed little since. At Oxford he was a cross-country 'blue' and he still walks with a pile of books under his arm as though he were limbering up for a marathon. He is clean-shaven, fresh-complexioned with short sandy hair. Nowadays he wears a fantastic conglomeration of scarves, pullovers and cardigans, but then he dressed reasonably, in uncreased grey flannel trousers, a pullover and sports coat, a soft collar and a Vincent's tie. He talks at the top of his voice. He is breathlessly alive.

He hit Sherborne like a whirlwind. Anything he taught became dramatic. In mathematics in the lower forms he awarded marks by the thousand. It caught the imagination of his pupils. They enjoyed announcing that as the result of the morning's work they had amassed 35,000 marks and the winner at the end of term proudly informed his parents that he had collected over ten million marks. The book-keeping of these astronomic sums presented no problem for Mais; he knocked off the noughts and entered in his book Smith 35, Jones 33.

In the teaching of literature he interested his classes in the personalities of the poets. Boys are partisans. They like championing a cause, they like adversaries. He encouraged debates on Byron v. Wordsworth, provided the boys had read the poets they despised or adulated. He made Shakespeare live, by treating the plays as drama. His lectures and essays when published in book form were not well received in the serious reviews, but the very characteristics that made him an unsound critic for adult readers inspired the young.

He got boys reading, and one of his great merits as a teacher was that he inspired what is called 'the average boy' with a desire to read. He had his special pupils—at Rossall he 'spotted' J. R. Ackerley and Desmond Young—but he did not concentrate upon them to the exclusion of his middle-brow pupils. During his four years at Sherborne not only did he not cane a single boy but he did not give a single imposition. He did not need to exert authority; the boys enjoyed their hours in his classroom.

As an athlete he had his special niche. We had good cricketers and footballers on the staff, but he was the only runner. His second term he trained one of the house sides (the Green) for the point-to-point cross-country race. Three men made a team. The best runner was in another house. But the Green's team won, by coming in second, third and fourth, the runners side by side, in step. Perhaps it was partly as a result of his influence that Sherborne has produced since a succession of fine runners—Milligan, Stallard and Chris Chattaway.

§

The headmaster—the Chief—of Sherborne in my day was Nowel Charles Smith;[1] a fellow of New College, a man of letters, the foremost authority of Wordsworth and at the end of his life the editor in a large two-volume edition of the letters of Sydney Smith. He came to Sherborne in 1909 and left in 1927 having raised the numbers of the school from 200 to 400, and having placed the school, in the public's esteem, among the first dozen in the country.

In my time the headmaster was also the housemaster of the School House, so that I was in constant contact with N.C.S.

A few years ago, a certain number of old boys were invited to contribute their personal reminiscences for purposes of archival reference. I sent in this.

When I went to the School House in September 1911, N.C.S. was starting his seventh term, and the House had not yet made up its mind about him. The seniors had been groomed under another ruler, and Canon Westcott had been much loved. Westcott was a better housemaster than

---

[1] N.C.S. died in 1961.

The Author as Hamlet in the nursery, aged about six

The Author in a sailor-suit, aged about eight

The family in 1904

a headmaster. In the late 'nineties when the school's stock stood low, the House, relatively, kept up its numbers, and it was possible for a headmaster to regard the outhouses as subject colonies. N.C.S. saw himself as a headmaster first and a housemaster second. The House sensed this change.

In other ways, too, Westcott was a hard man to follow. Westcott with his height, his white hair, and thin ascetic features, was an impressive figurehead, he was also a good speaker. N.C.S. was neither. His short introductory speeches at prize-givings and lectures were not effective and though his sermons read well and the intrinsic material was so excellent that they frequently made a powerful impression on the school, his delivery was hesitant. He was not the man to capture the loyalty and imagination of schoolboys with a vivid first impression, and in 1911 he was too recent a newcomer to have founded a tradition.

It was by slow degrees that he won the loyalty and allegiance of my generation. Boys respect, admire and are attracted to a strict disciplinarian and we learnt that N.C.S. was a man who knew what he wanted and how to get it. I can quote two examples. It was our practice in the School House changing-room to adopt a communal attitude towards each other's clothes. If you wanted a scarf or corps belt you took the nearest one. As someone invariably was in the sick-room there were enough clothes to go round. N.C.S. objected to this practice, and appointed a captain of the changing-room who was instructed to 'deal severely' with anyone caught wearing someone else's clothes. The room was periodically examined, and if the corps cap of someone known to be on parade was discovered, its owner received six. I was one of those who did. We resented this interference with a custom but within two terms we were all wearing our own clothes.

When I arrived it was the practice of the 'bloods' to wear grey flannel trousers in the summer. N.C.S. sent round a notice stating that the wearing of grey flannel trousers was not the privilege of a few persons. The notice had no effect. Before the following summer parents were encouraged to supply their sons with grey flannel trousers. When the weather grew hot, the matron put out the trousers and the boys were told that they had to wear them. Only a few boys had brought back trousers and those few endured a certain amount of mild persecution. But it was the thin end of the wedge; within two years everyone during the summer was wearing grey flannel trousers. We came to realize that when N.C.S. said a thing, he meant it. We liked him for that.

When a schoolboy has made an ass of himself, he expects to be 'come down on like a ton of bricks', and N.C.S. could be very formidable when he was angry. In November 1913, a scandal broke out in one of the houses, and he caned in the library in a single afternoon eight or nine of the delinquents. A group of us from the School House stood in the entrance to the cloisters while others leaned out of the study windows, shouting and mocking at the victims as they came down the steps. We created a considerable din. Suddenly to our consternation we saw emerge through the library door, not a stricken scholar rubbing his seat, but N.C.S., his face flushed both with exercise and fury. He strode down, abused us roundly, then returned to complete his task. We had no idea he was capable of losing his temper to that extent. We were impressed.

I am stressing this aspect of N.C.S. as a disciplinarian because so many tributes have been paid to his Christian gentleness and the very real sweetness of his smile, that those who did not know him might very well think of him as mild. He was anything but that. He had great personal charm but he also had a genuine capacity to make one feel very small. There is nothing that a schoolboy resents more than sarcasm and N.C.S. was never sarcastic. I once, to rag a master and in imitation of P. G. Wodehouse's Psmith, bought myself an eyeglass. I was practising the use of it in front of the studies when N.C.S. went by. 'I didn't know you had trouble with your eyes,' he said. I hadn't, I told him, I had bought it as a joke. 'If you suffered from bad sight,' he said, 'you would not make fun of what is for some of us a very great misfortune.'

In the sixth form we were allowed to learn our own repetition, and once in a mood of bravado I memorized the first seven stanzas of Swinburne's *Envoi* to *Poems and Ballads*. N.C.S. glanced at the book I handed him, then returned it to me. 'We'll take that as heard,' he said. Next time I learnt *The Scholar Gipsy*.

Once when he put me on to construe, I excused myself on the grounds that we had already passed the thirtieth line. 'You are now in the sixth not the lower fourth,' he said. 'If you have not the time to prepare as far as this, that is all you need to say.' N.C.S. never needed to implement his authority with punishments.

There was another aspect of N.C.S. that won him our respect—the position he held in the big world. He was a frequent contributor to the correspondence columns of *The Times*, and when we went back for the holidays and mentioned that we were at Sherborne our fathers' friends would say, 'That new headmaster of yours is a brilliant person.' We had imagined that the first name that would occur to anyone in connexion with Sherborne was A. W. Carr.

In the summer of 1913 when the Duke of Westminster attempted to raise a fund to train athletes for the Olympic Games, N.C.S. wrote a letter to *The Times* that served as the text for the first leader. He resented the suggestion that national prestige depended on the performances of a few professionally trained athletes, remarking at the end of his argument that schoolmasters were first accused of paying too much attention to games, and now were blamed for not producing Olympic athletes. He enlarged his theme in an article in one of the monthly magazines. The article, as the letter, attracted notice. We were surprised that N.C.S. should be so well documented about sport. One of the books that S. P. B. Mais recommended to the sixth was Arnold Bennett's *Literary Taste*. It contained a reference to 'that eminent Wordsworthian Mr. Nowell Smith'. That, too, impressed us.

July 1914 saw the departure of the last of those who had known the Westcott régime. When the school reassembled in September on the brink of a new world, a new generation was wholehearted in its allegiance to one who was ceasing to be described as 'the new chief'. N.C.S. had, we now realized, indentified himself with Sherborne. Sherborne was his life's work.

My own relations with N.C.S. were coloured by his friendship with my father. They had much in common. When my father wrote to enter my name, N.C.S. answered, 'I did not know you as an O.S. for I have not yet had time to familiarize myself with the O.S. list, but of course I know you well as a member of my college, and a winner of the Newdigate.' Friendship can be a one-sided business. Often our friends mean more to us then we do to them and vice versa. But I know for very sure that of the friends my father made in the second half of his life, N.C.S. was the one to whom he was most attracted.

I cannot pretend that after my fourth term my presence in his house caused N.C.S. much satisfaction, and it must have been, I recognize it now, a source of considerable regret to him that so much of the time he spent with my father had to be occupied with the discussion of my misdemeanours. During my last week at Sherborne N.C.S. said to me, 'I was particularly anxious to make a success of you, but I don't really see what else I could have done.' That struck me even at the time as a remarkably modest remark for a headmaster.

§

In addition to these three men there was my father. Each holidays brought us closer; and my increasing absorption in poetry imperceptibly but deeply altered our relationship. During my first fifteen years, he had lived in me. He continued to do so, but during my last five terms at Sherborne, from the point when I reached the sixth, I began, if not to live in him, at least to see him from another angle. I had always been very proud of him, but less for his achievements than for their adjuncts, for the figure he cut in the world, for his position as managing director of an important firm, for the respect people paid to him and to his opinions, for his popularity, for his geniality as a host, for the way people laughed at his jokes, for the way that he made a party go, the success that he was both with my contemporaries and my masters. Most schoolboys are terrified of being made conspicuous by something that their parents may do or say or wear. I never was. Wherever we went I knew that my stock stood higher because I was his son.

I had seen the effects, but now I was to appreciate its causes. I had by now extended the range of my reading to include the minor poetry of the 1890s, Dowson, Symons, Lionel Johnson and Le Gallienne. My father had glamour for me as the friend and associate of my new heroes. Had he not contributed to the first number of the *Yellow Book*; had he not attended the dinner in which the Rhymers had invested the royalties on their first *Anthology*? My mother, in her early days of marriage, had pasted his articles into a press-cutting book. I began to read them with avid interest. My father was surprised and touched; he also began to take a new interest in them himself. For ten years, running Chapman & Hall, reviewing for the *Daily Telegraph*, making this and that addition to Underhill, looking forward to week-ends at Sherborne, arranging holiday treats for his sons, he had had little spare time and no inducement to indulge in free-lance writing. Now he had a son reading his old articles.

Practical encouragment was to come at the right moment, from a lucky quarter. That excellent bookman, J. G. Wilson, who later took over the management of Bumpus's, wanted to publish a volume or two of *belles-lettres*, under his own imprint, and asked my father if he would prepare a collection of his essays. The volume appeared in March 1915, under the title *Reticence in Literature*. It had an excellent Press, and for that kind of book, sold well. It was dedicated to me and my delight and pride in it, the excitement with which I read the reviews, made him wish 'he could write another book for me'.

§

The Loom of Youth is autobiographical, the story term by term of my four years at Sherborne. One or two critics objected to my omission of any reference to my hero's holidays. But if I had, I should have had to write a different novel. My school-days were so interwoven with my father's reaction to them that I should have had to write a father and son novel and it was not that kind of novel that I wanted to write. I wanted to write about school, exclusively.

I had good reasons for doing so. Ordinarily the life of school is so sharply divided from the life of home that the two do not fuse. I was exceptional in that my relationship with my father was so close, and that my father through being an old Shir-burnian was himself so closely connected with the school. *The Loom of Youth* may have presented a partial picture of my own schooldays, but I think it was a true record of an average boy's experience.

Moreover, my own holidays were singularly eventless. In retrospect one year merges with another. I can remember the summer holidays. There was cricket to watch at Lord's and at the Oval. There were my visits to Somerset, where boys' cricket matches were arranged. But I do not quite know how I passed the daytime in the winter. My brother was too young to be a companion for me. He was at a local day school. He had made friends with a family that lived a quarter of a mile away and organized what he called 'The Pistol Troop' to repel in-vasion when the Germans came. He constructed a cache in a disused building site—'the clay heap' was his name for it— where the troop kept the cocoa, biscuits and fireworks with which to sustain a siege. Grown-ups were allowed to join in an honorary capacity, as doctor, Chaplain or printer to the troop, but I was considered too old to be an active and too young to be an honorary member.

Evelyn was always busy during his holidays, but I had no friends in the neighbourhood with the exception of two fellow Shirburnians, one of whom was a year junior to me, the other a year and a half senior, and protocol decreed that I should advance cautiously towards these friendships. The younger of the two was H. S. Mackintosh, who is now well known as a writer of light verse, particularly in the ballade form. Twice a week, when the programme changed, we went to the Bijou cinema in Finchley Road. One Christmas holidays we went to a dancing-class; that was in 1913. I was then fifteen and a half and was beginning to feel a need for feminine society. Mackintosh who was extremely precocious in terms of gallantry had assured me that the best way to meet girls was to go to dances; so after Christmas I persuaded my parents to give a fancy-dress dance at Underhill. It was a successful party and Mackintosh bribed Evelyn sixpence to switch off the electric light at the main so that he could embrace a young person on the stairs. But that is the only festivity I can recall during my four years at Sherborne.

My holidays were happy ones, but I realize now that their particular character accentuated for me one of the most real problems of adolescence. Doctors tell us that most adolescents acquire the habit of masturbation. The approach to it today is more sensible, because it is medical, than it was in my time. Such information as we received was absurdly incorrect. We were assured that it would have physical consequences as serious as those of syphilis. The victim would grow bald and blind. He would lose control over his limbs. This misinformation bred in a boy both fear and an exaggerated sense of guilt, which were increased by its being a solitary habit. A boy was fighting against himself. The sense of failure was magnified by each fresh lapse.

During term-time this was not an acute problem for me. I was busy; there was the necessity of keeping fit for games, but at home where I was so much alone I was particularly susceptible to the influence of what I read.

I thought about this during the trial of *Lady Chatterley's Lover*. The prosecution claimed that certain books harmed an adolescent. The prosecution was not explicit. What kind of harm? Did certain books undermine an adolescent's belief in virtue? Would a certain kind of book encourage a young man to assault the virtue of a sister's friend? I can hardly believe it would. Most young men are timid; they are more likely to be seduced by an older woman than to seduce a younger one. It is possible that a book might paint the pleasures of love in such glowing colours that a young woman would say to herself, 'If it is as wonderful as all that, I had better try it,' but against that argument must be set the fact that every other hoarding, every other advertisement in the Press is a direct or indirect embellishment of the delights of love; an incentive to falling in love, and through using a certain preparation, wearing a certain garment, to meriting the rewards of love. When I went to Russia in 1935, one of the first differences I noticed between the capitalist and the Communist worlds was that gallantry was not advertised, that the hoardings proclaimed instead the achievements of the five-year plan; so many cars rolling off the assembly line, so much pig-iron smelted. In Russia love was regarded with suspicion as a deterrent to the social obligations of the Soviet citizen. But in the capitalist world, most adolescents are in love with love at a very early age.

Those who favour a stricter censorship are on stronger ground when they argue that certain books raise lecherous images that make it harder for a young man to resist the temptation to masturbate. In my own case, as a solitary boy, with little to do during the holidays except read, this was admittedly the case. Certain books did make more difficult for me the fight against this temptation, but such books are not necessarily those to which authority would object.

I was most subject to this temptation during my sixteenth year, the winter of 1913–14. During that autumn two novels were published that were banned by the circulating libraries. One was *The Woman Thou Gavest Me*, by Hall Caine, the other Compton Mackenzie's *Sinister Street*. There was a good deal of correspondence in the Press about the action of the libraries and I imagine that many schoolmasters would have confiscated those books, had they found their pupils reading them. I read both, Hall Caine's novel without much interest, but *Sinister Street* with the highest excitement and admiration. I found neither book inflammatory. I did, however, find inflammatory a novel called *Joseph in Jeopardy* by Frank Danby (Pamela Frankau's grandmother). It described how a large healthy cricketer, married to a negligible wife, fell in love with an elegant society woman. No adultery took place, but there were two luscious descriptions of embraces upon a sofa. There were no anatomical details. In 1945, I came across a copy in a Y.M.C.A. library in the Middle East. It would be hard, I felt, to find a more blameless story. No housemaster could have objected to a boy reading it. Yet so inflammatory did I find it, to such an extent did it make more difficult for me the carrying out of the good resolutions with which I began each holidays, that on my return from Sherborne in April 1914, I tore out and burnt the dozen offending pages.

Thirty months later, when I was at Sandhurst, the staff sergeant asked us to contribute any novels we did not need to a collection for prisoners of war. I asked my father to send down a package. He included *Joseph in Jeopardy*. Before sending off the package, the staff sergeant browsed through them. *Joseph in Jeopardy* was one of those he read. He was as surprised as he was disappointed, he told me, to find that the lurid pages had been removed. If he at any later date came across a copy of the novel, and eagerly turned to the missing pages, he will have been sadly disappointed.

My other source of temptation was Marlowe's *Hero and Leander*. The Everyman volume of Marlow's plays in which it appeared was compulsory reading for me in the sixth.

Censors waste their time in trying to decide which books will harm an adolescent. Different boys are affected by different books; you can no more tell which ones will prove an aphrodisiac than you can foresee who will fall in love with whom. (What *did* he see in her?) Parents and schoolmasters can, I believe, best help their charges not by locking books away, but by keeping them occupied so that they have little time for brooding. In retrospect, I feel that my parents would have been wise to make plans for me during my winter holidays. But it is the only point of criticism I have to make—the one debit entry in a ledger on whose credit side is a long, long list.

§

At the age of fourteen and a half I was confirmed. I saw confirmation as something to be taken in my stride, as the next thing upon the list. I had learnt my catechism at Fernden, section by section, every Sunday. 'It will save you a lot of trouble to learn it now, instead of having to bother about it at your public school.' The ceremony had no spritual or emotional significance for me, except in as far as it strengthened me in my belief that I was almost adult. Two days before my confirmation, while I was ragging in the studies, my wrist got caught in a door and was broken and dislocated. I had to wait in the Chief's drawing-room for an hour before the doctor could be found to set it. The Chief's wife looked at me with sympathetic disapproval. 'I should not have thought, Waugh, that you would have been ragging at such a time.' For a moment, I did not know what she meant.

I accepted religion without belief. In retrospect I am surprised that this should have been so. I was brought up in a church-going atmosphere. At Underhill we had morning prayers before breakfast, read by my father, attended by the servants. My maternal grandmother's second husband was a parson. My aunts on both sides supervised Bible classes. When I visited them during the summer holidays I attended matins and evensong on Sundays. I enjoyed the atmosphere of the quiet country churches, the familiar prayers and hymns, the white surplices of the choir, the sunlight colouring the stained-glass windows. In London my father and mother communicated two or three times a month and went each Sunday morning to high choral celebration first at St. Augustine's, Kilburn, later at St. Jude's in the Hampstead Garden Suburb. As a young man my father had had doubts—as many English Anglicans had in the 1890s as a result of Darwin's theories. He was worried about survival after death. Speaking of that period, he would quote William Watson's poem 'The Great Misgiving':

> and, ah, to know not while with friends I sit . . .
> whether 'tis ampler day divinelier lit
> or homeless night without. . . .
> There is, O grave, thy hourly victory,
> and there, O death, thy sting.

By the time I was old enough for him to discuss such problems with me, he had reached a harbourage of acceptance. I do not think that he believed in the actual survival of personality after death, but he thought it possible. In the meantime he drew comfort and consolation from the observances of the faith.

Myself I had no such period of doubts, because I had no faith to lose. I am surprised at this because I do not think I am without a religious sense. I am a regular communicant, and I do not feel that I am a hypocrite in presenting myself at the altar; any more than I feel myself a hypocrite when I attend the ceremonies in a Masonic temple. It is necessary for us to meditate on death. The man who is not at all times subconsciously conscious and at times actively aware of the fact that he will one day die, that he is a man condemned to death with an indefinite reprieve, walks through life blindfolded. He loses the full dignity of manhood. 'Not to discriminate every moment some tragic dividing of forces on their way, is on this short day of frost and sun to sleep before evening'; and not to be aware of death robs us of that so needed amulet against disappointment and disaster—the knowledge that there is a limit set; that all things seen under the light of eternity are ultimately trivial. Anyone who reads in *War and Peace* the account of Peter's initiation into Masonry, will recognize that the object of Masonry is a preparation for death. Is it not possible to view in the same light the communion service of the established church? Are we wise to seek precise definitions? Are we not wiser to veil and interpret the mysteries of life and death in allegory and symbol.

I have sometimes wondered why I should never have had any faith in the religious instruction of my youth, whereas my brother, with the same upbringing, should have been deeply religious from the start. I have asked myself whether it was because I was, I will not say more susceptible to the literary atmosphere in which I was brought up, but readier to identify myself with the heroes of whom I read. I have suggested that through French literature I acquired a Latin rather than an Anglo-Saxon attitude to sex; in the same way Classical mythology and history may have combined with Shakespeare to give me a pagan attitude towards religion. Shakespeare it will be contended was a Christian, but his earlier influences were Classical. His similes are drawn from Greek and Latin authors. How old was he when he first read the Bible? What Bible did he read? His ideals are Roman. His heroes fall upon their swords rather than that the windows of great Rome should witness their abasement. Hamlet may regret that the Almighty has

45

'set his canon against self-slaughter', but he has no conventional piety; he has no clear conviction as to what awaits him beyond the grave. Even Hamlet's cast of mind is pagan, and I, absorbing Shakespeare, saw the drama of life through his eyes. The 'noble words' that rang through my brain and lit my thoughts found kinship with the High Gods on Olympus; the thunderbolts thrown into the plain, the fates weaving their threads; *si qua fata aspera rumpas*; 'the white implacable Aphrodite'. Seeing life in those terms, I saw it on a level of high courage.

§

As I said, I had happy holidays, yet I was never sorry to go back to school. My real life was there. My ambitions were centred there. My ambition was not yet focused; I did not know what exactly I was to make of my life, but I was confident that I was to make something. It was through what I did at school that I should achieve that something. Home was the harbour where I rested; replenished my stores, and was careened. One needed a harbour every now and then but I was soon impatient for the hazards of the high seas.

The drama and fascination of those days was heightened by their setting. I have seen no place more beautiful than Sherborne. If an American visitor were to ask me where he could best get a sense of the history and charm of southern England, I should say, 'Go to Sherborne.' Its school was originally attached to a monastery that was put down during Henry VIII's reign. Edward VI established the present foundation. The School House studies were once the Abbot's quarters. The library was once his guesten hall; the cloisters that support the chapel were built in the fourteenth century. The School House dining-hall, once the Big schoolroom, was built in Charles II's reign. But it is not its antiquity alone that gives Sherborne its special magic. Many schools contain old buildings. Nor is it even the golden warmth of the stone in which it has been built. It is the happy grouping of the buildings that makes the town unique, so that the Abbey, with a lawn running up to it, flanks the quadrangle in which the classrooms, the big schoolroom, the chapel, the School House dormitories are set. The proportions are perfect. The atmosphere is of a welded whole. It looks as though one man had planned it. The view you get as you stand in the north-west corner of the courts and look towards the low two-storied School House studies and see the square, squat Abbey tower framed above their roof, has no equal.

Sherborne lies in a valley, with the wooded slopes rising to the south. If you drive through it, on the main Exeter road, you will pass above it and be unaware of its nature. But if you go through by train you will see the Abbey and the playing fields and you will recognize its charm.

It is not only the actual school buildings and the Abbey that are beautiful. The town itself is charming. It is a market-town, with a main shopping street running from the railway line to the hill, with side streets that are flanked by Georgian houses; many of which possess sheltered brick-walled gardens. During my schooldays I had not the opportunity of visiting many of these gardens, since they belonged to housemasters. It was only when I came down as a parent to see my sons, and was invited to their masters' houses, that I realized how many delightful corners Sherborne owned.

I had the luck to be in the School House. I lived therefore under the constant influence of the Abbey. After my first term I left the day-room and was promoted to the studies. I absorbed the beauty of Sherborne through my pores.

How many pictures crowd my memory when I close my eyes. November rains dashing across the courts, when one ran for the shelter of the cloisters; bland autumn mornings with the beeches browning on the slopes and a bite in the air that made one impatient for the football field; lazy summer afternoons, lying on a rug watching a cricket match, with a bag of cherries at one's side; strolls down to the station between tea and first hall to buy an evening paper—there was no radio in those days— and read the latest cricket scores in the stop-press news; the race in winter, at the end of afternoon school, to get into the dining-room early and make a piece of toast at the large fire that burnt in the centre of the room, before a member of the sixth-form table came. Chapel on Sunday evenings was at a quarter to seven. The school was in its pews by twenty-five to. The long, free day had dragged a little. There was a sense of peace, waiting for the familiar prayers and hymns in the high dark chapel, with the lights gleaming on the memorial brasses. Then, shortly before the quarter to, one or two of the bloods would arrive, almost late. One of my chief memories of my first term was watching A. W. Carr stride down the aisle to take his seat in the choir, a bare minute before the service started. I watched him in blind hero-worship. Would I one day be important enough to arrive late for chapel?

I loved school life. I might well have seemed the very boy for whom the public school system was designed—gregarious, sociable, as keen on his work in form as on his prowess on the field, a boy for whom the fifteen hours of the day seemed too narrow a casket for all that it contained. It is strange that I of all people should have been in constant conflict with authority, that I should have left under a cloud, that within two years of leaving I should have been struck off the list of the Old Shirburnian Society for writing a novel of which an influential critic said that it was likely to prove 'the *Uncle Tom's Cabin* of the public school system'. Nowell Smith, when he wrote my first report, 'Could not have had a better first term,' can have had no prescience that six years later he would be writing, 'I take my leave of you, but I cannot help wishing you well, however you may contemn the thought.'

§

Why should it have turned out so unexpectedly? What ill-intentioned fairy at my christening poisoned the dish for me, or rather poisoned for authority the dish that I presented? Why should I have rebelled so fiercely against what I really loved?

In part it was a hatred of conformity, a resolve not to be turned out to pattern; a loathing of pomposity which has inspired me always to take the minority point of view, to argue the case of the minority. As a novelist one of my chief concerns is to show how an honourable person can behave dishonourably, through an inevitable process of effect and cause. The first false step taken, one thing leads to another. I have sided with those who are out of favour. I would have been one of the first Athenians to weary of hearing Aristides called 'the just'.

As a corollary to this instinct has been the impulse to expose

48

popular conceptions, and when I went to Sherborne the English public school was a popular conception. It was one of the 'two main pillars vaulted high' which supported the British Empire. Kipling was the uncrowned laureate of the Empire. To criticize Kipling was to impeach the crown, and 'the Brushwood Boy' was accepted as the ideal type which the perfect educational system was endeavouring to produce. I knew that the average public school boy was not in the least like 'the Brushwood Boy'.

The Brushwood Boy is a fine short story, but it is indicative of the causes for the anti-Kipling reaction during the late 'thirties, the 'forties and the early 'fifties. The balance is adjusted now. We can recognize that Kipling was a supreme short-story writer; we can also recognize that there was far more to the credit balance of the British Raj than it was possible for those of us to realize who were exasperated by the narrowness, the intolerance, the arrogance of the retired Indian Army officer and official. The things that Kipling stood for seemed the very things that were limiting our self-development. As a schoolboy I was in no position to react against his imperialism, but the ethics of *The Brushwood Boy* were the cause, in my opinion, of most of the misunderstandings that hampered the schoolboy of my day; 'the Brushwood Boy . . . whose training had set the Public School mask upon his face and had taught him how many were the "things no fellow can do". By virtue of the same training he kept his pores open and his mouth shut.'

I knew that the public school boy was not like that. I knew, for instance, that cribbing was the general practice in certain forms. I knew that it was not considered dishonourable to tell a lie to a master. I suspected that the public schools code of Honour was a unilateral deal invented by masters for the benefit of masters. A master had no right to demand that the boys who had broken out of the boot-hole window and gone to Pack Monday fair should 'own up'. It was up to the housemaster to catch them when they were half-way through the window. Most of all I resented the conspiracy of silence that existed towards the inevitable consequences of herding together monastically children of thirteen and men of eighteen, for two-thirds of the year.

The situation is very different now, and my generation is responsible for the fact that it is different. When I went to Sherborne, 'bated breath' is the only cliché with which the official attitude towards that subject can be described. Every now and again there would be a scandal and a familiar face would be missing in the chapel-pews; and perhaps in the following Sunday-evening sermon there would be a veiled reference to the occurrence. But there was no medical approach to the problem.

I should, I think, make in this respect an exception in the case of the Chief. In the autumn of 1913, in a new house, there was a scandal that involved a considerable number of boys. On the next Sunday the Chief announced that there would be no sermon in the conventional sense, that ladies and visitors would leave the chapel after the second hymn, but that the masters, the school and the preparatory school would remain. He then himself delivered an address on the subject. In the course of it, he said, 'I do not want you to think that I am speaking of your temptations from a theoretical appreciation of them. When I was quite young, I was myself corrupted by a very bad man.' That speech required courage of the highest order.

§

A boy at the age of fifteen is emotionally and physically ready to fall in love. At a public school he is for eight months of the year cut off from feminine society, so he falls in love with the nearest approach to the feminine ideal.

A younger boy can be prettily good-looking in a girlish way. He is—at least he was at Sherborne in my day—differently dressed, wearing an Eton collar instead of the usual double collar worn inside the coat which you could not wear till you were five foot four in height. He is weak and stands in need of protection. He has the glamour of strangeness, since he moves in a different world; lower in form, playing in a different league, with different friends; sometimes in a different house. The majority of schoolboys experience such emotions, though it is a minority who are the objects of them. I never was myself.

These friendships colour the life of a public school boy in the same way that love colours life for the adult male; and indeed

Arthur Waugh at Underhill, 1910

The Sherborne courts

it is love; a particular type of love; an idealistic, un-self-seeking, Platonic love; a love that is based on service and devotion, that has a kinship with the love practised by the troubadours in the medieval courts of love. The very nature of the emotion precludes all possibility of personal satisfaction. Such satisfaction, such gratification would be a desecration of one's own high feelings. Such malpractices as one might enjoy were on a different level of emotion. A visit to a brothel would not, in ancient Spain, contaminate the pure fount of adoration that a hidalgo cherished for the damsel he hoped to marry. It was in such terms at that time at Sherborne that we saw ourselves. We would not 'sully the sad splendour that we wore'. Usually we expected as little from these emotions as the Arthurian knights who wore their ladies' tokens in their helmets. Nothing was expected from these high fervours. There was an exchange of notes, through an intermediary, which gave the whole intrigue a conspiratorial aura; there would be an exchange of glances. Occasionally there would be walks on Sunday afternoons, or rather, there would be meetings on walks on Sunday afternoons. Eastwards out of Sherborne run two parallel roads that gradually approach each other a mile out of town; a sunken road joins them. It was the practice for two senior boys to walk out by the lower road, two junior boys by the upper road. They met in the sunken road and each couple retired behind a different hedge. Little could have been more innocent than these rendezvous. We sat and talked, but that at that age was happiness. For the younger boy it was no doubt high boredom. But I never take the train through Sherborne without looking northwards at those converging roads, that sunken lane and the hedge running from east to west.

In my whole fours years at Sherborne, I only took three such walks. Others were less fortunate. The official attitude against such friendships was very strong; and there were those who did not wish to expose themselves to the risk of official censure. A fellow-prefect in the School House was attracted to a boy in another house. He felt that the difficulties of seeing him were insuperable, but he acquired from other boys in the boy's class an exact timetable of his curriculum. He knew where he would be at any given moment of the day. He knew for instance, that he would at 11.45 on every Tuesday be crossing the courts between the lower fourth French set and the remove mathematics set. He would place himself so that he could watch the crossing. Each day had for my fellow-prefect its own adventure.

The official attitude towards these friendships varied with each housemaster. Some took them more seriously than others; but without exception every housemaster when he became aware of such a friendship, put a stop to it, his expressed view being that he could not run the risk of such a friendship developing into immorality. This attitude most of us resented strongly since we were in a romantic idealist mood. In a case where love was involved, immorality was impossible. We wanted to be of service to the object of our affections. Authority also argued that it was bad for a young boy to have friends older than himself; particularly if this led to favouritism. It would make the boy unpopular with his contemporaries. He would have a lonely time when his protector left. On this point authority was on surer ground. There *was* that danger; but we felt that by being on our guard against it we could circumvent it. We could not believe that there could be anything 'wrong' in an emotion that we knew was more spiritual than physical; that raised us to a heightened sense of living. We felt that, through the conspiracy of silence that veiled the realities of school life, authority had got the situation wrong.

On Sunday evenings in chapel, I used to listen with irritation while sermon after sermon presented and adulated the public school code of honour in terms of 'the Brushwood Boy'. 'We aren't like that,' I thought. 'One day I'll show them what we are really like.' I was never against Sherborne, but the popular conception of Sherborne.

§

My spirit of rebelliousness was also fanned by an intense partisanship for my house. The School House with seventy to eighty boys in it was twice as large as any other. It was a world of its own. For the cricket and sports cups, we divided ourselves into two parts, A–K and L–Z. But in football we played as a house, taking on the two best of the outhouses in junior matches and three in the senior football. We only played in the finals when the outhouses had fought out between themselves which ones should have the right to challenge us. The Three Cock, the School House against the three best outhouses, was the final match of the year. A special card was printed for it. During the Easter term, when the shouts of 'house' and 'school' rang down the touchline, it was not hard to feel that there was more than ordinary rivalry between the two. The oldest buildings of the school were ours, the editor of the *Shirburnian* was always a School House boy. It was easy for us to think of ourselves as the aristocrats of the school and the outhouses as the commoners.

This feeling of superiority was exacerbated during my first terms there by the fact that School House athletics touched a low level during my second year. This often happens to a house or school when a predominant athlete leaves. For two years A. W. Carr had carried the house, as he had carried the school on his shoulders. In the autumn of 1911, there were thirteen challenge cups on the mantelpiece in the School House dining-hall under the statue of Edward VI. By the summer of 1913, we had lost every one. It was at this point that a number of School House old boys presented a loving-cup so that never again should His Majesty suffer such an indignity.

Most of the cups had gone to the house run by G. M. Carey, an old Shirburnian, an Oxford and England captain, whom I christened 'the Bull' in *The Loom of Youth*. Most schools at that period had an equivalent for the Bull—the old boy who returns to his old school wearing the laurels of distinction, who devotes his whole life to the service of his school; who identifies himself so completely with the traditions of the school that he regards anyone who disagrees with him as being disloyal not to him but to the school itself. 'The Bull' was a fine man; but he was fierce and difficult; mellowed by a tactful and most charming wife who was the housemaster's wife in Warren Chetham-Strode's play *The Guinea Pig*. Chetham-Strode, though older than myself, was a contemporary of mine and we played in the colts together.

Between the autumn of 1911 and the summer of 1913 Carey's enjoyed an incredible run of success. During this period they lost only one house match, the junior cricket in 1913. The success of Carey's naturally aroused the envy and hostility of the house. There was a resolve not only to get those cups back upon the mantelshelf but to do Carey's down. The attitude of the fifteen-year-olds like myself was, I regret to confess it, not unlike that of the Nazis. Smarting under defeat, we were resolved to recover our lost prestige by dragooning the less athletic-minded into conformity. It is a part of my life that I look back on with no pride at all; but it is as well that we should not forget that we have, many of us, the seeds of Nazism within us. Might we not have been tempted, had we been Germans, to become Nazis during the slump of 1930? Was it not the same instinct that made some of us, during the autumn of 1913, threateningly interrogate those who had not represented the house in any game? What good were they doing here? we asked. What contribution were they making to the house's fortunes? If they couldn't play cricket or football, couldn't they train for something in the sports, putting the weight, for instance? Mercifully this period did not last long; firstly because most of us in growing older started to make sense, secondly because cups soon reappeared under the statue of Edward VI, and the house could resume its attitude of superiority without aggression.

This period, though, had its consequences for me; I was in constant contact with 'the Bull' on the cricket and football fields. I saw more of him than any single master; and a criticism of his methods came as an inevitable corollary to my crusade. Nothing could have been more silly and illogical. For the misunderstandings that there were between us, I have only myself to blame. He stood for all the things that I admired. He could have been the friend I needed on the staff; instead I made an adversary of him.

V

My Last Year at Sherborne

When Sherborne broke up on the last Tuesday of July 1914, I was just sixteen. I was buoyant with high spirits and self-confidence. As a cricketer I had earned a place in the first XI, finishing second in the batting averages. As a footballer I had won my house cap during the Easter term and stood a good chance of getting my 'firsts' that autumn. I was in the sixth and hoped to be made a house prefect in September. I had definitely found my feet, and for the public school boy who had done that, the future in the days of imperial Britain was wide with possibilities.

There were no clouds on my horizon during those long July evenings, and when the Chief in his farewell speech spoke of the bad news in the morning papers, I thought he was referring to the threat of civil war in Ireland. For myself the papers during that last week had been mainly exciting because of Middlesex's progress in the County championship. On the Saturday my father was taking me to the Rectory Field at Blackheath to see Kent play Surrey; they were the two leaders, with Middlesex lying third to them, and the match was crucial. I had been looking forward to it eagerly, but when that Saturday came it was hard to believe that I had ever worried about a County championship. With war inevitable there was everywhere a taut, nervous expectation.

Most young people hoped for war. There was none of the reluctant but resolved acceptance of an unwelcome fate with which twenty-five years later the country listened to Chamberlain's final broadcast. There was on the contrary the spirit of crusade that was to find expression a few months later in Rupert

Brooke's 'Now God be thanked who has matched us with his hour.'

After lunch we were joined by the *Daily Telegraph* cricket reporter Major Philip Trevor. He had published several books with Chapman & Hall and his son was an old Shirburnian. He was a short, red-faced, cheerful man, a good judge of the game and an even better judge of the part that personality played in it. He was one of the first sports writers to insist that a man's batting or bowling was an expression of his individuality. At this time he preferred to watch from the ring, because in the pavilion players would bother him with explanations of how the catch which they had appeared to miss had been out of reach and how they had played the ball to which they had been given out leg before. As a schoolboy I often sat beside him in the mound at Lord's. He maintained a constant flow of comment: 'Twopence to pay,' he would say as the ball sped wide of cover 'No, threepence,' he would correct himself as he remembered that mid-off could not throw.

To more than one player that afternoon was brought the orange envelope of a telegram. 'Calling up orders,' the major said. 'I know where I'm to go, what I'm to do. The machine will start to function over the week-end. I shan't need to report this match. By Monday there'll be no room in the paper for anything but war news.'

It had been a bright and sunny morning when we set out from Hampstead, but the sky clouded over in the late afternoon. It was raining when stumps were drawn with Surrey taking three points for a lead on the first innings; a result, in terms of championship percentage, disabling for both sides' prospects; precisely the result that I, as a Middlesex supporter, had prayed for a week earlier. Nothing seemed less important now.

For me, as for many thousand others, boyhood ended on that grey July evening. Day after day during my summer holidays, I received news of this and the other Shirburnian who had joined the army and would not be returning in September. I was only a month over sixteen and could not join up for at least a year. I was impatient at the delay. It infuriated me that a boy who had been my junior on the football field should be a commissioned officer while I was still a schoolboy; was I not his physical superior even if he was seventeen to my sixteen? Through those hot August days when the British troops fell back from Mons to the Maine, there was for me one absorbing question, the same question that was exasperating my contemporaries all over Europe—'How soon could I get to France?'

§

It was very strange going back to Sherborne in September 1914. The school was a different place. There was scarcely a boy over eighteen left; and not so very many of over seventeen and a half. Most of those who were, were waiting for their commissions to come through.

It was an altogether different atmosphere from that of 1939. In 1914 the voluntary system was in operation. The hoardings were covered with recruiting posters. Kitchener's face stared out at you, with pointing finger, 'Your King and country need *you*.' It was dramatic to join the colours; sneers were delivered to the hangers back. Women gave white feathers to men not in uniform. Public school boys, from the nature of their training, were the first to go. The government had made few plans to cope with the rush to the recruiting stations. New battalions were formed hastily and officers with no military training were commissioned from the local gentry. The impatient ones enlisted in the ranks and put in their papers for commissions. Gentlemen cadets at Sandhurst had their training curtailed and headmasters were invited to recommend cadets who could go straight to the R.M.C. Three-quarters of my senior friends had left. I found myself fourth prefect in the house and captain of house football. On the first evening in hall, sitting at the high table, under the statue, in the wide armchair which was reserved for the captain of the house, I looked down at the day-room table, remembering how three years back I had sat there on my first night, looking up at A. W. Carr, wondering if I should ever be sitting in his chair. Was some new boy looking up at the high table now, with the same thoughts? Yet even as I thought that, I realized how dissimilar the situations were. How puny I must seem in comparison with Arthur Carr. I was only here because better men were at the front. I was here by proxy.

That night after supper the Chief summoned the new prefects to his study. There were four of us. 'In the same way that Kitchener has called up his reserves, I have called up you. I do not suppose that in the ordinary course of events any of you would have been prefects, but in the same way that, in the army, captains have become colonels overnight, so have you been raised to a position of authority. I know that you will prove worthy of it.'

It was a warm September night. The sky was cloudless. The Great Bear wheeled high over the school gate. I walked slowly across the courts and stood in the gateway to the cloisters. I looked back towards the studies. The curtains over the games study windows were glowing softly. Thirty years ago it had been my father's study. His name was cut on the large window table. Three years ago as a new boy I had wondered if it would ever be mine. It was my study now. How quickly it had all come about.

§

It had come about too quickly. A year too soon. I was not ready for it. I could not feel that I had really earned it. I was in someone else's shoes. Nothing seemed quite real.

I fancy that that feeling of unreality pervaded a good deal of English life during the autumn of 1914. No one could guess how long the war would last, no one could guess at the kind of war that it would be. We had not got adjusted to war as a permanent and stable background. It was extremely difficult for a schoolboy to continue his studies in the same spirit that he had six months earlier. He could not tell whether he would continue his education to its end. Would he ever go to a university? Would he indeed be alive after the war? There seemed a basic pointlessness about everything that we were doing. I felt that we were marking time.

In another respect too, authority had come to me too soon. I had needed another year of discipline. I was still too close to the Nazi mentality that a year earlier had made me interrogate the non-athletic members of the house. I was still aggressive and belligerent. I still had a feud with Carey's and as captain of the School House I had a nuisance value which I could not resist the temptation to exploit. The following episode will provide a typical example.

Before the war, the school O.T.C. had one parade a week and an occasional field day. After September 1914 we had two parades a week; we also had squad drill three days a week between morning school and lunch. We had very little spare time to ourselves. The forms below the sixth had during the week, as part of the school curriculum, an hour period each week at P.T. in the gymnasium. One or two serious-minded outhouse members of the sixth felt that they needed P.T., and suggested to 'the Bull' that he should give the sixth P.T. on the three mornings when they were not doing squad drill. 'The Bull' was willing and he asked the head of the School House whether the School House would be prepared to co-operate. The head was a school prefect and one of the two boys whom I saw during the holidays. We discussed the problem. None of the sixth wanted to do P.T. We had enough on our hands already, so we devised a scheme by which I, as captain of the house, should arrange to have boxing practice at that hour in the School House changing-room. The head could therefore tell 'the Bull' that the School House members of the sixth would be otherwise occupied at that point. I posted a notice on the board saying that there would be boxing practice in the changing-room between 12.30 and 1 on Mondays, Wednesdays, Fridays.

Later that day 'the Bull' sent for me. Would I use my influence to get the members of the sixth to attend these P.T. classes? If the School House did not co-operate, there would not be enough members available to complete a class. He had, he explained, gone to the head of the house instead of the captain of the house, because he had wanted it to be an exercise in terms of form not of games. He would be very grateful if I would help him. He could not have been more friendly. I would have given anything to say 'Yes', but I was not ready to lose face to that extent. I was sorry, I said, but I had arranged those boxing practices. We thought these practices more important than P.T. in view of the house boxing competitions at the end of the term.

'The Bull' was furious. He drove his fingers through the back of his hair, as he always did when he was roused. 'I only

want to do a keen thing for Sherborne, and you won't help me.'
The P.T. project was abandoned.

That was typical of the kind of incident in which I found my-self involved. Another example of my rebelliousness. After I had been given my first–XI colours, I went out to field in a school match wearing my house cap, to show that I was prouder of being in the School House than in the first XI. I was told by 'the Bull' to take it off. So I went out to field after lunch bare-headed.

Another year's apprenticeship and I should have made better sense. The friends whom I have made in recent years may read this section with surprise. They regard me, I imagine, as an amenable and accommodating person. But I fancy that at root I am the same person now as then. I rarely do anything that I do not want to do, but I have learnt how to get my way without putting other people's backs up. I have learnt that if you want to get your way in this world, it is as well to let other people have their innings too. Co-existence, in fact.

Authority had come to me too soon, but that does not mean I did not enjoy authority. I liked having fags; I liked sitting in the big chair below the statue; I liked initialling notices on the house board; I enjoyed holding the destinies of others in my hand, being the one who gave house colours to others. It is agreeable to be the most important person, even in a small community. And apart from that, there are many privileges attached to prefectship in a public school.

I was in the history sixth. I was allowed to do my reading in my study. I had a fire-place in my study; and the masters who were giving tuition to the specialists of the literature and history sixths used to take their classes there. How good it was on a late November afternoon, after a hard game of football to come back to that study in which a fag had set the fire ablaze, to wait till the other specialists from the outhouses came across. We would read our essays aloud to our special tutor and he would discuss them with us. I should be physically exhausted after football but mentally alert. The Abbey clock would chime the hour. Five o'clock; the master would have another class. The other two specialists—one of them was A. Cortesi, the *New York Times* correspondent in Rome—would leave and I would be left alone. An hour in which to read history or poetry, as I chose.

In the sixth we worked as we thought fit. We had served an apprenticeship. It was now up to us. If we wanted to get a scholarship, we knew the way to set about it. If we preferred to be idle, it was our own look out.

In those days it was easy to get into Oxford, provided your father could afford the fees. I had taken the school certificate and had therefore no need to worry on that score. Oxford seemed a long way off; between it and Sherborne lay the Flanders fields. Would I not be wiser to make the most of these fleeting moments that were spared me, and enrich them with poetry rather than with Lodge's *Modern Europe*?

I saturated myself with poetry through those months. I was also pouring it out indefatigably. Every prose writer begins by writing poetry. George Moore said that there was something wrong with the novelist who did not produce one volume of verse. In addition to that, the love of poetry is a particularly English thing. It is the last thing that you would expect of this staid, formal, seemingly conforming race. A. G. Macdonell, a Scot, made great play of this in *England, Their England*. Every Englishman is a secret poet, that was his ultimate conclusion. Every man has a locked drawer in his desk. In a Frenchman's locked desk, there would be love letters, or braided locks; in an Englishman's there are unpublished poems. The Englishman is at heart incorrigibly romantic. There is a constant battle in his heart between the Cavalier and Roundhead; on the one hand there are the prim precisians of Whitehall, but on the other there are the sailors who put their telescope to their blind eye; and both are typical Englishmen. When I have lectured to foreign audiences, I have always stressed this point. When you see the Englishman with his stiff collar, his rolled umbrella and his bowler hat, never forget that locked drawer in his desk and his unpublished sonnets. During those winter evenings, looking out on the cloisters, I covered 'reams in the shade', just as my father had done, thirty years before.

§

'You will be making here,' so I was told from the pulpit on my first Sunday at Sherborne, 'friendships that will last you all your life.' I did; but far more important than those half-dozen or so friendships was the discovery that friendship is a fair-weather business. On three separate occasions my friends deserted me, for reasons of self-interest.

The first occurred when I was fifteen and a half. A prefect in the School House and I had both contracted one of the romantic friendships of which I wrote in a previous chapter for a boy in another house. The prefect in a mood of jealousy decided upon revenge. He persuaded the head prefect that I was a bad moral influence in the house and that I deserved a prefects' beating. I was summoned before them and lectured on my behaviour. I was then asked if I would take what they had to give me or appeal to the Chief. I very naturally put myself in their hands. I received two strokes from each of the six prefects. Two of them were close friends of mine, but they did not intervene on my behalf.

The second episode came in the following term. It might surprise anyone meeting me for the first time today, a short stocky man, grey-haired, balding and mild-mannered, to learn that I was on the Rugby field an extremely fierce forward whose vigour earned him at Sandhurst the nickname of 'the Tank'. At Sherborne I was perhaps too fierce; but that was in the tradition of Sherborne football. And I had been picked out for special praise in a match for the colts, against Clifton, when I was myself guiltily conscious of having crossed the dividing line between rough and foul play.

My trouble came in the final of a house match in which I played the game of my life and was presented with my house cap afterwards. It was a match in which no try was scored, fought out on a muddy field, with the play on both sides very fierce. I was leading the School House scrum. It was my voice that exhorted the players to fiercer efforts, and to some of the masters on the touchline I seemed the embodiment of the spirit of rough play. They felt that a public example must be made; they invited the games committee to deal with me. I received two strokes from each of the seven members of the committee. Two of them were School House prefects. They had both congratulated me after the match and had told the captain of the house, who was sick in the sanitorium, that I deserved my house colours. Neither of them intervened in my defence.

The third occasion occurred in my last term. Fifty years ago, as I have already said, a conspiracy of silence shrouded the main moral of school life. Today the danger is recognized with frankness; and I wonder how many ex-public school boys would deny that at some point in their schooldays they indulged in homosexual practices; practices that had no lasting effect, that they instantly abandoned on finding themselves in an adult, heterosexual world. I was not the immaculate exception, and I had the bad luck to be found out. A scandal started, a number of names were involved, and a chapter that had been long closed was opened.

Expulsion from a public school was highly dramatized in the school story of my day. It was referred to in hushed tones in sermons. It was held as a perpetual threat over our heads. The boy who was expelled was ruined for life. Fathers said, 'If this disgrace befell a son of mine, I should give him fifty pounds and a ticket to the colonies and that is the last that he would hear from me till he had redeemed himself.'

For a few hours in that hot June of 1915, the danger of this fate hung over me. I learnt during break at eleven o'clock that the scandal had broken. A fag brought a message over that 'the Bull' wished to see me in his study after lunch. The particular boy involved was in his house. During those three hours of suspense I was acutely concious of dramatic irony. Here was the life of the school continuing unchanged about me. Everything looked the same; I looked the same, indistinguishable from the others who were crossing from one classroom to another, lunching in hall, changing into corps clothes. Yet how different my own position was. A murderer must have the same feeling, when he reads in an evening paper of the crime which in a few hours will be attributed to him. He looks round the familiar pub. This is how it was yesterday, this is how it will be tomorrow, with these same people at the bar discussing his arrest.

I had an overriding sense of being apart from the whole issue, of looking down on it, as though it were happening to someone else, very much the same feeling that I have had when some unexpected good fortune, the sale of a serial or a film, has altered the immediate structure of my life. As I walked across to 'the Bull's' study to that fateful interview, I could not believe that this was happening to me.

I need not really have had such qualms. Not only had the particular chapter been long closed, but it was not a very lurid one. My prominence in the school, however, gave it notoriety, and the Chief suggested to my father that I should leave at the end of the term.

I was far from popular with a certain section of the staff, and some of the masters felt that I should have been expelled. What particularly irritated them was, I subsequently learnt, my behaviour afterwards. I should, they felt, have gone about in sackcloth and ashes, but the tide of my fortune was running high. I had just won the English verse prize and on the cricket field I was heading the batting averages. Three days after the scandal broke, against an M.C.C. side that contained the two Essex professionals Mead and Reeves, I hit up a score of 96 in under an hour. I could not help feeling pleased with myself, particularly as I was glad to be leaving at the end of term. For six months I had been badgering my father to let me join the army as soon as I was seventeen. My behaviour not surprisingly exasperated certain masters whom I had already antagonized by my general air of rebellious arrogance. They felt that it was time that I was taught a lesson.

The lesson took the shape of a boycott. Two of the disapproving members of the staff were housemasters and they instructed their house prefects to prevent any members of their houses being seen in my company except during the fulfilment of school duties. The idea spread to other houses and I was eventually presented with a manifesto beginning, 'You who are a member of the VI, XI and XV have shown yourself indifferent to the moral standards of the school . . .' and ending, 'We do not any longer wish your company among us.' The letter was offered for signature to every member of the Sixth, XI and XV; I do not suppose that any of them had imagined my private morals to be ranged on an austere level. They guessed me to be indifferent honest. But there were only three abstentions on the list.

The term had still seven weeks to run, and it might be imagined that they would be seven of the worst weeks of my life. They were not, however. The XI, having signed the document, proceeded to ignore it. You cannot very well put in Coventry a man with whom you are playing cricket, particularly if you like him. The three abstentions were in the School House so I had company in the studies. Mentally what I then needed most was the stimulus of an adult mind; there was S. P. B. Mais, there was also the sixth-form tutor, a brilliant scholar, just down from Cambridge, whose study was lined with glass-covered shelves of books bound in morocco, vellum, calf. I spent many hours there, taking first one book down from his shelves and then another. Many Shirburnians and many Cambridge scholars cherish warm memories of Geoffrey Morris. No one does more than I.

I was not lonely during those seven weeks. I did not feel myself an outcast. And I fancy that my vanity was flattered by my being the centre of attention. Criminals are supposed to enjoy the notoriety that attends their trials. Certainly I was amused by the predicament in which on two occasions my isolated status placed my adversaries. As I have said, I had won the English verse prize and I should normally, with the other winners of school open prizes, have received it at the hands of the Chief at the final prizegiving, but authority considered that I should not be the object of public acclaim. That part of the ceremony had therefore to be cancelled; and the winners of the English essay, the Greek and Latin prose and verse were not able to walk up to the dais to accept what Compton Mackenzie has called 'a calf-bound memento of their industry'.

A similar situation was created by my finishing at the top of the school batting averages. If the batting cup could not be presented in public, nor could the bowling belt, the fielding trophy, and the various track events that had been won in the spring sports. Again the ceremony was cancelled. The signatories of the manifesto were thus deprived of public honour. I thought that funny.

At the age of sixty-three, looking back towards one's boyhood and one's childhood, one asks oneself, how one has become the person that one is. In a period of psychotherapy we wonder what scars have been left on our subconscious nature by incidents that at the time seemed trivial. Were I to learn that an acquaintance had been exposed to an experience such as I have described, I might well exclaim, 'Ah, that explains it. Now I understand why that man is so suspicious, so on his guard, so unforthcoming; yet on occasions he is so importunate in his demands upon a friend, over-demonstrative, jealous and possessive, resolved to bind to himself with bonds of steel the one person who he feels will not let him down.' To have ninety-five per cent of one's friends dismiss one from their company might be regarded as a shock. It has had no such effect on me. I could appreciate their point of view. It was a question of the practical ordering of their lives. A boy, particularly one in another house, would have put himself in an uncomfortable position by refusing to sign. Why should he do that on my account? Would I have in his place? In one, two, in three cases possibly; but not more; not for a mere friend. Those of us who have axes to grind—and most of us have—are not grateful to those who hinder our grinding of them. This was a very useful lesson to have learnt at seventeen.

I have had right through my adult life three recurrent dreams and I dream every night. The one concerning N.G.B. I have described already, the second is staged during my last term at school when I am involved in a scandal and threatened with expulsion. In the third, I am in battle, about to be taken prisoner. Nothing that has happened to me since the age of twenty has provided me with material for a recurrent dream. I must suppose therefore that these three experiences left scars of some kind, but I cannot see that they have had a crippling or limiting effect. On the contrary the first two experiences have made my life a good deal easier to live.

Fernden was so tough, that everything since it has seemed tame. Sherborne, by teaching me not to demand too much of friendship, had enabled me to relish congenial company. I am grateful to my *Almae Matres*.

§

A boy's last week at school, particularly his last Sunday chapel, has been the subject of innumerable essays. For four, five years he has listened to that good-bye hymn: he has looked across the aisle at those who are about to leave, wondering how they are feeling, wondering if one of them will cry. Now it is his turn.

> May thy father hand be shielding
> Those who here shall meet no more.
> May their seedtime past be yielding
> Year by year a richer store.

And on the following evening at the concert, he will join in the choir's singing of the *Valete*:

> We shall watch you here in our peaceful cloister,
> Faring onward, some to renown, to fortune,
> Some to failure—none, if your hearts are loyal,
> None to dishonour.

They are sentimental moments, but they are exciting too. One is standing on the brink of adult life. One dramatizes the future; picturing how the 'peaceful cloister' will be roused by one's feats in the big world; foreseeing the moment when a form-master will say, 'Ah, yes, I remember him, an inky-fingered little boy, always blotting his exercises; now he has been knighted; well, well, well.' That feeling was heightened by the war. Within twelve months we would be in the trenches. It was not a question of the 'peaceful cloister' waiting thirty years to acclaim a public honour. The very boys who sat around us now might be granted a half-holiday in honour of our gallantry or they might read our name in the Roll of Honour.

The hero of a school story invariably rounds off his career with a spectacular performance on the cricket field. This boon was granted me. On the last Saturday of term School House L.Z was playing Carey's, as always our chief rival, in the final of the Senior House cup. At no point during the series had we felt that we had a chance of winning. We were an unbalanced side with only two first-XI colours and no bowling. We had been lucky to scramble through the first two rounds. Our only hope was that in view of the bad weather there might not be time to finish the match before the end of term; in consequence the School House would have the cup for half the year.

The first day's play was on a Wednesday. We won the toss.

I failed, so did the captain—the only other colour—but to our surprise the tail by rustic methods hit up their fives and sevens, while a stylish player, who for three years had shown grace at the nets but never reached double figures in the middle, batted through the innings. Our total reached 125. It was more than we expected, but it was not enough. To our delighted astonishment, however, our enemies collapsed; the pitch was very slow; the light was very bad and a number of good batsmen played too soon; balls were skied and fieldsmen pounced on them. They were all out by half-past six and we had a lead of 43.

But even so, we had no hopes of winning. Carey's would not collapse again. We were lucky to have made so many runs. How often does not the weaker side lead on the first innings; the balance is adjusted in the second. That was on Wednesday night. It rained all Thursday. The term ended on Tuesday. If the rain continued the match could not be finished. On Friday it was raining still; and the corps parade was cancelled. Our hopes ran high. But though on the Saturday the sky was grey, the rain had stopped. Even so, it may begin again, I thought, as I went out to bat that afternoon.

I went in second wicket down. The captain was already out. 10 for 2. Carey's were jubilant. For the last month I had been out of form. I was barely expected to reach double figures. But therein lies the mystery of cricket. You never know when you will run into form. On a morning when your head is clear, and you are bouyant with good health, you convert half volleys into yorkers. But on the day after a heavy alcoholic night, when your head is splitting, you see the ball like a balloon. That happened to me then. I felt the first ball right on to the centre of the bat, and my soul exulted. The second ball was straight but short and it soared over square leg's head. Every nerve quivered and relaxed. I'm here to stay, I thought.

The wicket was dead, the outfield sodden, but I was the kind of batsman who could make use of such conditions. A player who strokes the ball along the carpet would have been hopelessly bogged down, but I had strong wrists. My motto was, 'Hard and high and often.' Within an hour I had hit up 77. How often have I not in memory relived that hour: at the other end the usually ineffective stylist kept up his end for forty minutes.

Then once again the rustics contributed their fours and sevens. We totalled 171. Not an immense total; a small one indeed on a dry, fast ground; but on such a wicket, in a grey poor light, and with a lead of 43, with our spirits up and their spirits down, it was a foregone conclusion. It was all over by six o'clock, and a fag was bicycling to the post office to send my father my last Sherborne telegram.

PART 2

The Loom of Youth

I

Inns of Court O.T.C.

When I left Sherborne at seventeen, the age limit for officers in Kitchener's army was eighteen and a half, but the Territorial Army and the Special Reserve still retained their pre-war age limit of seventeen.

In August 1914, ex-public school men had been granted commissions without previous training and they and their men learnt soldiering together; the spirit of those days has been excellently described by Ian Hay in *The First Hundred Thousand*. But now a year later it had been decided that it was desirable that a newly joined officer should know more than a recruit. I had had a certain amount of training in the O.T.C., but it was of an elementary nature, and though the colonel of the 6th Dorsets was prepared to give me a commission, it was decided that I should spend a few months first in the Inns of Court O.T.C. The suggestion came from the Chief, who would as my ex-headmaster have had to sign my commission papers, and I suspect that his recommendation was partly a punishment for my irresponsibility during the previous year. It was a decision that was to have considerable consequences for me. Had I taken a commission straightaway, I should probably never have written *The Loom of Youth*. When should I have had the time? And certainly I should not have met W. W. Jacobs, whose eldest daughter Barbara I was to marry four years later.

I was enrolled in the Inns of Court in mid-September. I was given the number 6139. I have always since given that number to any of my heroes who saw service in the ranks. How surprised I should have been that September morning if I could have foreseen that forty-two years later, on the opening night of my film *Island in the Sun*, with Princess Margaret, to whom I had been presented, as the patron, I should hear Stephen Boyd announcing himself as Private No. 6139.

The pattern of training in the Inns of Court was as follows: First there was two weeks of preliminary training at the depot at Lincoln's Inn. The recruit was then sent to camp in Berkhamstead, for a further period of training with a company. This period lasted about two months. He was then posted to a month of concentrated training in an instruction class; his eight weeks in the company had not done much more than turn a civilian into a soldier; the instruction class trained him to be an officer. At the end of the instruction class he put in his papers for a commission. I expected to be gazetted early in 1916.

On the whole I liked army life. I enjoyed its comradeship and the sense of physical well-being that came from a life in the open air. But the weeks of company training at Berkhamsted were for me as dull as they were strenuous. In terms of instruction I was covering ground with which through the Sherborne O.T.C. I had been long familiar. There were night operations twice a week; there was a battalion field-day every week. There were company exercises. We marched miles; taking with us a haversack ration consisting of a damp slice of bread, a piece of stodgy cake and a wedge of tasteless cheese. The nature of each exercise was explained to us; and afterwards there was a lecture pointing out the lessons to be learnt from it, but we knew as little of what was happening as the average private soldier does in battle. We marched, then we deployed; we took cover, we advanced or retired, in short rushes, under covering fire.

Between the members of my sections there grew up the sense of comradeship that attends any group activity. It would be pleasant, I thought, to go to war as a private, without responsibility, with congenial companions. But I was bored by the monotonous routine of drills and musketry and the endless footslogging. I could not help comparing my present life with that which I had been leading ten, eighteen, thirty months ago. As I marched over Ashridge Park, I remembered that a year ago I had been bicycling down to the football field for a puntabout or an upper; as I listened to a lecture on the establishment of an infantry brigade, I pictured the sixth form sitting under Nowell

Smith to a discussion of the Romantic Revival; in the evenings on my way to night operations, passing Berkhamsted school and looking at the lighted windows, I would think, 'At Sherborne now they are sitting round the games study fire waiting for the bell to ring for hall.' Day by day, hour by hour, I pictured myself back at school. And I might still be there, I would tell myself... I had no one but myself to blame. . . .

There were, of course, compensations. After a first ten days' highly uncomfortable sojourn in a woodshed, on a hard floor without a mattress and a lack of blankets, I was placed in a billet in the town. I enjoyed the privacy of a room to myself, in which I could read and write at night. I had, moreover, friends in Berkhamsted. My cousin, Henry Cockburn, who had spent much of his life in the Far East and was known in the family as 'China Harry', had retired there because the two schools offered an opportunity for educating his son and daughter. He invited me to dinner every Wednesday evening. He was the father of Claud Cockburn and I first met that wild firebrand, who has been, lo these many years, one of my closer friends, as a bright-eyed, eager twelve-year-old.

W. W. Jacobs had also settled in Berkhamsted, because it offered easy educational opportunities for his five children. I do not know how much he is known to a generation of modern readers. I believe that *The Monkey's Paw* is an anthology short story. But it is not typical of his work. He wrote half a dozen macabre stories, but he wrote a century of comic stories about Thames-side characters and a country poacher called Bob Pretty. He was a master of the short story. In 1915 his reputation stood very high. He was one of the pillars of the *Strand*, in the days when the *Strand* was as important a magazine as *Punch*. He had a guaranteed contract at £350 a story; higher than any English writer except Kipling was receiving then. At Fernden during the winter evenings N.G.B.'s partner had read his stories aloud to us. In the holidays my heart had bounded when I had seen his name on the cover of the *Strand*. I was thrilled when I learnt he lived at Berkhamsted.

My second week-end there my father and mother came down to see me. As we were walking down the High Street after lunch, my father suddenly stopped. 'Hullo, Jacobs,' he called out. Under a straw hat was a small, weasel-shaped face with a long pointed nose. A pair of watery blue eyes inspected me. 'I can offer,' he said, 'my invariable hospitality—a hot bath.'

He invited us to tea. He had a large modern practical house, Beechcroft, half-way up a steep hill on the way to the school playing-fields, up which I had frequently marched on my way to exercises. I was excited at the prospect of meeting an author I had admired for so long. My memories of that afternoon are focused exclusively on him. I do not remember his wife or his children. Barbara was fourteen then. Was she there that day? She made no impression on me. My father and Jacobs had not met for several years. They had seen quite a little of each other once, through having had a close mutual friend. They discussed him that afternoon. He was a painter, of talent but improvidence, with a wife who wrote poetry of a delicate charm that had never caught the attention of the critics. They talked of the publishing situation, of how the war was affecting the sales of books. We talked of modern novelists; Jacobs did not think very highly of them, particularly of Gilbert Cannan, who had always been the bad boy in the Georgian nursery. I was surprised at the virulence with which Jacobs spoke against him.

'It's not surprising,' my father said, as we walked afterwards down the hill.

He told me something of Jacobs' background, of how his father had married a woman older than himself who had proved a termagant. He was resolved to profit by his father's mistake and do the exact opposite. In his late thirties he married a girl twenty years younger than himself, resolved to bend her to his will. For a year or two she had been a docile spouse, then, her mind lit by the advanced writing of the day, she became a Socialist and an eager champion of women's rights. As a suffragette she had broken the window of a post office at Charing Cross and served a four weeks' gaol sentence. Her rebelliousness had increased Jacobs's natural conservatism and intolerance. They had exaggerated certain extreme tendencies in each other. H. G. Wells had been a close neighbour, and Mrs. Jacobs was the heroine of his novel *The Wife of Sir Isaac Harman*. I looked forward to seeing more of her on my next visit.

§

Every other week-end I had thirty-six hours' leave. Berkhamsted was only fifty minutes away from London. My father would meet me at the barrier at Euston station and we would go to Tottenham Court Road to see a cinema. The days of the big feature had not yet come. D. W. Griffiths's *The Birth of a Nation* was the one exception; but Chaplin was breaking into popularity. That summer troops had been singing on the march

> His little baggy trousers will want mending
> Before we send him
> To the Dardanelles.

Most weeks there seemed a new two-reel. Chaplin was advertised in large lettering CHAS CHAP. We would be back at Underhill by six o'clock. How good it was after the hard seats of the Y.M.C.A hut to loll back in a comfortable chair before a fire, and how good to browse along the library shelves, taking down one favourite book after another; and how much more than good after dinner to listen not to a lecture on tactics but my father reading poetry.

I doubt if father and son could have been closer than we were during those months at Berkhamsted. We wrote to each other every day; it seemed to me perfectly natural that after supper on Sunday, a hard-worked man in his fiftieth year should come all the way down by tube from Golders Green to Euston station to have a few extra minutes in his son's company. I took it as a matter of course.

I never needed any company but his. A young man in his eighteenth year who would probably be in the trenches within ten months might well have been expected to spend a portion of his leaves in an atmosphere of night clubs and bright lights. I never did. I wanted to be alone with my father and talk of poetry, and of the writers he had known as a young man.

One Sunday W.W. invited my father to spend the day with him. He was there at the station to meet his guest; in the evening he accompanied him to his train; in the afternoon he took us for a drive in Ashridge Park. During a nine-hour visit I was not alone with my father for five minutes. I was indignant. Surely W.W. must have realized that we should want to be together. I did not realize then how exceptional our friendship was. On the Tuesday morning we each received letters opening with the sentence, 'As a visit to the Jacobs family, Sunday could not have been pleasanter, but as an opportunity of seeing one another it was a disappointment.'

My father's letters every morning were the chief event of my day at Berkhamsted. When I had been at Sherborne, he had written about my life there, mentioning only those incidents in his own life that were likely to be of interest to me; mutual friends at Hampstead: news of Evelyn; Chapman & Hall plans to publish a book of cricket reminiscences. But now there was no aspect of his day's routine in which I was uninterested. I wanted to know about *all* the books that he was publishing, the authors whom he had met, the books that had been sent him for review, the articles that he was planning. I took the same pride in his writing that a few months earlier he had taken in my cricket scores. And his was writing in which any son could have taken pride.

For several years, on the invitation of W. L. Courtney, he had done regular short unsigned reviews for the *Daily Telegraph*, which brought him in £50 to £60 a month. On the outbreak of war the proprietors of the *Daily Telegraph* not unnaturally instituted as many economies as they could. They removed outside contributors and my father had not been on the staff. The literary columns had of course to be continued, to attract advertisements, but the quality of the material that filled these columns was not considered to be important. Realizing that their golf correspondent would now be idle, the proprietors made him Courtney's second string, and after a year of curtailed contributions my father's connexion with the paper ended till the war was over.

A year earlier this would have been financially a shock to him, but he had no longer to meet school bills on my account, and with Evelyn still at a day-school where the fees were low, he welcomed the release from routine reviewing. Once again he could write upon subjects of his own choosing. He had also leisure in which to read the kinds of book he liked.

On the *Daily Telegraph* he had been confined to novels and biographies, with Courtney choosing the best books for himself. Without realizing that he was doing so, my father had lost touch with modern trends. On account of his asthma he had gone out in the evenings less and less. On Gosse's advice he had joined the Savile. But the Savile, then on the site of the present Park Lane Hotel, was twenty minutes away from Henrietta Street, and he lunched instead at Gatti's—usually with Gerard Meynell.

It was a pity he did not join the Garrick where he had many friends and would have enjoyed the talk about the theatre. For ten years my father had seen few writers, apart from those who were published by Chapman & Hall, and Chapman & Hall was not *avant-garde*. He had, for instance, not heard of Georgian poetry till he received from the *Daily Chronicle* in November 1915 a copy of the second volume for review. Gosse coming out to lunch on the following Sunday was astonished to be asked who E. M. was. 'But, my dear Arthur, surely you must have guessed, our dear Eddie Marsh. The Maecenas of the young, the final arbiter. Occasionally I dare to call to his attention the work of some poor protégé of mine, but he will shake his head. "Not good enough," he will squeak, "not good enough."'

That autumn and the following spring were a period of discovery for my father. After seven years' hibernation the literary scene made a new impact on him. He returned with fresh zest to the pleasure of writing. His essays on Lionel Johnson and Stephen Phillips were sent first to me before going to their editors. When I re-read them the other day, they seemed as fresh and vivid, as sound in their judgment and generous in their appreciation, as they had when I read them as a private in the Inns of Court.

August 24, 1916, was his fiftieth birthday. In that year he had articles in the *Fortnightly*, the *Nineteenth Century* and the *Quarterly*. In the spring he became the chief literary critic of the *Outlook* and contributed a signed two-thousand-word article a week on a book of his own choice. By Christmas 1918 he had written a sufficient number of articles to fill a volume that he called *Tradition and Change*. It received a very favourable press and Chapman & Hall made money on it.

§

Georgian Poetry 1913-15 was accompanied by a slim volume of poems, with a black and white Vorticist design on the cover. It was entitled *Catholic Anthology 1914-15*. It contained, in addition to poems by Ezra Pound, T. E. Hulme and Orrick Johns, *The Love Story of J. Alfred Prufrock*.

In *Enemies of Promise*, over twenty years later, Cyril Connolly was to write,

> I have often wondered what it must have felt like to discover those opening lines of Prufrock in *Blast* or the *Catholic Anthology* in 1914-15, with Rupert Brooke's poems, Kitchener's Army and 'Business as Usual' everywhere. Would we have recognized that new sane, melancholy, lighthearted and fastidious voice?
>
> Surely we would have noticed it, would have 'lingered in the chambers of the sea' and experienced that exquisite sensation, the apprehension of the first sure masterful flight of a great contemporary writer. But how few of us did.

I can answer that question for him as regards myself. I missed it altogether. So did my father. So did Edmund Gosse. I can remember Gosse that day after lunch, reading Flecker's 'The Dying Patriot' in his mellifluous voice . . .

> West of these out to seas colder than the Hebrides
> I must go
> Where the fleet of stars is anchored and the young
> Star captains glow . . .

but the slim volume with the Vorticist cover, which is now a landmark in the history of poetry, lay disregarded on the window seat.

§

I passed out of the instruction class early in January. My training was now complete, and I forwarded my papers for the colonel's signature. I returned to my company to wait for my gazettement to come through. I was at a loose end, traversing familiar ground. Now surely, I thought, was the time to begin the project I had long planned, of writing a novel which would show the public school system in its true colours. I should not have time to finish it, but I could make a start.

Before I was a third of the way through, however, I learnt that the War Office had raised the age limit for commissions in the Special Reserve and Territorial Army to eighteen and a half. What was going to happen to me now I could not guess, but it meant that I would have time to get my book finished if I hurried.

I wrote *The Loom of Youth* in seven and a half weeks, which included a week off half-way. I got up at half-past four in the morning and returned to my manuscript at night after the day's parades. I wrote five days a week. I posted it section by section to my father, who corrected the spelling and punctuation, interjected an occasional phrase and sent it to be typed. I never revised it. As the manuscript shows, it was printed as it was written, paragraph by paragraph. It is 115,000 words in length.

My mood was mixed. As I have already said, all that autumn I had kept comparing the present with the past, reliving term by term my years at Sherborne. I was homesick. The impulse that dictated me to write the book was in very large part a need to relive the past on paper—a need which, though I did not at the time recognize it as being that, is the writer's particular medicine, the capacity to cure an ailment by lancing the abscess with his pen and letting out the pus. It was in part a nostalgic book; yet at the same time my nostalgia was tinctured by resentment. I need not have been here at all. I could either be still at Sherborne, or I could have taken a commission straightaway, as so many others had, but for that scandal. I was partly to blame, but only partly. I was the victim of a system which encouraged the myth of *The Brushwood Boy* and created a conspiracy of silence to conceal the reality of the public school boy's life. The cult of athleticism was a corollary to that myth.

I was impelled by a need to explain and justify myself. It is in such a mood that a man at the end of a long and intense love affair writes to the mistress whom he still adores, but nonetheless holds largely responsible for the rupture. 'Isn't it your fault,' he cries, 'here, and here and again here? We might be together still.' Perhaps in the last analysis that is what *The Loom of Youth* was—a love letter to Sherborne.

I finished it in the middle of March. A week later I learnt that the hundred or so members of the Inns of Court who were under eighteen (we were known as 'the war babies') were not, as most of us had hoped, to be returned to civilian life until we had come within range of being commissioned, but to be transferred to the 101st Provisional Battalion which was stationed on the east coast at Southwold; *The Loom of Youth* had just slid under the fence. If the age limit had not been raised, I do not suppose I would have finished it. As a subaltern, I would have had no time. When I did have the time, I should have been in a different mood. That is what I meant by saying that chance decreed that I should learn I had the knack of narrative.

§

The 101st Provisional Battalion was in charge of coast defences. In 1914 the possibility of invasion had existed as a menace, but at this stage of the war no one seriously imagined that the Germans had so few irons in the fire that they could risk an invasion across the Channel. Our chief job was guard duties; our spare time we spent digging out from the sand some barbed wire entanglements which had been set too near the sea and had been submerged by a heavy tide. The battalion was a ramshackle concern. It was manned by troops who were too old, too young or too infirm for service in France. It contained a number of 'old soldiers'. I was grateful for the six weeks I spent there. If you have served in the ranks, you see soldiering through the private's eyes, and though in the Inns of Court I had been No. 6139 Private Waugh, A.R., being in an O.T.C. was not being in the ranks. I hope I was a better officer for the experience of those six weeks.

I was only there six weeks because I was able to persuade my father that an indefinite period—it looked likely to be a year—guarding the east coast would not get me anywhere. He did not need much persuading. Fearing that an idle summer on the sands would see me helplessly involved before June was past in an unfortunate liaison with a local shop girl, he welcomed my suggestion that I should fill in the gap by sitting for a cadetship at the R.M.C. Sandhurst. The next examination was in early July. I could apply for leave to study for the exam.

I had no intention of making the army my career, but the end of the war was a long way off. Time enough to make plans when it was over. I could always, I presumed, send in my papers. The fact that by going to Sandhurst I received a regular instead of a temporary commission was to have important repercussions for me later. At the end of the war instead of being demobilized, I was transferred to the R.A.R.O. (Regular Army Reserve of Officers). I had to report to the War Office in writing every year. I was liable to recall at a moment's notice, and indeed was recalled in April 1921 during the coal strike. Every few years I received instructions as to what to do in the event of a general mobilization, and in September 1939 I was recalled as a lieutenant to the Dorsets. I was then forty-one. At that age, had I not been on the R.A.R.O., I should have found it difficult to get back into the army. I might have joined the Ministry of Information. I might never have found myself as a security officer in Baghdad, where I acquired the knowledge of police methods that has proved so useful to me in the writing of my later novels; certainly I should have had a very different second war.

In early May I returned to Underhill on leave and enrolled at a Kensington crammer's—Carlisle & Gregson. It was a happy period. I was out of uniform. I had felt self-conscious a year earlier walking the streets as a civilian subject to white feathers, and shouts from passing troops of 'Kitchener wants you'. But now that I was a soldier, I did not care. I enjoyed the domestic routine of catching a tube every morning, spending my mornings in the classroom, lunching frugally at an A.B.C., returning to a couple of hours in the classroom; then back to Underhill and a walk over the heath with my father before dinner. I had a little homework to do, but not very much. The Sandhurst standard in wartime was below that of the school certificate which I had taken thirty months before. I had to read up a special period in history, but my history grounding was solid. I did not anticipate any real difficulties. The only possible danger points were mathematics, which I had not done since I passed into the sixth, and geography, which I had never studied as a subject either at Fernden or at Sherborne. I was supposed to have picked it up as I went along. Carlisle & Gregson concentrated on these two subjects. From the way they handled the geography, I appreciated the technique of 'cramming'. A candidate had to get thirty-three marks to qualify, in a paper graded to one hundred marks. The paper always included a map. Draw a map of South America, Germany or Italy, putting in the following towns and rivers. The map rated twenty-five marks. Carlisle & Gregson said, 'We will guarantee that you will get full marks for the map. You can pick up the other eight marks out of your general knowledge.'

They fulfilled their promise. They had a system of measurements that you memorized, by which you could draw the outline of any country and graph its rivers; the rest was simple. I went into the examination confident that I should get my twenty-five marks. I had forgotten it all within a month. But that did not matter.

In the meantime *The Loom of Youth* was going the round of London's publishing houses. Martin Secker was then the publisher of the *avant-garde*—Compton Mackenzie, Hugh Walpole, Gilbert Cannan, Frank Swinnerton, J. E. Flecker—and I asked S. P. B. Mais to take the manuscript to him. It was returned after a month with a friendly letter saying that though he found much on which he could congratulate me, he did not believe that in wartime enough people would be interested in the real life of the public school boy to justify its publication. He hoped that if I did not find a publisher for it, and wrote another 'first novel', I would remember him.

I did not offer it to Chapman & Hall because I did not want the world to say that I had only got it published because I was my father's son. Nor did I ask my father to recommend it to his friends in the trade. I wanted to do this on my own. I sent it to Constable, Methuen, Mills & Boon; to be rewarded with formal rejection slips. My father then suggested that he should send it to Frank Swinnerton who was Chatto & Windus's reader. Swinnerton said much what Secker had; and I decided that I had better put the book away for the duration. This decision was not as big a disappointment to me as might have been expected. I was confident that it would be published one day; I had written it; I had said what I had to say; having got the thing off my chest, I had in part lost interest in it. I was far more interested in my poetry and wondered how soon I could hope to qualify for Georgian poetry. I was far more disappointed when S. P. B. Mais showed some of my poems to Eddie Marsh, and E. M. replied that I was no good yet, though I might be one day. Moreover, with the comparative certainty that my days in the Inns of Court were over, with Sandhurst ahead of me, I had begun to enjoy life again. A crested wave was mounting. Once again I was finding that fifteen hours between dawn and sunset was too narrow a casket for the day's good things. *The Loom* could wait. I did not realize then how important timing is. If *The Loom* had not been published till after the war, it would not have caused the sensation that it did.

I sat for the Sandhurst exam in early July. The results would not be published till the end of August. Until then I had to return to duty with the Inns of Court. Without enthusiasm, I re-assumed khaki and caught a train for Southwold. On my arrival there, I learnt that 'the war babies' had been returned a week earlier to Berkhamsted. I caught the next train to London. On the way down I had eaten a packet of sandwiches that my mother had cut for me. I felt that the occasion merited a proper meal. I went into the dining-car. A gunner captain seated himself opposite me. The head waiter came up to me. 'Are you travelling first-class, sir?'

'No,' I said, 'but I want to eat a first-class dinner.'

'Certainly, sir,' and he conducted me to another coach, where I ate in a proletarian setting, a dinner with one extra course—sardines on toast—at an additional cost of three and six—at that time three days' pay.

I returned next day to Berkhamsted. The corps was under canvas. I found my fellow 'war babies' in a disgruntled mood. They had gone contentedly native in the sands at Southwold, learning the 'old soldier's' technique. They were not too glad to find themselves again treated as future officers. Six months would have to elapse before they could go to an O.C.T.U., and they were riled at being told by their officers that though they had had ten to eleven months in khaki, they were by no means ready to be officers. 'Damn it all,' they said. 'Way back in January we passed out of the instruction class and had our papers signed.'

Their morale was low. Mine would have been, too, if I had been in their position; but I could not believe that I had failed to pass into Sandhurst. I relaxed to a lazy summer, dozed through lectures, evaded responsibility, read *Tess of the d'Urbervilles*, wrote romantic sonnets. Leave was now granted every week-end, because it had been found that the mess was running at a loss and by sending the corps home over week-ends, and drawing their ration allowance, the mess could get back into the black. A few miles away, along the Somme, military mismanagement was taking its high toll of youth. But it was possible for a young soldier to accept his good fortune with a clear conscience. His time would come; and indeed thirteen months later there was Passchendaele.

II

Barbara Jacobs

One of my first acts on my return to Berkhamsted was to renew my acquaintance with the Jacobs. I went up to Beechcroft on a warm July afternoon. It cannot have been the first time that I met Barbara, but it was the first time that I had noticed her. She was then fifteen and a half. She was of medium height, brown-eyed. Her hair was long, parted in the centre, tied in a bow behind. Her parents were there, and one or two members of the corps. We were in the garden and she was sitting a bit away from me. I cannot remember anything she said. Perhaps she did not speak at all. But I was very conscious of her dark, brooding beauty. After a while, she got up and moved away, without saying good-bye. I watched her walk across the lawn, her hands behind her back. She had grace and dignity and pride. Her aloofness was a challenge. Next week, W.W. told me, the family would be going to Studland for their summer holidays. By the time they were back, that was to say, I would be at Sandhurst. But there would be plenty of time before I sailed for France.

On August 24, my father's birthday, the list of successful candidates for Woolwich and Sandhurst was published in *The Times*. About three hundred had passed in. I started reading from the bottom. I was Sixty-seventh. I had had little doubt that I should pass. But my heart bounded all the same. I was back at Underhill by lunch-time.

§

In wartime, the two-year course at Sandhurst was compressed into eight months. I enjoyed those eight months as much as I had disliked my seven months at Berkhamsted. I was with young men of my own age and background. The training was professional, interesting, progressive. We were drilled on the square by staff-sergeants from the brigade of guards; we were lectured by staff college graduates. There was no footslogging. We bicycled out to our exercises. We lived comfortably. I had a room to myself and a servant to shine my buttons. We were well fed. Dinner was a parade and we wore dinner jackets. I was a teetotaller in those days and I cannot remember whether it was possible to order beer or wine in college. I fancy it was not.

Sandhurst was run on the public school pattern. Work in the mornings, games in the afternoon, work in the evenings. It was good to be playing Rugby football again. I did not get into the college XV, but I was prominent in the company side. When my term became seniors, I was made a sergeant, which allowed me the privilege of one week-end leave a month.

On one of my monthly week-ends, I went to Sherborne and stayed with S. P. B. Mais. I little thought that nineteen years would pass before I again sat in the school chapel. Every Saturday I took a pass. Usually I went to London; but one of the cadets in my company lived at Rickmansworth. That was not far from Berkhamsted. He was a rich young man, destined for the cavalry and agreed to let me share his car for a nominal contribution. W.W. was, I learnt later, very surprised when I wrote to invite myself. "What's he after? You?" he asked his wife. He could not believe that his fifteen-year-old daughter had a suitor.

I arrived at half-past three. W.W. and his wife were resting. I was entertained by Barbara. It was the first time that we had talked together. We talked of poetry and painting. By the time her parents joined us I knew my mind.

It was a symptomatic afternoon. Mr. and Mrs. Jacobs and myself, joined by an officer in the Inns of Court who was billeted at Beechcroft, were caught up into a tense argument about conscientious objectors, Mrs. Jacobs and myself insisting that it needed a great deal of moral courage to flout popular opinion. Mrs. Jacobs was very deaf, and W.W. had to raise his voice. 'I have to shout to make her hear,' he said to me afterwards, 'and when you start shouting it is hard to keep your temper.'

At that time, the relations between the two were very bad. They scarcely agreed on anything. Mrs. Jacobs was, then, in her middle thirties. She had been very pretty as a girl, and she should have been in the full summer of her beauty, but constant ill-health and deafness gave her face an expression of anxiety and strain. She was always trying to hear what was being said. Even so, she was a strikingly attractive woman. She and Barbara were taken for sisters sometimes.

Her ill-health was mainly the result of nerves, the outcome of unhappiness. Feeling that her personal life was spoiled, she was resolved that her children should not be sacrificed to their father's narrowness. She was prepared to oppose him on every issue where their education was concerned. He was, as I have said, a violent reactionary, and she, as a disciple of Shaw and Wells, goaded him to extremes. H.G. had had an unfortunate influence on Beechcroft. W.W. cannot have enjoyed the picture of himself as Sir Isaac Harman, and the scandals of H.G.'s private life peopled W.W.'s mind with terrors. Barbara wanted to study painting, but W.W. was convinced that London in general and the Slade in particular were filled with embryo H.G.s waiting to exploit his daughter's innocence. That autumn Gilbert Cannan's novel of the Slade, *Mendel*, with Mark Gertler as the hero, and Augustus John as one of the chief characters, had confirmed W.W. in his intransigence.

As I drove back that night, I recognized that I would be wise to make an ally of Mrs. Jacobs. She was very likeable and I was in sympathy with most of the things she stood for.

Next day I wrote her a long bread-and-butter letter in which I amplified some of the arguments that I had presented the night before. She replied at greater length. She was an excellent and indefatigable correspondent. Letters were, because of her deafness, her easiest means of communication. We wrote to each other two or three times a week, six- to eight-page letters. She had an acute, warm, vivid mind. I enjoyed the exchange of ideas. Yet, at the same time, these letters were for me part of my campaign. I referred often to Barbara. I wondered what she was reading, what her plans were. I knew that a part of these letters would be read to Barbara. I wanted Barbara to think of me as someone who was thinking about her.

I was also through these letters becoming increasingly conscious of the feuds and problems that were shaking Beechcroft. I recognized that W.W. would never let Barbara study at the Slade, but I had an alternative idea. Why should not Barbara stay at Underhill, and take lessons at another art school? My parents would be her chaperones. W.W. could not question their credentials. At Underhill Barbara would hear constant talk of me. She would be around when I came back on leave. My father had always regretted not having had a daughter. Here was his chance of one. I could see nothing against this scheme. I had only to play my cards carefully and wait. Every third day a letter in my handwriting would be delivered in the Chesham Road. Time was on my side, and I suggested that I should spend a day at Beechcroft during the Christmas recess.

The professor of history at Sandhurst was Thomas Seccombe—a distinguished and well-loved man of letters. He was an old friend of my father. He kept open house on Sundays. Half a dozen or so of us would go up in the early afternoon. He had a seventeen-year-old and attractive daughter; and a schoolboy son, Lionel, who was in the 'thirties to make a name for himself on the B.B.C. as a reporter on athletics. We would have a solid tea and play nursery games like 'Up Jenkins'. It was a congenial counter-atmosphere to the R.M.C.

There were others at his house besides G.C.s. There were men of letters like R. A. Scott-James and left-wing publicists like E. D. Morel. I often used to desert the nursery playground to listen to my elders and betters. I told Seccombe that I had written a novel. He was generous enough to ask to see it. He was enthusiastic. He thought he might be able to find a publisher for it.

Grant Richards, in his autobiography *Author Hunting*, says that it was through S. P. B. Mais that he received the manuscript. It is difficult to remember the exact sequence of events over an interval of nearly half a century. I daresay that both versions are correct. It is possible that Mais's first wife, Doris did say to Grant, 'Petre, why don't we show Mr. Richards

Alec's book?' But my recollection is that Seccombe said to me, 'I have links with two publishers, Fisher Unwin and Grant Richards. To whom shall I send it first?' My father had had some difficulties with Unwin—he was known in the trade as 'Fishy Unwin'—and I knew that S. P. B. Mais was now being published by Grant Richards. So I plumped for Richards.

§

The Christmas recess at Sandhurst was usually ten days long, but this year it was extended to three weeks because some structural repairs were needed. S. P. B. Mais and his wife came to Underhill for a long week-end. His wife went down with 'flu and the week-end lasted for ten days. Chapman & Hall had in the press a novel by S. P. B. Mais called *Interlude*. It was the story of a married schooolmaster employed at a West Country school that was obviously Sherborne, who has a love affair in London with a girl at the Times Book Club. It was dedicated to his wife in a long letter in which he expressed his dissatisfaction with his selfish hero; but it was she, he said, who had encouraged him to write *Le Shelley de Nos Jours*. I had assumed, as my father had, that Mais had used a familiar background for an imaginary plot, but his wife during her illness told my mother that *Interlude* was not fiction and that there indeed was a girl at the Times Book Club. This was my first realization that 'things like that' happened to 'people that one knew'.

Mais's energy was phenomenal. He arrived with the first fifteen thousand words of a novel. He had finished it before the end of his visit. He wrote it in tubes, in odd half-hours before lunch or dinner, in the intervals of rushing round London from one meeting to another. It was 70,000 words long, and was published by Richards in August with the title *Rebellion*.

I went out with Mais on a number of these expeditions. He took me to the mirror-hung domino room of the Café Royal. There was a fancy-dress dance somewhere in London and a number of young people in *travesti* were shouting to each other across the tables. They invited us to come on with them. I felt no envy because in my pocket only a few shillings remained out of my weekly pound. In a few months I should be an officer drawing seven and six a day. This time next year I might be on leave from France, with the swollen bank balance that had accumulated in the trenches. I should then be able to wave back acceptance of such casual invitations.

The war had now been in progress for nearly thirty months. We had come to accept it as the normal framework for our lives. Rolls-Royce ran an advertisement, 'One day the war will end as suddenly as it began. You will then need the best car in the world. Place your order for a Rolls-Royce now.' We knew that this would happen, that this must happen, but we could not completely credit it. Pre-war was another world. Post-war would be another world. We were living in the present and making the best of it. London had great glamour in 1916; there was only a partial black-out, with the tops of the street lamps darkened and faces coming out of shadow into sudden cones of light. There were no security precautions as we knew them in the Second War. There were good-bye parties for the men who were going overseas, men who would, if they were still alive, be back within four months resolved to settle in two weeks the accumulated debt of twenty weeks' boredom, squalor, horror. Rationing had not yet touched the restaurants. Everyone was making money; there were things to buy with it. *Chu Chin Chow* was running at His Majesty's—'Any Time's Kissing Time'; the Bing Boys were at the Hippodrome with George Robey and Violet Lorraine—'If you were the only girl in the world.'

There was talk of peace that Christmas, with the costly Somme offensive petering out in failure, and it is hard not to believe now that it would have been better to have made peace then, before the Russian revolution, before America came into the war, before 'the *dictat* of Versailles' had left Germany with a heritage of rancour, and before the waste and slaughter of Passchendaele had deprived Europe of the young men who should have been its leaders in the 1940s. But no one really believed then that peace would come so soon. There was the feeling that we owed it 'to the fallen' to continue fighting until victory was won. 'Take up our quarrel with the foe. . . . If ye break faith with us who die, we shall not sleep, though poppies blow in Flanders fields.'

Those of us who were under nineteen that Christmas joined with our elders in the discussions about peace, but we kept to ourselves the consideration that weighed most with us. We did not want the war to end before we had reached the trenches; we dreaded having to sit silent after the war when men only a few months older than ourselves compared front-line experiences. Our dearest hope was for a mild 'blighty', a wound that would send us back to England with a gold stripe on our sleeve, that would prevent us going out again, but that would have no crippling, no maiming after-effect.

I had met, through S. P. B. Mais, Desmond Young who had been a pupil of his at Rossall and who was after the Second War to produce a bestseller in *Rommel*. He had been badly wounded at Ypres in 1915 and had been drafted into staffwork. He had a charming small house in Chelsea. I visited him there once or twice. With an open fire blazing, with his books round him, with modern pictures on the walls, he seemed a very enviable person. He had earned his comfort and his safety. I would rather have been him than anyone.

Siegfried Sassoon wrote a sonnet ending with the line, '"Thank God," he said, "they had to amputate."' One could not foresee in 1916 how one would feel in 1919. Arthur Hogg, one of my best Sherborne friends, lost his leg at Passchendaele. He did not think himself unlucky when he lay in hospital, with friends coming to see him, knowing that he was 'out of it'. But when he went up to Oxford and saw the others hurrying down to the football field after lunch, he realized all that he had lost. He wondered from what source he would draw the courage to continue living.

§

I had hoped that the Christmas recess would give me an opportunity to continue my campaign at Beechcroft. I sent Barbara a book for Christmas. I re-read her letter of thanks many times, hoping to detect some inner meaning. It was signed, 'Love, Barbara,' but it was a very formal letter. I could draw no hope from the use of the word 'love'. I decided that she signed all her letters that way.

I suggested to Mrs. Jacobs that I should come down early

in the New Year. A day was fixed. I counted the hours to it. But on the very morning that I was preparing to set out to Euston a telephone message came that Barbara had developed measles. 'Well,' I thought, and resumed my correspondence with her mother.

§

A G.C. sergeant at Sandhurst was only liable to find himself in trouble with authority—unless he was particularly negligent—on a single count. He could run into debt. One paid money in to the paymaster, one signed for minor purchases, and every evening a book showing the extent of one's credit was placed in the company anteroom. Debt was a crime. It was easy to get into debt because some branches of the R.M.C. were slow in presenting their chits and an unexpected chit might place one in the red. This happened to me at the end of January. I was twopence in the red, and on a charge. I waited disconsolately in the anteroom after breakfast. A sergeant could only be punished by a reprimand. But a reprimand was a punishment and would cancel my privilege of a monthly week-end leave. The morning mail came in. It contained a small green envelope. In the top left-hand corner was printed 'Grant Richards Ltd.' I tore it open. The letter was a page long. My eye ran down it quickly. One thing alone was clear to me. *The Loom* had been accepted.

The orderly sergeant put his head round the door. 'Your turn, Tank.' With my hat off I was marched in, as I had to be, as a sergeant, between two other sergeants. My crime was read out. I was asked for an explanation. A chit at the lake had been held back, I said. The major deliberated. 'Very well,' he said. 'This one time we'll look over it. Case dismissed.'

My week-end pass was safe. Surely this was a good omen for *The Loom*. I was marched out. I turned to the senior sergeant. 'Pearse,' I said, 'my novel's been accepted.' He grinned across his face. 'That's wonderful.' In the anteroom he tapped with his swagger cane upon the table. 'Listen, all of you. The Tank's had a novel accepted. We ought to wish him luck.' There was a burst of clapping. I wonder whether in the long history of the R.M.C. there has been another occasion when an anteroom has wished a fellow G.C. good luck on the acceptance of a novel.

94

In his letter of acceptance Grant Richards made two suggestions, that I should cut out the three or four Greek words that
I had included in the text, since the sight of them might put
certain readers off, and that I should call myself Alec Waugh
and not Alec R. Waugh. I accepted both these suggestions. He
also stipulated that the book needed to be sponsored and that he
would invite Thomas Seccombe to write a preface.

This was a sound idea and Seccombe's preface proved to be
an excellent piece of writing. He divided it into two parts. In
the first he talked about me, how he had come to read the book
and what he thought of it. In the second he wrote of the public
school system, 'You may say that the Public School system got
us out of the mess of 1914, yes, but it helped largely to get us
into it.' He made *The Loom* his text for an attack upon the
system. Seccombe's opinion carried weight not only in literary
but academic circles. His preface pin-pointing the attention of
reviewers made the book controversial.

Richards planned for publication in July.

§

I have referred already to the effect that sheer chance can
have upon one's life. In the spring a notice was posted on each
college board. 'Will any G.C. who wishes to apply for the
Heavy Machine Corps (Tanks) write his name below.' The
senior sergeant said to me, 'You'll have to put down your name
for that, Tank. If you don't, we'll put it down for you.'

If I had not had that nickname, I should never have put my
name down on that list. If I had not, things might have turned
out in one respect very differently. If I had been posted straight
to the Dorsets on passing out of Sandhurst, I should probably
have been in France within a month; and I might not have been
able to bring my courtship of Barbara Jacobs to a head before I
sailed. And if I hadn't then, I might never have. As it was, I
had after leaving Sandhurst an extra two months' training as a
machine-gunner. That gave me the time I needed.

In March there was an outbreak of mumps at Sandhurst and
the college was closed for three weeks. During that three weeks
there was a dance at Beechcroft, for the Inns of Court. Barbara
was not considered old enough to take part. I spent nearly the

whole time sitting beside her in the gallery. It must by now have been apparent to W.W. what I was 'after'. My correspondence with Mrs. Jacobs did not slacken but it was interspersed with letters to her daughter.

I had two weeks' leave after passing out at Sandhurst. I had now a bank account and a cheque book. I invited Barbara and her mother to lunch with me in London and see a matinée— Gerald du Maurier at Wyndham's in *London Pride*. I spent a day in Berkhamsted and Barbara and I went for a long walk on the common over which I had deployed with such depression eighteen months before. The Machine Gun Corps Headquarters were at Grantham. Week-end leave was rarely granted to subalterns. But by getting up at 4.30 on Sunday morning and walking two miles to the station, I could catch a slow milk train that got me to London by eight o'clock. I could spend a whole day at Underhill, and an eleven o'clock train would get me back to camp by 2 a.m. In wartime such a journey seemed well worth while. On one of these Sundays, W.W., Mrs. Jacobs and Barbara came up to Underhill for the day. After tea Barbara and I stayed in what had been my nursery and declined to join the others on the lawn.

All this is over forty years ago. Galsworthy wrote of the burgeoning of first love, as an emotion that is universal and which time transmutes into 'a fragrant memory, a searing passion, a humdrum mateship and once in many times into a vintage full and sweet with a sunset colour on the grapes'. It is an emotion that it is impossible to recall. I can remember times and places, I can remember tones of voice, and I can remember during that summer of 1917 a sense of bounding vitality, of heightened living. Part of that feeling came through Barbara, but part of it came from life itself, from the excitement of widening horizons. Every third day I was receiving a small package of proofs, and there is little more exciting than the first sight of one's work in print; there was in addition the last-minute sense of drama that the imminence of France presented. I have sometimes wondered whether I am not too much in love with life, to have ever been completely in love with anyone.

I even find it difficult to remember what Barbara was like, though I can see her so clearly and can recall so many of her hats and frocks. She had her father's quick sense of humour, but not his acidity. I never heard her say a mean or spiteful thing. She was lively company, though I think that in those days she was not very happy. Her outlook on life was clouded by her parents' friction. She suspected that conflict awaited her, and she was not belligerent. This sadness accentuated her poetic wistfulness. Her father was devoted to her. She was his first and favourite child. They had lived for a while at Epping, and as they walked through the forest he would tell her his Bob Pretty stories. He used to take her up to London to an occasional matinée, and now in late middle age I can appreciate, as I could not then, how pathetic was her impatience, sitting at a table, while he lingered over a brandy and cigar, terrified lest they would be late for the play. Of course they never were.

W.W. was punctilious in punctuality as in so much else. The ten minutes of lingering over a cigar is for a man an essential rounding off of a good meal. It is a masculine trait that women should have the wisdom to indulge; too many women never realize how important to a man it is, and Barbara had been trained by her mother to resent masculine autocracy.

When I hear people say, 'They had to stay together for the children's sake,' I think of the Jacobs family. It would have been better for everyone had there been a separation; certainly it would have been for Barbara. Her genuine love of her father was confused with her absorption in her mother who was, she felt, the victim of the inequalities in the social system and the inferior position occupied by women in it; a system of which her father was a bastion. The aloofness in her which was such a challenge to a man, and the brooding beauty which was so hauntingly attractive, were the products, both of them, of an awareness of this conflict and a deep hankering to be quit of it. I have not seen her since the summer of 1922. As the wife of a distinguished professor in Mill College, California, she has led, I have been told, a happy life. She is probably as different a person now as I myself am. But in her teens, if my diagnosis is correct, the constant conflict which enriched her personality saddened her inside herself.

§

At the end of June, I finished my machine-gun course and was transferred to a depot company awaiting posting overseas and was granted a week's embarkation leave. On my last morning I was given a T.A.B. injection. This was the kind of cheeseparing meanness that only a Whitehall bureaucrat could cook up. A first T.A.B. injection makes one feel so ill, that in the Second War troops were given forty-eight hours off duty after it. To drink alcohol during that period is disastrous. For at least ten per cent of the officers going on embarkation leave, those seven days were the last that they would spend in freedom upon this earth. Why spoil two of them? I had not then learnt to enjoy wine and the lack of alcohol was no deprivation for me. But I can imagine how I would have felt at twenty-seven. As it was, feeling considerably under par, I cherished no gratitude to the Establishment. Even condemned criminals are allowed a final dinner.

Most of this final leave was spent with Barbara. On the Saturday she and her mother came up to Underhill for the week-end and we went to that excellent comedy *His Excellency the Governor*. On the Tuesday I went down to Beechcroft for the night. I returned to Underhill the following evening. On the Saturday Barbara and her mother came up for the day to see me off to camp.

Barbara and I considered ourselves now engaged. There was no proposal. There is no need for that when two young people recognize that they are in love with one another. They assume that they will marry as soon as circumstances permit. But most very young people are not in a position to translate that assumption into a practical programme. I was barely nineteen, she was sixteen and a half. Nowadays, particularly in America, that is not an absurdly young age to talk of marriage, but it was then in England, and in retrospect I am surprised that our parents fell in so readily with the assumption that we would marry one day. They would not, I suppose, have done so had there been no war. Clearly there could be no marriage till the war was over. No one could tell when that would be, or what the postwar world would be. At the moment our material prospects

Barbara Jacobs in 1916

The Author's father and mother in 1917

could not have been less immediately encouraging. My father
had no money except what he earned and that was not a lot.
W.W. had saved a certain amount but he had four other children
to educate; he would be in no position to make us an allowance.
Barbara had in her own name a few Government shares that
brought in £50 a year. When the war was over I should have
to find myself a profession. I might need to take a university
degree. I was unlikely to be self-supporting for several years.
Our parents could protect themselves with the mental reservation, 'It may come to nothing.' In the meantime, they did not
want to present opposition to a young man who was shortly
going to the wars.

§

The first sight of one's first book. Life has not many richer
thrills. I saw mine during my embarkation leave. I had paid a
call at Grant Richards' office. Richards was out, but a copy of it
was lying on his desk. I picked it up, turning it over in my hands
caressingly. It looked so beautiful, with its bright jacket; a
schoolboy in white flannels and a blue and gold blazer, reading
in a deck-chair on a lawn, with the square abbey tower in the
background. Who could resist buying it?

'Can I take it away?' I asked. His secretary shook her head.
'We need that copy for the travellers.'

'Oh, but, please,' I pleaded.

She hesitated, then yielded to my eagerness. 'Very well,' she
said.

I hurried round with it to Henrietta Street to show my father.
On the way, in Garrick Street, I met Warren Chetham-Strode
who, thirty years later, was to write the Sherborne play, *The
Guinea Pig*. I showed him the book. A staff-sergeant on his
way past drew himself up stiffly and saluted. In the First War
salutes were acknowledged by the senior officer. Chetham-
Strode was a captain; I waited for him to salute, but he had not
seen the sergeant; I was so absorbed in showing him my book
that I did not realize that he had not seen him till it was too late.
The staff-sergeant looked indignant. I felt bitterly ashamed.
That unanswered salute is still upon my conscience. Was it a
bad omen for *The Loom*, I asked myself?

Ten days later I received in camp my six complimentary copies. One of them I sent to Bumpus to be bound for Barbara. I had sent her the proofs, but W.W. had confiscated them. He did not want his daughter to be informed about the disgusting habits of small boys. This was the first indication I received that the book was likely to be considered shocking. I did not feel, however, that he would be so firm about a volume bound in calf. I wrote inside it:

Four years of wandering more or less,
Of struggling ignorant why I strove,
The odyssey of selfishness,
And yet the prelude to our love.

Publication date was July 20. There was no week-end leave from Clipstone, but I felt confident that after I had been there three weeks I could apply for U.P.A. (Urgent Private Affairs) leave. Was I not publishing a book? Did I not need to consult my publisher? It was arranged that Mrs. Jacobs and Barbara should come up to Underhill for the week-end of July 28. By then there might be some reviews to read.

I have rarely looked forward to anything as much as I did to that week-end leave. I was impatient to see Barbara again. The tempo of our courtship had quickened rapidly during my embarkation leave. On its last Saturday at Underhill, the day of the first daylight raid on London, there had been an electric tension in the air. I had a sense that our love was still in bud, that it would come to flower during the next week-end. I counted not only hours but minutes to that Saturday.

On the Thursday morning I noted that my application in the leave book had been initialled. At lunch-time there was a telegram from my father, 'Congratulations on splendid send-off *Times Literary Supplement*.' Immediately after parade I drove into the town to buy it. Yes, there it was, a third of a column, in big type, starting off . . . 'A most promising first book. Mr. Alec Waugh has something definite to say, the ability to say it and an appreciation of the subtler causes of action and inaction.'

I had managed to get a little cricket during my three weeks at Clipstone. There was a net practice that evening. I saw the ball as big as a balloon. Only thirty-nine more hours. On the notice-board in the mess was a message telling me to report at once at company office. I hurried round anxiously. Had my leave been cancelled? No, it wasn't that. I was to proceed to France at once.

All next day, with my valise packed, I hung around company office, waiting for instruction. 'At once' does not mean the same thing in the army that it does in civilian life. I still hoped that I might be able to spend at least a few hours at Underhill with Barbara. But after tea the final orders came. I was to take the next train to London and catch the 7 a.m. from Victoria the following morning. There was no telephone at Underhill. I could not call up my parents. I caught one of the last tubes out to Golders Green.

That long walk up the hill, in view of the desolate news that I was bringing home. . . . My parents were expecting me back for a gay week-end, instead I had come to say good-bye. I threw some earth up at my mother's window. 'The key's under the mat,' she called down. 'I'm going to France,' I answered. It was after one. We sat talking, the three of us, for an hour or so, then I went up to bed to get three hours' sleep.

It was a bright summer morning. As the tube ran into the tunnel, one could glimpse for three seconds the scaffolding on the empty building plot next to Underhill. I craned my neck to make the three seconds five.

Barbara and her mother arrived at Underhill in time for lunch. I have wondered sometimes whether there would have been a different outcome to it all if my posting had come three days later and I had had that week-end leave. Things were never the same between Barbara and myself again. A current had been switched off.

III

Passchendaele

The Flanders offensive that has been as much criticized as any operation undertaken by British arms opened at the end of July. On the same day it began to rain. It continued to rain right through that week. I was at the M.G. base at Etaples, waiting to be posted to a forward company. It was too wet even for P.T. I sat in the mess, eagerly turning to the book page of the London papers. In practically every daily and weekly paper *The Loom* was the novel of the week. Everywhere it was welcomed warmly, as a fresh, vivid piece of narrative. E. B. Osborne in the *Morning Post*, Gerald Gould in the *New Statesman*, J. C. Squire in *Land and Water*, Ralph Straus in the *Bystander*, all of them hailed the book as an astonishing achievement.

On 7 August I was posted to the Third Division which was then holding a quiet sector on the Somme, north of Bapaume, where the Germans had made a strategic withdrawal in the spring. There were, at that time, four machine-gun companies in a division. Three of them were allotted to the brigades, the last was used according to the divisional general's own requirements. I was in this company—the 233rd. It was a cosy assignment. In a quiet part of the line, one was usually stationed behind brigade H.Q., in greater comfort and in greater safety, while in action one was usually given something interesting to do. A cosy assignment and a machine-gun company was a cosy unit. One was on one's own. There were ten officers, a captain in command, an adjutant, a transport officer and seven subalterns, two to each section. A section was a very different command from a platoon, if only because its fire-power was so much greater and because the four guns were scattered over a wider front. During my eight months with the company, I rarely had an independent command. I was a kind of section adjutant to my section officer. That too was cosy.

§

In Flanders the rain fell steadily, but southwards on the Somme the sun shone as it should in August. My company was in a very quiet sector. No-man's-land was a mile deep. There was a little token shelling, but I doubt if there was a casualty in the division during the entire month. We were employed on digging machine-gun emplacements to guard against a German breakthrough, but no one imagined that there would be one. The division had not been heavily engaged since April. We should probably be moved north soon. We presumed that the object of all this digging was to keep the men occupied and fit.

Soldiering under such conditions in summer is a kind of picnic. I was in excellent health. I enjoyed the *camaraderie* of the mess. I liked the being in France at last. For two years I had been training for this. It was exciting getting to know one's men. And ahead there was the imminence of drama. I should learn what it was like. I should not have to sit silent during the 1920s when my contemporaries talked of the Somme and Loos. I should be able to interject, 'I remember a night in '17.' And in the background of all that was the increasingly large mail that reached me every night; letters about *The Loom*, press-cuttings of *The Loom*, the day-to-day drama of success. For by now it had become clear that the book was a genuine success. Early in August, my father had lunched with Richards. 'Do you think,' he said, 'it will sell five thousand copies?' Five thousand was a big sale in those days, and long experience had taught my father that the main sales of a novel were over in ten weeks, by which time the circulating libraries would have sufficient stocks. But *The Loom* was following a different graph.

Timing is all important, in nearly everything. It certainly is in the rarefied atmosphere of the bestseller and *The Loom* could not have appeared at a luckier time. It had an immediate news-value. There was a boom in soldier-poets. Robert Graves, Siegfried Sassoon, Robert Nichols, W. J. Turner had recently made their debuts. Here was a soldier-novelist, the first, and in his teens. As always in wartime there was a demand for books, and there was that summer a dearth of novels. A spirit of challenge and criticism was in the air. The war after three years was still 'bogged down' and public opinion attributed allied failings in the field to mismanagement in high places. The rebelliousness of *The Loom* was in tune with the times.

At the start, it had been reviewed in the literary columns of the Press, but it soon ceased to be 'just a novel' and became the focus of a controversy. In large part this was due to Seccombe's preface, and H. W. Massingham, the editor of the *Nation* and a very influential journalist, wrote in his Wayfarer column:

> I have read few books that have interested me more than Mr. Waugh's *Loom of Youth*. It is in one respect an almost miraculous production. Here is a boy of eighteen who discusses his school life, reproduces its talk and atmosphere and builds up a merciless memorial of its evils and short-comings. It is a most straightforward account, it cannot have been invented, and yet I thought it sufficiently deli-licate. . . . It seems to me that it is a revolutionary work—if only the parents of England will read it and having read it, act on it. If they do the one without the other, it is on their conscience that they risk the ruin of their children's characters and minds. So I urge them to do the one and the other.

All this of course made a considerable difference to Barbara and myself. In the early summer it had been easy for her parents to think of our attachment as something that would blow over. But now, with *The Loom* a bestseller, I had become, precarious though the career of authorship may be, somebody of whom the father of a daughter could think as a possible match, and the scheme concocted by Mrs. Jacobs and myself, of Barbara entering as a student at Bedford College and staying at Underhill, now became feasible. Apart from *The Loom*'s success, W.W. would have been reluctant to have his daughter connected so closely with the Waughs, making ties that she might find it difficult to break later on. As it was he became amenable. Barbara came up to Underhill in October, to be welcomed there as the daughter of the house. This gave our understanding an official status.

§

In early September the Third Division was taken out of the line and after ten days of intensive battle training was moved north to Flanders. The July offensive had failed in all its main objectives, but the attack continued. Every week fresh divisions were poured into the battle and a few hundred yards were gained at the cost of many thousand lives. It has been argued since that the higher command persisted in the offensive to relieve pressure on the French, whose morale stood very low, after the long-drawn-out defence of Verdun. There had been, indeed, more than a threat of mutiny after the failure of Nivelle's offensive in the spring. But the troops who were sent north were not told that. We were assured that the German troops were failing, their reserves exhausted; one more push and we should be through into the open.

We went north in one of those familiar railroad trucks— eight horses, forty men. We entrained in the early evening. For the last six weeks we had been living in a desolate world of roofless houses and gutted farms. The Germans had destroyed everything when they withdrew. We woke on a sunny autumn morning, in a world of well-tended gardens, carefully planted fields, neat cottages and villages surmounted by church spires. As we marched down the cobbled streets, women and children waved at us from their front doors. 'Back to civilization again,' we thought. It was ironic that we should be restored to civilization as the prelude to an experience that was the supreme negation of civilized existence.

At this period of the war, machine-guns were used in attack as a form of light artillery, that laid down a barrage in front of the advancing troops. Machine-gun fire was more accurate than artillery, bullets were unlikely to land among our own troops; and in terms of personnel more lethal. On the Somme a year earlier, the British higher command had believed that it would be impossible for any defence to survive the barrage preceding an attack; but the German machine-gunners stayed down in their deep dug-outs while the barrage pounded above them and had just time to man their guns and mow down the advancing infantry. The more accurate machine-gun barrage could keep closer to the advance and prevent their doing this. Three of my company sections were to fire a barrage on the morning of the attack. The fourth section, my own, was in reserve.

The object of the attack was to capture Zonnebeke, then, if the Germans faltered, sweep through into the open. We captured Zonnebeke all right, but one glance at the terrain over which we were expected to advance convinced us that there would be no breakthrough into the open. The rains had ceased for the moment—later through October they were to fall ceaselessly—and the sun shone out of a bland autumnal sky, but the ground was waterlogged after the early rains, the irrigation system had been destroyed by cannon fire; tanks were bogged down; there was no trench system, only a waste of shell-holes connected by duckboard tracks.

We wondered whether the staff officers at G.H.Q. had any idea what the ground was like. There were no helicopters then. It was only six years since the first aeroplane had flown from London to Paris. It would, I suppose, have been possible for a general to have flown low over the ground, but it would have been very risky. Some generals at some point must have come up by horse and foot to make a personal reconnaissance, but during my eight months in France I did not see a single officer above the rank of lieutenant-colonel. I pictured the staff, well back from the line, examining their maps, working out gradients and contours and deciding how far the first wave would reach in the first two hours.

The generals of the Second War showed that they had learnt the lessons of the Somme and Passchendaele. They saw to it that their men knew them, that their men felt they were being led by them. We had no such feeling in the First War. There was a marked antagonism between the staff and the fighting man. Raymond Asquith refused a staff appointment because he wanted to stay with his men; he did not want to be in safety.

In the Second War, such an officer would have felt that he should go where he was needed most. Staff officers in the Second War shared many of the dangers and discomforts of their men. There was no equivalent in the Western Desert for the satires of Siegfried Sassoon: 'When I am old and bald and short of breath, I'll sit with scarlet majors at the base. . . .'

§

The third Division was in the line eight days at Ypres. Of the seven line officers in my company, three were killed. One of them was Jackson, the partner in the publishing firm of Sidgwick & Jackson, the second was Knight, a schoolmaster at Bishop's Stortford, in whose honour stand today a pair of memorial gates. There have been many descriptions of Passchendaele, of its waste and horror. If it is to be ranked as a British victory, it may be questioned whether it did not exhaust the victors more than the defeated. There is little new to be said about it, except that for each individual soldier each battle is an individual thing, a little different from every other's; in the same way that each individual's life is for him different from everybody else's. If it were not, there would be no novels written.

For me, Passchendaele was quite different from what I had expected. I had not realized how much of the time I should be doing nothing, how much of the time I should be out of danger, nor how the routine of trench life would continue, with the daily reports sent back to company headquarters, and the nightly arrival of the mail and rations, just as though a battle were not in progress.

My section was in reserve and as the junior officer in the company I was assigned to a number of different jobs. On the first day, I was attached to the divisional machine-gun officer, a major, to help him with the barrage charts. I arrived with a heavy haversack. He looked at it with disapproval. 'How on earth do you think you are going to advance eight or nine miles on Wednesday, carrying a great thing like that?'

'I didn't know that I was going to, sir,' I answered.

He frowned. 'Always assume that you'll advance.'

The greater part of my kit was sent back to details.

Because I had been attached to that major, I was under cover when the relief took place, and the Germans, presumably pre-warned, had shelled the extension of the main Ypres–Potije road right through the night. During that night, Jackson and Knight lost their lives. Twenty-four hours earlier, I had shared a tent with them. That morning, in the mail, I had received a copy of Matthew Prior's poems. I had read in *The Oxford Book of English Verse* his poem to a girl of four, and had asked my father if he had a collected edition of his poems. In sending it out, he wrote, 'It is a volume in a set, so if you can, do send it back.' The book arrived with several others. Jackson, watching me unpack them, said, 'Can you lend me the Prior?'

I learnt of Knight's and Jackson's deaths as I was directing the loading of a crate of ammunition near the Cloth Hall in Ypres. It was an exquisite September morning. Jackson and Knight were by training and temperament the two officers in the company with whom I was most in sympathy. I had a sense of overpowering loss, mixed with a blind impotent rage against the Germans. That *they* should have killed *them*. Then I remembered, Prior's poems. In Jackson's kit. One of a set. My father wanted it back. But no, I thought, I can't write to the adjutant and say, 'There's a book of mine in Jackson's kit.' He'll think, 'There's Jackson dead, a commonplace in wartime, but we're feeling pretty bad about it, and all that bastard's worrying about is a volume of Prior's poems.'

Fourteen years later, in the Welcome Hotel in Villefranche, a highly irresponsible young woman tried to commit suicide. For thirty-six hours nobody had seen her. Her door was locked. The management decided to break into her room through the balcony. We found her, naked, in a coma; we hurried her to the local hospital. It was an afternoon of stress and strain. In the town there was a young tourist who had lent her a couple of *New Yorkers*. He pestered me for their return. I was furious—Florence had nearly died, and here was this wretched creature fussing about a couple of *New Yorkers*. Then I remembered Prior's poems. That is the kind of thing that makes each man's battle individual.

'Going over the top' may be the crucial moment in a soldier's life; the supreme test of manhood; but it is a test that is reserved for the infantry and cavalry. The actual day of the assault was for a machine-gun section in reserve a day of calm. During the previous night we had, under fire, supervised the unloading and despatch of small-arms ammunition boxes. Among the men detailed was one man from another unit; he was in the late thirties, small, thin-chested and asthmatic; his knees sagged under the weight of the boxes. 'Come on, come on,' I urged him. He looked at me with a pathetic lack of guilt. 'I'm sorry, sir, I'm doing my best. They're sending over chaps they wouldn't have two years ago.' I felt a swine. I thought of a county-class fast bowler who had been discharged from the army for bad feet.

The first wave went over at half-past five; we were perched in a slit trench a few yards in front of a battery, whose guns wheel to wheel were thundering their barrage above our heads. I have never heard more noise. There was no enemy reply. King, my section officer, said, 'The Boche is concentrating on our front line now. He'll hit back at us this evening. It won't be any fun.'

By seven the barrage had ceased. The infantry had taken over. We sat in the mild September sunlight, resting, dozing, supervising the care of guns, checking spare parts, waiting for news of the advance. By noon little driblets of walking wounded and prisoners started to come down the road. The attack had not failed. No spectacular seven-mile advance, but an achievement of first objectives. None of us believed any longer in a breakthrough. There was intermittent shelling, from big guns. One of these guns was so powerful that you could actually see the shell. I remember watching one shell turn over and over in the air; it was due to pitch half a mile away. It fell with an immense explosion. When the cloud of dust settled, a group of ant-like figures could be observed scurrying round the debris. A small party came down the road; two wounded men and an unhurt escort. The escort shouted out, 'Lucky bastards, aren't they? Cushy blighties.'

That afternoon my section was moved forward, in advance of the gun emplacements from which the other three sections had fired their barrage. I did not know what was the purpose of this move. Presumably way back at divisional H.Q. a colonel had said to a G (3), 'Now, what precautions have we taken against a counter-attack on the left?' The G (3)'s pencil had poised over the map. 'I was thinking, sir, of arranging a strong point here.' 'Excellent idea, Frobisher, excellent idea,' and a yellow pencil encircled a strategic point; lines of protecting fire were marked out and King and Waugh were despatched to a line of linked shell-holes without any field of fire whatsoever.

We got there in mid-afternoon. At half-past five a barrage burst about us—the prelude, we presumed, to a counter-attack. Every other second, a shell pitched just in front of us or just behind us. Fountains of mud and iron plunged upwards on every side. It seemed impossible that a barrage such as this could continue any longer without a shell landing in the trench. We dismounted the guns; the men leant close against the parapet. King and I walked up and down the trench, gossiping and laughing, trying to keep their spirits up. I was not frightened, not in the sense that I was in May 1940 during the evacuation from Boulogne when I lay on the docks, waiting to embark, while the dive-bombers circled over us, but I felt dazed and helpless. Man was at the mercy of the machines that he had constructed for his safety and his comfort; an order was given two miles away and a curtain of steel descended. The individual was powerless. He had surrendered the dignity and independence that should have been his heritage at birth.

For half an hour or so the shelling continued, then ceased as suddenly as it had begun. Had the counter-attack come? Had it succeeded? We did not know; there was no means of knowing. We remounted the guns, posted sentries, set about brewing tea, waited for the rations.

The mail contained a letter for me from Gilbert Cannan— my hero of the moment. I had sent him a copy of *The Loom*. He wrote:

I have read it with an eager pleasure for it is exactly what I have been hoping for from the younger people—the flat and simply sincere declaration that they cannot stomach the world as the nineteenth century made it. Passionate sincerity brings with it a skill that no plodding or study can achieve and so the book is well done.

I had anxiously awaited a letter from him. Receiving it as I did I might have been expected to shrug, 'It doesn't mean much at a time like this.' But I did not. I was delighted. That is one of the curious things about a battle; the routine of life goes on although one may be blown to pieces in half an hour.

Three hours later a runner came up from details. A subsection of two guns was to go forward under my command to the edge of the front line. The instructions were precise. I was to proceed down the main Zonnebeke road, to the point where it cut the Ypres–Roulers railway. I was then to proceed north on a compass bearing of 60° for half a mile till I reached Van Diemen's farm where I was to mount my guns in a position from which I could bring enfilading fire to bear on a German counter-attack. The staff officer who drafted these orders was thus able to draw a yellow circle on his map and assure his colonel that every reasonable precaution had been taken. There was, however, no recognizable point at which the Zonnebeke road cut the Ypres–Roulers railway. The ground had been shelled continuously for seven weeks, and had been fought over three days before. Among the debris that littered the waste of shell-holes were one or two crumpled pieces of railway track, but there was no more indication of a railway than there was of a road. King had been instructed to guide me to my new position. The runner accompanied us, so that he would know where to bring up messages and rations. King was seven or eight years older than myself. He took stock of the desolate scene. 'It's as likely to be here as anywhere,' he said. 'Let's take that bearing.'

It is never easy to take a compass bearing in the dark; it is impossible to be accurate when there is iron about, and a broken tank was stranded a few yards away. We did our best and started off; some fifteen of us weighed down by guns and ammunition boxes. Every few minutes we were challenged from a shell-hole. Were we the relief? No, we were not. How was the war going? We had no idea. We progressed very slowly; and it is hard to march on a compass bearing when you cannot go straight forward, when you have to be skirting shell-holes. King said eventually, 'We must have gone half a mile.'

We had no idea what Van Diemen's farm would look like.

The only thing we did know was that it would not look like a farm. At this point of the war the Germans were concentrating on defence in depth. On the Somme, where the ground was firm, they had placed their machine-gunners in deep front-line dug-outs; but at Ypres where there was water a few inches below the surface they relied on small concrete forts, known as pill-boxes, which would survive an enemy advance and provide a focal bastion for a counter-attack. We saw a dark rectangular shape upon the skyline. 'This may be it,' said King. No one challenged us. 'It's empty, anyhow,' he said. Its foundations lay below the level of the ground. Advancing troops could not have been aware of its existence till fire was opened on them from the rear. It measured about twenty feet square. We looked inside. It was divided into two compartments. There were three dead Germans there. 'It's as likely to be here as any-where,' said King. 'Anyhow, no one's going to come here to find out.'

We moved out the corpses and moved in. 'At least we know where you are,' said King. 'Good luck.'

I never saw him again. Next day a shell did pitch in that slit trench, killing his batman and himself.

§

I was four days in that pill-box. Nothing happened. I was never sure where I was; I had no idea where the German line was. I did the routine things, lay low during the day and by night made contact with the infantry on either side. They had no idea either where the Germans were. There had been no counter-attack on this immediate sector. I was afraid of going too far forward lest I should stumble into an enemy patrol. One night I fell into a shell-hole and shivered in damp clothes for thirty hours. I have inherited to a mild degree my father's asthma. I cannot think why I did not catch a cold. We were shelled at dawn and dusk; but the cement offered us pro-tection. The opening of the pill-box faced the Germans. Our only danger was of a shell landing in the doorway. None did.

The rations came up next night. The runner told me of King's death. When was the relief due? He did not know.

Nobody knew anything. There was a large mail for me. It contained a copy of Mais's novel *Rebellion*, written at Underhill after Christmas. There was a bottle of rum. To counteract the chill of my soaked clothes, I took a tot. It was the first time that I had tasted spirits. It scorched me and I spat it out. I did not try rum again during the campaign. Next night the rations did not come. Had the runner been killed on the way up? If the runner as well as King was dead, how would anyone know where we were? Van Diemen's farm indeed! If no rations and no orders arrived, how long did I have to stay here? A relief must be due within three days; could I after four days assume that orders had been mislaid? Would I be justified in taking my men back; or would that be a court-martial offence? Desertion in the face of the enemy? The enemy were, I knew, only a couple of hundred yards away but I was less concerned, far less concerned about anything that they could do to me, than with what my captain at H.Q. might do if I did not carry out his orders.

For the next twenty-four hours we were hungry and very grateful for a box of apples that we had found, only quarter-eaten, in the pill-box. A letter lay on top of them, written in German, that none of us could read. I pictured the woman, wife or mother or fiancée, packing this box with loving thoughts. When had the box arrived? On the eve of the attack before he had time to thank for it? Was his one of the three corpses that we had shovelled into the nearest shell-hole? Was some woman thinking in Bavaria at this moment, 'I wonder if Franz has got those apples yet?'

I read *Rebellion*. It contained a satiric description of a Sunday lunch in a west-country rectory. The heroine's sophisticated palate was revolted by the thick greasy soup, the stringy, fat-lined mutton, the custard and stewed pears. Mais had lingered over the description; my mouth watered. If only I could be set before a meal like that, right now.

Next day the rations came up as usual. On the previous day the ration mule had slipped into a shell-hole. An extra supply of rum had been sent up. There was a spate of rumours. No. 1 section had had heavy casualties. We were due to be relieved at any time.

§

Nothing happened during those four days in the front line in one of the biggest battles in history. We did not see a German, we did not fire a shot, we did not have a casualty. The morning and evening barrages thundered round us; we were safe under the cement. It was quiet at night; I took an occasional short stroll maintaining contact on my left and right. Very-flares lit the horizon. There would be the dull thud of shell-fire, a random bullet would spit into the mud beside me. I cannot remember if there was a moon. I think there must have been. It was not very dark. The waste of shell-holes stretched on every side. I could distinguish, now and again, a soldier 'souveniring', searching the dead bodies for watches, cigarette-cases, fountain-pens. So this was war, I thought; how far from the fluttering pennants of Agincourt and Crecy; from 'the bannered broidery that covers crime and calls it history'.[1] How different from the idealized picture presented by the pulpit and the Press. 'Blessed Banners', indeed; 'the cup of sacrifice'. Man had been robbed here of his innate dignity, reduced to the lowest level of existence; huddled in the primeval mud, waiting for the 'brazen frenzy'[2] to churn him back into it. Standing there looking over the carnage-strewn morass, the need rose in me to dedicate my pen to the portrayal of war as in itself it was; to expose the popular, conventional idea of war. The politicians in their Whitehall offices, the manufacturers pocketing their dividends, the publicists and the apologists of war mouthing their telling periods must be made to face the Gorgon; too many people were doing well out of the war; the common man was being exploited for their gain and glory. Never again, I vowed, never, never again. The young men of my generation must see to that.

[1] D. S. MacColl's Newdigate Prize Poem, 1882.
[2] Julian Grenfell's 'Into Battle'.

The Author and Milton Hayes as prisoners of war

"LITTERATOOR"

A cartoon in the prisoner-of-war camp magazine.
Left to right: the Author, Hugh Kingsmill, Gerard
Hopkins. The resemblances to Hopkins and Kingsmill
are so close that I fear I must have looked like this

IV

Winter in the Trenches

From Ypres we went south, to the desolate landscape of the Somme; the broken villages, the uncoloured downs, the long, straight roads with their poplars that dwindled to stumps as the road approached the line, re-emerging as trees again on the far horizon behind the German trenches; not a sign of civilian life, not a field being ploughed, not a garden tended; not a shop or café. Our hearts were glad though to be back. The salient was behind us; we would not be in serious action again for several months: and we had now in the company a feeling of solidarity. We had survived our test. We had been blooded. The long pause of routine trench warfare between the nightmare of individual shows was by no means unpleasant; if one liked soldiering, and I did.

We were guarding a stretch of line in front of Bullecourt. My section H.Q. was under the embankment of a railway line, in a deep, well-built German dug-out. I had plenty of leisure to read and answer my immense correspondence from readers of *The Loom*.

Every night at half-past six I would go down to the ration dump with my runner. We would stand, shivering in the cold, exchanging gossip with the fatigue-men from other units, waiting for the tinkle of the mules' harness down the road. 'Any letters for me?' I'd ask. I was greeted with a guffaw. 'I think you must be writing to yourself, sir.'

I would spread out the letters on my dug-out table, as though they were a pack of cards. A third would be addressed in a script I had not seen before. I would not have time to read them before I went round the guns.

I

At night there was a melancholy beauty about the undulating barren waste of that bleak battle-scoured countryside. On the horizon there would be the flash of guns. Now and again a Very light would climb into the sky, to hang, lighting the landscape with its incandescent glow. The broken, roofless houses, their bases in shadow, would appear to be suspended above the ground, ghostly and unsubstantial habitations. Then the light would fade and the houses vanish. I enjoyed those evening tours, thinking of the letters awaiting me in my dug-out.

§

Some of them were from other novelists who had written to my father. From two of them I would like to quote, not out of vanity but because they are interpretative of the divergent points of view of H. G. Wells and Arnold Bennett, two important writers whose names are often linked.

> Wells wrote: Your son is an astounding young man, and I've rarely read a first novel with so much interest. He writes easily and unaffectedly and he's got a sense of character beyond his tender years. . . . I hope he won't become a novelist (or only a novelist incidentally or a sociological novelist if he must be one). I want to see a rush of the young men into power after the war. I don't think we can spare them for art. But I've been trying all my life to get the art tradition out of literature.

On the other hand, Bennett said:

> I think it is a staggering performance for the author and would be a fine performance for nearly anybody. I am not primarily interested in the public school altercation and I don't much care whether the institution of the P.S. can successfully survive your son's presentation of it or not. What interests me is the very remarkable narrative gift of this man. . . .

As I read such letters in my dug-out, I had the sense of being welcomed into an honoured company. At the same time, I could not resist a sense of being cheated; what a time I should be having if I were in London; meeting the men and women whose work I most admired. A success like this could only come once in life, and I was being robbed of its fruits. Actually I was very lucky. If I had been in London then as the literary lion of the hour I do not see how I could have helped having my head turned—2nd-Lt. Waugh, A.R., Dorset Rgt., attached M.G.C., was an altogether different person from that dashing young iconoclast, Alec Waugh.

§

By no means all the correspondence that I received was on a note of welcome. The schools had now been back a month, and every housemaster in the country had returned from his summer holidays to find his desk littered with letters from anxious parents demanding reassurance that their Bobbie was not subject to the temptations described in this alarming book. In self-defence the schoolmasters hit back and within a few weeks the book became the centre of violent controversy.

Canon Edward Lyttleton, the ex-headmaster of Eton, delivered himself of a ten-page attack in the *Contemporary Review*, at that time an important monthly.

No one in 1914 [*his article began*] could have foreseen that with the war still raging in 1917 and the fabulous expenditure in full swing there would be found enough purchasers of a book like *The Loom of Youth* to run it through three editions in three months. It is an inexplicable phenomenon. The book is written by a very young author, but the fact remains that it is uniformly dull, occasionally unpleasant, and, in my judgement at least, almost wholly untrue.

The *Spectator* ran for ten weeks and the *Nation* for six a correspondence filling three or four pages an issue in which schoolmaster after schoolmaster asserted that whatever might be true of 'Fernhurst', wherever that might be, at his school things were very different. Grant Richards adeptly fanned the conflagration. He had initiated that summer an original style of advertising. He inserted each week in *The Times Literary Supplement* a half-column of gossip about his books and authors. It was set in small, heavy, black type, and caught the eye. Richards was a good writer and it was readable. He was, I think, the first publisher to exploit the publicity value of unfavourable comment. Richard Hughes, at that time in the sixth form at Charterhouse, wrote, as his weekly essay, an attack on *The Loom*. His form-master Dames Longworth, a fine old Tory, sent it up to the *Spectator*, as a counterblast to such 'pernicious stuff'. Next week Grant Richards quoted him: 'Mr. Dames Longworth called the book "pernicious stuff", but Clement Shorter prophesied in the *Sphere* that it would prove "the *Uncle Tom's Cabin* of the public school system".'

In many schools the book was banned and boys were caned for reading it. Censorship usually defeats its own purposes. Cecil Day Lewis was then a fag at Sherborne and in his autobiography *The Buried Day* he wrote:

> It was difficult in any case to dissociate chapel from adult cant and hypocrisy when sermon after sermon introduced comminations against *The Loom of Youth*. . . . Those of us who had smuggled copies knew that it was true, so we took a poor view of those elders who proclaimed that such things could not happen in Sherborne, or if they did, should not have been written about; and their blindness, or hypocrisy, or moral cowardice—as it seemed to some of us—devalued in our eyes the religion of which they were spokesmen.

In retrospect, I can understand why Sherborne was so indignant. During the 'nineties it had suffered grievously from unfortunate publicity; the story of the episode has been excellently told in A. B. Gourlay's *History of Sherborne*. Now just when it was recovering its strength under a new headmaster, its weaknesses were being exaggerated and exposed, and by an ex-boy of whom it had officially thoroughly disapproved. But at the time I was surprised and angry.

When the book had been accepted, my father had decided not to send Evelyn to Sherborne because it would be awkward for him to sit under masters who had been satirized in print, but

I had not anticipated so violent a reaction. I was unwise enough to write a letter of protest to the *Shirburnian*.

The editor was one of the three boys who had not signed the Grand Remonstrance. He replied that at the beginning of the term the Chief had told him that the *Shirburnian* must contain no correspondence about the book; he had, therefore, taken my letter to the Chief. The Chief's letter to me said, 'You say that you have been attacked, but you have not been attacked by the *Shirburnian*, and you will not be. . . . Your letter is a repetition of your libel on the school. . . . I presume that you will want to resign from the O.S. Society, which I cannot think why you ever joined.'

I had put myself in a weak position by coming into the open. I should have waited for Sherborne to make the first move. I replied that I did not wish to resign from the Society which I had joined because I loved Sherborne. I sent the Chief's letter to my father. He wrote at once resigning his membership of the Society. I learnt later that both our names had been removed from the list before the correspondence began.

It was not till 1933 that we were re-instated, through the efforts, largely, of Cecil Day Lewis and V. C. Clinton-Baddeley.

§

A modern reader will wonder what all this fuss and indignation was about. Several years ago a friend was reading the book in my presence. 'When do I reach *the* scene?' he asked.

I looked over his shoulder. 'You've passed it ten pages back,' I told him.

Two points must be remembered. First, that before the First World War, Britain's imperial destiny was rarely questioned, and the public school system as a bulwark of Empire was held sacrosanct. Second, that no book before had accepted as part of the fabric of school life the almost inevitable emotional consequences of a monastic herding together for eight months of the year of thirteen-year-old children and eighteen-year-old adolescents. On that issue as I have already pointed out such a complete conspiracy of silence had been maintained that when fathers were asked by their wives, and schoolmasters by parents who had not themselves been at public schools, whether 'such things really could take place', the only defence was a grudging admission. 'Perhaps in a bad house, in a bad school, in a bad time.'

The book has never been out of print and during the Second War was issued as a Penguin. It is read today in much the same spirit that *Tom Brown's Schooldays* was at the turn of the century, as a human, realistic study of school life. The fact that it was once the centre of such violent controversy is the proof surely that the writing of it was badly needed. A tin god had to be dethroned.

§

The late autumn and early winter of 1917, how the rains lashed across Northern France and Flanders! In the salient only mules could get the ammunition to the guns; tanks were bogged down but the attack continued, and the slaughter with it; every week a few yards of swamp land were recovered, at the cost of many thousand men. Haig, to the end of his life, believed that the attacks were justified, that they drained and exhausted the German machine and brought the end of the war nearer. Who am I to question his opinion? To the soldier in the line it seemed an impossible enterprise, a stalemate; he did not believe that the higher command had any conception of the conditions under which he was being forced to fight. In that, I believe that 'the man on the spot' was right. In November Lansdowne wrote a letter to *The Times*, urging a negotiated peace. Most of the troops agreed with him. The Austrians and Germans broke the Italian line at Caporetto and several British divisions were moved to the Italian front. We prayed that we might be one of them. But we were out of luck. Revolution again shook Petrograd and Russia checked out of the war. In late November the tanks broke through at Cambrai and joy-bells were rung in England, but a few days later the Germans counter-attacked and staff officers were captured in their pyjamas.

We were on the extreme left of the Cambrai attack. We fired a barrage on the first morning and waited for orders to advance, orders that never came. The first morning was memorable. The secret of the attack had been well kept. We were set to dig a series of gun emplacements in a sunken road. Tanks were rumoured to be around. But from the orders we received it all sounded like a routine exercise, designed to keep the men alert.

Zero hour was at 6 a.m. It was a quiet night, a little token shelling, a Very light or two, a night like any other; then suddenly the sky was filled with noise and flame. I have never seen such a firework display, star shells, Very lights, S.O.S. signals. My section officer and I watched it, transfixed, like children on Guy Fawkes day. Then sumultaneously, to our horror, we realized that we were making our individual contribution to the spectacle; one of our guns was firing a belt of tracer bullets, thereby giving an exact map reference of our position to the enemy observation posts. We rushed down the slippery road like Rugby forwards after a ball that is bouncing in the open. Apparently, mercifully, the Germans were too busy to be concerned with us.

We fired our barrage for half an hour, then knocked off, started on the cleaning of the guns, waited for breakfast and for orders. I cannot remember how long we waited. At one point the rumours became news; then rumours began to contradict each other. The first news was buoyant; a complete breakthrough. We must be ready to advance at half an hour's notice. We were to move through Bullecourt to Hendicourt. It was no good looking for roads, there were none. At Hendicourt we would get fresh orders. The day wore on. Our excitement ebbed. It was very cold; there were no dug-outs. The men fixed up a covering of groundsheets; machine-gun officers needed a dry clean place where they could work out range charts. We dug out a shelter in the side of the road. It was dismally inadequate. The night passed; and then another day; rumours filtered through that the attack was checked. A tank had slithered on a bridge and broken it, so that the infantry could not cross the river; a German officer single-handed at his anti-tank gun had held up the entire attack for half a day. The order still held, to be ready to advance at a half-hour's notice. It was cold and wet and windy. When the final order came, cancelling that readiness to advance, was I relieved? I hope I was not. But I suspect that within part of myself—I hope a very small part—I thought, 'That's that.'

Christmas 1917: as grey a Christmas as Britain has ever known; a long grim year, three major attacks—at Arras, Ypres and Cambrai with nothing tangible to show for them; and the German armies who had been released from the Russian front were massing now in France and Flanders, waiting for the spring offensive. We might have consoled ourselves with the knowledge that the vast American machine was geared for action, that the summer would see their troops in the line, that within a year the Germans would be outnumbered. But we had come to think of the war as something between France and our-selves and Germany; anyhow the menace of the spring offensive lay across the gap before the American arrival.

In the middle of February I went home on leave. The Second War had no equivalent for that fourteen days' leave from France. There was no leave from the Middle East. I do not know if there was any leave from France after D-day, but it cannot have been on the same scale. And England in the Second War was a very different place to return on leave to. London was under bomb-fire; there was tight rationing and the strain of five years' austerity. England was too exhausted to spread red carpets under the feet of returning warriors who had been having in many instances a less dangerous and strenuous time than had those at home. In the First War Britain in general and London in particular were geared to the tempo of the leave from France. I have known few better moments than the surprise with which I received one morning in my dug-out the news that I was to return to H.Q. and proceed on leave.

It was one of the best fortnights of my life. A few weeks earlier the Jacobs' had agreed to the official announcement of my engagement and my first act in London was to drive to Regent Street and buy an engagement ring. My return was unexpec-ted. That made it the more exciting. The announcement of our engagement appeared that week in *The Times*; and there was the pile of congratulatory letters; the visits to photographers; in addition there was the thrill of seeing piles of my novel on the bookstands.

In the trenches I had resented being deprived of the fruits of my success. I had brooded on the lunch parties I was missing, the big names I was not meeting; now I was back in London;

but a fortnight is a very little time. I wanted to spend as much of it as possible with Barbara and in the family circle. I might be a widely discussed personality, but I was only nineteen, a very unsophisticated nineteen. I did not drink, I had seen nothing of adult life; not only had I not mixed in the big world, I did not know that it existed. My idea of a good party was a nursery one, 'Up Jenkins', charades and letter games.

I did, however, make a few contacts with the world of letters. I lunched with Gilbert Cannan. C. K. Scott-Moncrieff, with whom I had begun a correspondence as a result of his review of *The Loom*, gave a lunch party for me at the R.A.C. where I sat next Ronald Knox and met Robert Ross. I called on J. C. Squire in his office. I had tea in Hanover Terrace with Edmund Gosse. I went down for the night to Tonbridge where S. P. B. Mais was now a schoolmaster, Sherborne having dispensed with his services after the appearance of *Interlude*. Not a great many contacts, but they were enough to show me that I had become, for many, a different person from the young subaltern who seven months earlier had craned his neck to get that extra two seconds' glimpse of the scaffolding south of Underhill. Up till then, as A. R. Waugh, I had been known only to the people who had actually met me; they had judged me on my appearance and behaviour, how I had looked, dressed, talked, moved, acted. But now as Alec Waugh I was known to a number of people who had formed an impression of me through my book, had wondered what I was like and assumed in terms of their reaction, favourable or hostile, that I was this or that. I did not then, naturally, fully appreciate the consequences of that recognition; with its corollary that for the rest of my life I should be two persons, myself and the author of my books; nor could I guess at how different those two persons might become.

'Never meet authors' has become an axiom, and it is very true that many authors are or seem to be very different from their books. Very few authors express their entire personalities in their books and very often if they have expressed adequately in their books a certain side of their characters, they do not need to express that side in their lives. It would be nearly true to say that the better the writer the more disappointing he is to meet, were it not that men of achievement invariably carry an aura round them, so that one says instinctively, 'I wonder who that is, he must be someone.'

I have met a good many men of prominence, and I have usually found myself wondering what they are like behind their masks. That is why, in London and New York, I have preferred small clubs to large, clubs like the Beefsteak, the Coffee House, and Pratt's, where it is easy for men of importance to relax.

A man who depends for his prominence on his ability to impress and convince his fellows on the platform, in the pulpit, in boardrooms, conferences and committees, develops an effective personality. A writer luckily does not need to. His ability to dominate a drawing-room does not enhance his literary prestige. His wit and charm may secure invitations for him, but he will not sell one extra copy of his books by having his attendance at a social function paragraphed in a gossip column. I am as anxious as anyone to deserve and if possible to earn the good opinion of my fellows, but I have always known that there was one way only for me to do it—through my books. I am not a man with a striking presence; I cannot imagine that any woman would look at me twice in a restaurant; I do not scintillate in conversation. I have no wish to impress my point of view on other people—except on paper. I am more interested in finding out what the other man thinks, and why. I have no wish to talk about myself; I want to know what other people are about. I prefer listening to talking, except on special occasions. I do not know what shyness is. I have never felt nervous as I knotted my evening tie before going out to dinner, wondering whether I should be a success or not. I have recognized my duty as a guest. It was up to me to help 'make the party go'. But I have never needed to impress anyone. I have never had an axe to grind. I have had only one concern—to write as well as I was able, and I have rated as secondary every consideration that did not advance that purpose. If my books could not earn me the respect of my hostess and her guests, what object could be served by epigrams across a table?

From the age of nineteen I have known that anyone who felt any curiosity about me could satisfy it by going to a library. I have known that for me success or failure depended upon the position occupied on the literary bourse by the name Alec Waugh. As a result I have been able, in august as in simple company, to be myself, even though that self was not quite the person that the reader of my books may have expected.

A writer is a lucky mortal to be able to do that, particularly if he is not extrovert, and the majority of writers have a brooding, reflective temperament. If I had not been a writer, if I had belonged to a profession that does not win its spurs till early middle age, had I been a barrister or a bureaucrat or, as is most likely, an officer in the colonial service, my ambitious nature would have forced me to develop a public personality, so that people who met me would remember me, thinking, 'That is a young man who should go far.' I am glad I did not have to.

V

The Big Retreat

I returned to France on March 5 to find that our company had
been moved north of Arras, with my section divided, and myself
in charge of a subsection whose two guns commanded a valley
west of the Arras–Cambrai road. The position had, on one
flank, a superb field of fire.

A curiously unreal calm lay over the line during the days that
preceded the offensive. The sky was cloudless. The dun-
coloured fields turned green. The air was mild and the sun
warm upon our faces; the kind of weather that in early March
surprises us into the belief that summer has already come. I had
nothing to do but wait. I had bought in Boulogne a yellow
paper-covered translation of Zola's *La Terre*. Across the cover
was printed 'Unexpurgated edition, not allowed in England'.
I had bought it for the unworthiest of reasons, but to my surprise I found myself reading it slowly, appreciatively, in long
sips, thirty pages a day, not as I had expected turning the leaves
hurriedly to reach the next salacious passage. This was the way
to write, I thought, the massive construction of a narrative, the
marshalling of scenes and characters, the monumental archi-
tecture of a theme. This was how I would build my second
novel. Although the big offensive was a few hours away, I had
no doubt that I should find myself one day seated at a desk.

One of my daily duties was to examine my men's gasmasks. I
was also supposed to examine my own. I had neglected to do so
for some little time. On March 18 I decided that it was time I
did. To my horror I discovered that the container was half
rotted away. I was terrified, and overwhelmed with guilt. I
sent the mask down to H.Q. accompanied by a letter explaining

that I must have taken the wrong gasbag when I had gone into the latrine of another unit. It was the most unconvincing piece of fiction that I have ever penned. Luckily H.Q. was too busy to send me the reprimand I merited. A new mask was forwarded without comment.

Fifty hours later I was thanking heaven that at last I had remembered my obligation to myself. On the morning of the 21st the valley that I was guarding was deep in mist, and shells were pitching round us with the dead 'phut' that proclaims they contain gas. An S.O.S. went up upon our right; we fired our barrage with our masks on. The Germans were as lucky with their weather then as they were twenty-two years later in the Ardennes. The rainless spell had dried the ground. Mist was shrouding their advance. Slowly the mist cleared. Would I see the valley dotted with field grey uniforms? My nerves were taut. But, no. It looked exactly as it had done for the last two weeks. What now, I wondered? Had the attack failed? Had it been a feint attack? The shelling on the right seemed a long way off and intermittent. Once again I waited for news. After lunch I made contact with the unit on my flank. They knew as little as I did. Slowly the day died, a bland mild evening with soft pastel colouring. Rations arrived on time. There was no message from H.Q. It was rumoured, so the runner told us, that a heavy attack had been beaten off. A couple of hours later, a confidential envelope confirmed this rumour. It contained a message from the general congratulating his division on the soldierly valour it had shown that morning. I was to read the message to my men. We were well aware that we had done nothing valorous. But the message pleased us. I slept well that night.

It was the last night on which I was to sleep with a mind at peace for several days. At noon a message announced that the Fifth Army was in retreat, that Bullecourt and Ecoust-St. Mein were in German hands. Twenty hours later, I received orders to withdraw, to join my section commander and proceed with him to a defensive position a couple of miles north of Neuville Vitasse.

Twenty-two years later, on May 9 1940, the eve of the German offensive, when I was stationed with G.H.Q. B.E.F. at

Arras, I walked on my afternoon off to Neuville-Vitasse to inspect the site. My section was placed on the side of a low hill, that commanded a long valley; a minor road ran a hundred or so yards below. On the far side of the valley a long poplar-lined road crossed the horizon. The village of Neuville-Vitasse was at its foot. In the side of the hill was a deep German dugout. There was a slit trench in which we dug our gun emplacements. Our company commander, a young captain, had guided us to our position. 'Your job,' he said, 'is to hold up the advance along that valley. Hang on here, whatever happens.' There was no organized trench system.

Apart from the fact that the hill was not dotted with shellholes, that there were no trenches, that the shattered village of Neuville-Vitasse had been rebuilt, it all looked very much the same twenty-two years later, except for one thing, and that surprised me. At the top of the hill, very close to our position, was a low martello tower. I could not think what purpose it served. It looked old, yet I have no recollection of it. Surely if it had been there, I should have remembered it. If it was not there then, why was it built since?

It was on the night of March 23/24 that we took up our position. When day broke, we recognized that we had a superb field of fire down the valley; but ours was not a strong point. In the first place, we had no bombs. The transportation of a machine-gun section is a bulky operation; we were a limber short and had had to dump what we did not immediately need. We could always get more bombs, we thought.

Once again we waited, resuming the trench routine, with the regular arrival of mail and rations, and the morning and evening situation reports to details. From the newspapers we learnt how the main battle was progressing up to two days before, but we had no idea of how it was progressing on our immediate sector. We did not know where the front line ran—if indeed there was a front line at all. We knew where H.Q. was upon the map, but we did not know where it was in terms of trenches. I very much doubt if we had large-scale maps of our immediate front. Field service regulations laid down that we should make contact with neighbouring units, but we did not know where they were. As far as we could judge there were no troops in the valley that we guarded. We had no idea how the land lay on the far side of the hill. We were afraid if we reconnoitred rashly of stumbling on an enemy patrol. Our job, we reminded ourselves, was to watch and guard the valley. What happened on the other side of the hill was the concern of others. From what we could judge from the newspaper reports, Arras was on the extreme north of the German attack. The main drive was aimed at Amiens. We were, we fancied, in the same position, in reverse, as we had been at Cambrai. On the night of the 27/28 a large mail came up, with a cake for my section officer. We were at peace with the world as we sat, munching the cake, reading our letters. Soon we would be relieved. We had certainly got off lucky. Five hours later, from the thunder in the air, and the flashes of star shells in the sky, it was clear that the offensive had been resumed.

Once again I had no idea of what was happening. One of our difficulties was that neither my section officer nor myself had any experience of open warfare, apart from what we had acquired on field days during training; and in a way all that happened during the next few hours had the unreality of a field day. Nothing at all happened in the valley that we were guarding, but we gradually realized that a good deal was happening on the other side of the hill. An infantry officer, wounded through the shoulder, on his way back to the first field dressing-station, told us that the Germans were through on our right in force. An infantryman on his way back to his unit had found the road leading to it blocked. Could he stay with us till he knew where it was? We were shelled first by light artillery, then by whizzbangs. A shell landed on a gun emplacement, destroying the gun, killing one of the crew. We could see, far away to our right Germans filtering behind us. We sniped at them, with rifles, but they were not machine-gun targets.

'We might get a target if we mounted a gun out there in the open,' said my section officer. But even there, there was not a target, and the gunner was shot through the wrist. As I bound it up I noticed how the skin puckered back, on the side where the bullet had come through, like stretched silk that has been released. The road to H.Q. was, I believed, still open and I sent him back. I never learnt if he got there.

The morning passed; no sign of activity in the valley, but all the time on our right the steady filtering behind us of grey-green uniforms, like a sea flooding slowly round us. We looked at the road that ran through the valley. We might find targets if we could get down there. We might be able to enfilade this encroaching stream. A dash across the open, then the cover of a shell-hole; but we had acquired the trench warfare mentality through months of immobility, of staying where we were put until we got new orders. We had to guard this valley. We might be court-martialled for desertion if we acted on our own responsibility. We were more afraid of our captain at H.Q. than of the Germans in the shell-holes opposite. None of it seemed real.

'If only we had some bombs,' said my section officer. We were not a strong point. We had no defence against an enemy who would advance up the trench, bombing us from behind traverses. The shelling became more persistent and more accurate. The incoming tide was stealing closer. We were cut off and we were defenceless. My section commander and I looked at each other. 'I don't see that there's anything we can do,' he said.

I nodded.

'We'd best destroy the guns,' he said.

By noon it was all over; and we were the wrong side of the line.

VI

Prisoner of War

A month later I was in an Offizier-Kriegensfagenlager, in a walled barracks above Mainz, one of the few parts of the city that survived the saturation bombing of 1943–5. As prison camps go, it was airy, comfortable, congenial. We had a view of the Rhine and the cathedral, from our upper windows. There was a large barrack square and there were chestnut trees. We were crowded but not overcrowded; ten of us to a room; about 600 in the camp. It was a pleasantly sunny summer.

A little while ago I was exchanging prisoner-of-war reminiscences with an American diplomat, Robert Gray, who was taken prisoner in the Second War. 'There's one thing to be said. I did a lot of reading. I read all the chief Russian novels. If I hadn't read them then, I don't know when I would have done.'

My experience was similar. My education stopped when I was seventeen. The gaps in my knowledge are numerous and wide, and I have had no chance, caught up by the demands of livelihood, of filling them. The only real leisure I have had since I left Sherborne was the six months I spent in the citadel at Mainz. It was there that I was introduced to Flaubert, Maupassant, Balzac, Chekhov, Turgenev and Dostoevsky—no, not Tolstoy, there were no copies in the camp of *War and Peace* or *Anna Karenina*—to George Moore and Walter Pater.

Life in a prisoner-of-war camp was much the same in the First War as in the Second. As most prisoners do, I arrived at Mainz covered with lice. I began to itch some days after capture. I took off my shirt and found some unsavoury creatures in the seams. I slaughtered them and trusted that I was through

with it. The itching began again next day. I made a more tho-
rough search, scrutinizing every garment. I had time on my
hands and I devoted an entire morning to it. Now, surely, I
was quit of the pest. But that night I was scratching again.

For two days more I waged my battle against odds; then I
surrendered; there was nothing to be done. I was pitted against
invisible foes. For three weeks I was verminous; there are few
conditions that demoralize one more; one is outside the pale.
As soon as I reached Mainz, I was put under a shower and my
clothes were stuffed in an oven.

As a prisoner, I was exposed to another experience that I had
never expected to have come my way; for three months I was
hungry. Germany was by then very short of food, and officer
prisoners of war who were not working, as O.R.s were, in field
and factory, could not expect more than the barest rations.
Twice a day, at eight and three, we received in our rooms a jug
of coffee that did not taste like coffee and had been made, we
were told, from acorns. At noon and at six in the evening we had
soup in the dining-room; the soup was thin and it was accompanied by a dish of vegetables. Always once a day and sometimes twice this dish contained potatoes. Each week the menus
for the week were published on the camp notice-board. Our
red-letter days were those when we had potatoes twice. *Sauer-
kraut* was served every day; none of us liked it—presumably
because the flavour was unusual to us. We never had any meat
or eggs; the fish was pungent. Every two weeks we were issued
with a paper cone containing a few ounces of coarse, brown
sugar. Most of us ate ours in a single sitting and felt rather sick.
We were also issued weekly with two loaves of brown bread.
We would mark off, on the crust, the limits of each day's
allowance. It tasted much better when it was new and the
temptation to devour it in two days was great. I rarely arrived
at the start of a loaf's last day with my full ration left. On the
last evening, as I looked at a small dry crust, deliberating
whether I should eat it now or leave it for tomorrow's coffee, I
knew the problem of a pauper with a shilling in his pocket, as he
wonders whether it shall purchase him a supper or a breakfast.
It cannot do both.

We could supplement our rations at the canteen, as far as our funds permitted, with fish and liver pastes, and packets of soup. One of these packets contained dried vegetables; you were supposed to soak it in water for six hours before heating it. I misread the instructions and left it in water for thirty minutes. The vegetables, in consequence, did their swelling inside me. It was most painful.

We thought about food most of the time, recalling meals that we had enjoyed, planning meals for our return to England. A great part of our conversation turned on food. There would be discussions of the best way to treat a chicken; and arguments about the respective qualities of baby lamb and beef. Some of us adopted a highbrow, puritan attitude, denigrating the pleasures of the table in comparison with the pleasures of the mind. 'What worried me during those first two weeks,' I would contend, 'was not that I had very little to eat but that I had nothing at all to read.'

That was, in fact, partially true. But I wooed sleep each night, as my lower-browed companions did, with memories of rich meats and steaming sauces.

By the end of June, food parcels had started to arrive, and we accepted the traditional prisoner-of-war pattern of existence, the crowded dormitory routine, the cooking over a small communal stove, the excitement over letters, the queueing up for parcels, the problem of getting money (in 1918 a subaltern was allowed to cash one five-pound cheque a month through a Swiss bank), the boxing competitions and theatricals, the long walks round the square, and the intolerably long evenings when one was confined to one's barracks after nightfall. There was also the organization of classes in foreign languages, history, economics. Every camp contained several schoolmasters. At the start there was a rush to enrol and fifty students would start to learn bookkeeping and shorthand, but the enthusiasm soon waned, and after a few weeks each professor found himself addressing a small but serious study group.

Every week at Mainz the head of the Educational Committee posted a programme allotting the rooms available for the separate classes. At the foot of the list was a note stating that when no classes were in progress the Alcove was reserved for authors, architects and other students. The Alcove was a small, first-floor room at the end of the series of rooms in which we ate. As a dining-room it could seat twenty at two narrow tables flanked by backless benches. It looked out upon the ramparts, which an ancient sentry patrolled with a slow dragging step. This room was my equivalent for a University. It was here that I met for the first time adult minds upon equal terms.

I was lucky in my fellow captives—in Sir Henry Lunn's second son, who later for professional reasons changed his name to Hugh Kingsmill; in Gerard Hopkins, the author of several novels and the translator of a number of French novels, in particular those of François Mauriac; in Milton Hayes, the author of *The Green Eye of the Little Yellow God* and a first-grade music-hall entertainer; in the musician Maurice Besly, and most markedly of all, John Holms, a man who came to nothing, who died young, but of whom I still think as one of the most brilliant people I have ever known, of whom I hope to write fully in a later book, of whom the curious may read in Peggy Guggenheim's memoirs and in William Gerhardi's. I owe more than I can say to those long hours in the Alcove.

Life in a prisoner-of-war camp is a strange experience. It is a period of suspension; there is nothing that one can do but wait. One's future and fortune lie in the hands of others. Officially one's duty is to escape; one is receiving pay from the home government; one should earn that pay by trying to get back into the fighting line. Even if one fails, each attempt to escape, forces one's captors to take greater efforts in security, thereby incurring a drain on their war effort. In retrospect I am surprised that I did not join one of the escaping clubs. Was I deterred by my ignorance of German and by the knowledge that in four years no successful break-out had been made from Mainz, or did my inertia spring from a need to lick my wounds, to recover my energies, to come to terms with myself?

Every unwounded prisoner of war must be afflicted by a sense of guilt. He did not join the army to languish behind prison bars. Should he be here at all? Was there not something he could have done to avoid this fate? Did he fail in initiative, did he fail in courage? Had he done this, had he not done that? I suppose that every prisoner has felt as I did then. It is pointless to brood over the past; one has to get on with the next thing. I am resilient. I was here, I told myself, and there was nothing more to do about it; I must take advantage of my good luck in being still alive; but would I have been human if it had not been with a sense of guilt that I thought of the men and officers of my company in France, in danger and distress, while I sat here in safety, waiting to be released by them?

I was asked when I got back to England how soon I realized that the tide had turned, that an Allied victory was imminent. I fancy that I knew as early as anyone did in Britain. Censorship in Germany was strict; but the Allied communiqués were printed in their papers. They were interpreted, in the leading articles, in terms of propaganda, suggesting that there were sound strategic reasons for the withdrawal; parallels were drawn with the withdrawal to the Hindenberg line in the spring of 1917, but the facts spoke for themselves. Moreover, we could sense in the way the Germans themselves received the news that they were at the end of their resources. They no longer spoke of victory but of peace. One of the officers in charge of the camp said, 'This is like the last hour of a long journey; you think that it will never end, but it will end.'

§

Richard Aldington, in one of his finest poems, written in 1919, describes the mood with which he looked forward to his return to civilian life. The war is over. He has the chance he longed for to live his life out to the end. He will return, a free man, to his wife, and his friends, to the work he loves, 'long quiet evenings by the tranquil lamp'. And yet he wonders . . . will he find it so easy to return to the old life; may he not find himself 'out of patience with the café chatterers'; will he be able to 'cajole his scanty pittance from the money vultures'? And love, how will he be welcomed after the novelty of his return has faded? 'Can a woman be both beautiful and loyal?' Perhaps this is his happiest moment, 'here in this cold little Belgian house'.

I thought of that poem in the summer of 1959 when I drove over to Mainz, from Frankfurt where the P.E.N. Club congress was in session. Mainz had been heavily bombed during the war. Had I been led blindfolded into the square, I should not, when

I had been unbandaged, have known where I was. Not a building that I could recognize was standing. The cathedral was a shell. But the citadel on the hill had not been touched. It had been converted by the French into a university. The square had been laid down in grass. Everything was very spick and span. From the outside it seemed unchanged, though the interior had been made over, with dormitories converted into offices and classrooms. Walls had been added, ceilings had been raised. The Alcove itself had gone, but the same window gave upon the ramparts. In what spirit had I looked through that window forty years before, during those autumn weeks when it became increasingly clear that the war's end was near?

Forty years on. 'When we look back and regretfully wonder . . .' My heart in those weeks was buoyant with anticipation. I am four years younger than Aldington. I had had no adult pre-war life. I was unmarried, I could not foresee the dangers that he did. There was no cloud on my horizon. Forty years on. The contrast between the promise of life and its fulfilment. In what shapes, what colours did I foresee my future? Would I have been shocked at the age of twenty could I have foreseen the sexuagenarian who in 1959 would stand looking up at the Alcove window?

In some respects I would have been. I have always been ambitious. But it was for fame, not fortune, that I was avid. I had never met a man of wealth; I had never been inside a rich man's house. The two classes of men I most admired were poets and first-class cricketers, whose feats are not recompensed in terms of cash. I visualized for myself the highest literary achievements. 'Balzac, get ready to stand down,' I thought.

Foreknowledge of the meagre outcome would have been very galling. If that is all that's going to come of it, I might have thought, are those forty years going to be worth the living? In that respect the looking back is melancholy; but in other respects, in terms of actual living, that twenty-year-old dreamer would have been astounded could he have foreseen the richness and variety of experience that awaited him.

I had no idea that life had so much to offer. How could I have? I foresaw manhood and the conditions of adult life in terms of my father's life and the life lived by my father's friends. I had had a happy childhood. I had been brought up in a happy atmosphere; I pictured myself making a marriage like my father's, living in a house of my own in the Green Belt of London. I saw myself catching the same tube every morning; lunching in my club, returning late in the day; changing into a tweed suit, taking an hour's walk; now and again entertaining guests, now and again going out to dinner, playing golf and cricket over the week-ends; taking a three weeks' summer holiday in France; seeing my children go to my own school, reliving my youth in them—a placid bourgeois pattern. I had no idea that there were different patterns, and how different my own would be. New landscapes, tropic seas, shadows on the horizon that take shape as mountains, the first slow evening stroll along a foreign waterfront; the stir of cities; the impact of fresh personalities; the dramatic ups and downs of a precarious profession—I knew nothing of all that; nor had I any conception of the varied and rich rewards with which the goddess Aphrodite can recompense her subjects. The twenty-year-old prisoner at the Alcove window had no idea that he was going to have so much fun.

§

Forty-four other boys went to Sherborne on the day I did. By the start of the Second War eighteen of them had died, and three more died during the Second War; the half of us did not reach their half century. The label 'Lost Generation' has been applied and is applicable to a number of different groups. Each group was 'lost' in a different way. In respect of casualties my generation suffered less than its predecessors because none of us were old enough to be posted to France before the battle of the Somme, and most of us did not go overseas until 1917. We were lost in two senses, firstly in that leaving school between seventeen and eighteen we were never fully educated; in consequence, a large section of the survivors earned their livings in the colonies and overseas—of my contemporaries, some older, some younger, only three made their mark and were knighted in the conventional, scholastic avenues, W. E. Beckett, D. O. Lumley and G. B. Todd-Jones. Secondly, in that we never became a generation. We were drafted straight from our schoolrooms into adult life. We never grouped ourselves at a university.

When I was young, the university seemed more important than the school. It may have been different in the cases of those who went to schools like Eton, Rugby, Winchester, but Tonbridgians, Shirburnians, Marlburians expected to make at Oxford and at Cambridge the friends who would last them throughout life. At school one was limited by being discouraged from forming friendships with boys of a different generation and in different houses. You made your pick out of a dozen or so boys. At a university you were not limited by your college or your term. You discovered yourself, deciding what kinds of thing you wanted to do in life and with what kinds of person you wanted to do them. That was the normal pattern. For the men of my generation it was broken.

On Armistice Day, 1918, the young man of my generation found himself quarter-educated, with expensive tastes, a sense of responsibility, and a certain practical efficiency, but handicapped by his lack of education. On the other hand he was exposed to far less competition that he would have been if there had been no war. The same number of posts were vacant and the men in quest of them were fewer. Twenty-five years later it was apparent in every country in Europe that there was a grave deficiency of first-class men of fifty. The U.S.A. were not in the same position, because their casualties were fewer, but in 1970 they will be.

On my return to England I had to decide what was the next thing on my programme. I was engaged to be married. I was not too old to go up to Oxford and a short course there would have been invaluable, but I was not in a position to finance myself. I should need the few hundred pounds that I had saved out of my royalties to set up my marriage, and now that I had achieved independence I did not feel justified in asking my father for assistance. As a Regular Army officer I could have stayed on in the army and that would have been the best thing for me to do; I should have been sent abroad, either with the army of occupation or to India. I should have enlarged my experience, and I could have written in the ample spare time that army life provided until I was in a position to take up authorship as a profession. But that would not have been fair to Barbara. I had, in fact, no alternative to applying for a transfer to the Regular Army Reserve of Officers, and discovering to what extent I could support myself by my pen.

It might seem that I was in an excellent position to do just that. But *The Loom of Youth* had not made my fortune. The public generally has no idea of how little an author can make out of a book that appears successful. *The Loom* was a best-seller, in that it was the most discussed book of the year, but its feminine appeal was small, except to mothers. It was not read by young women in their twenties. It was published originally at five shillings, on a flat ten per cent royalty with thirteen copies counting as twelve. My largest royalty cheque was for £250. Its American sales were minute, and although it has sold steadily over the years it has not in all earned me £1,000.

Nor was it the kind of success on which I could 'cash in'. It did not bring me commissions for well-paid articles in the women's magazines. If a schoolboy committed suicide, half the papers in London would ring up to request an article, but I could only write one article. For 364 days in the year the public-school system was not news. Moreover, the kind of article which that kind of 'news' required was then ill-paid. On my return from Germany the *Sunday Times* commissioned me to write an article on 'Public Schools after the War'. The article, in which I suggested a lowering of the school-leaving age, was featured and started a correspondence. I was paid three guineas for it. A theatrical agent suggested that I should lecture in the Aeolian Hall on 'Our Public Schools' on a fifty-fifty profit-sharing basis. The lecture was widely advertised, the hall was packed, applicants were turned away. Most papers covered it. My share of the profits was £11 8s. 2d.

In the Alcove, at Mainz, I had begun a novel of army life, but it was clear that for several years war books would be un-popular and anyhow I did not know how to end my novel. I had written a few short stories, in a mixed manner of Maupassant and Chekhov; they had no magazine appeal. I had, therefore, to find an alternative for army pay.

I suppose that at that time there were a number of possibili-ties open to me. I was young, I had talent, I had connexions.

Some magazine or paper might have found employment for me. Some publishing friend of my father might have offered me a post, as reader and adviser. But the easiest solution, clearly, was to join Chapman & Hall. It was to prove a considerable mistake, because once having publicly identified myself with my father's house, I could not switch my allegiance to another. It would have been too great a reflection upon everyone. But I could hardly have been expected to realize that at the time. It was natural for me to assume that my father and I would work in harmony together.

There was then an acute housing shortage, so it was arranged that Barbara and I should furnish two rooms at Underhill, taking our meals with my parents. That too was a mistake. My wedding-day was fixed for July 29 and after my honeymoon I was to join the staff of Chapman & Hall, as literary adviser, on a yearly salary of £200.

Why, the reader may well ask, was I in such an overpowering haste to get married, when reason must have surely counselled me to pause before taking so decisive a step? Why did not self-interest counsel me to caution? Was I so overmasteringly in love?

Was I? It is very hard to recapture the emotions of forty years ago, but of one thing I am very certain, that though I hurried on my plans for marriage, I had travelled a long way since the spring of 1917. I was a different person, the world was a different place—at least for me. Let me put it this way; would I as a prisoner have been overwhelmed with misery if I had learnt that Barbara had met 'the dream of her life' and wanted to return her engagement ring? My vanity might have been hurt, but would I have felt any such feeling of desolation, of the pillar'd firmament being rottenness and earth's base built on stubble, as I was to feel ten years later in Monterey when I heard a beloved voice say, 'I've met the lad again.' That question I can answer. No, I should not. I should have shrugged it off. Too much had happened between June 1917 and October 1918.

Why then was I in such a hurry to be married? For what reason other than my perpetual, persistent restlessness; my incessant self-demand, 'What is the next thing on the list?' I had fallen in love. I had become engaged. Was not marriage the inevitable corollary? Had fate intervened, I do not believe I should have minded. There was so much else to come. I had a hundred arrows in my quiver. But as it was and since a marriage had been arranged, no intervention came, and . . . I was excited at the idea of being married. . . .

§

On the last Saturday of July my father and I went to Blackheath, to see the last day of the Kent v. Surrey match. It all looked as it had done five years before. At the station there was the same horse-drawn four-wheeler to drive us out to the Rectory Field at 'a bob a nob'; Philip Trevor, now a colonel with an O.B.E., was on the train with us. Certain figures were missing from the scene. Hayward who had made a century then, had now retired. D. W. Carr who in 1909 at the age of thirty-three had made so sensational an entry into first-class cricket with his googlies, had bowled in that match with so little success, o for 134, that he had given up the game, then and there. Colin Blythe had fallen in battle on the Somme. But of the twenty-two players in the 1914 sides, fourteen were on the field today. Hobbs and Hardinge, Woolley, Troughton, Strudwick, D. J. Knight, Hitch and Ducat were still the chief performers.

So often during the war I had looked back to the last Saturday of peace, remembering how the game had petered out into a draw, with the light failing and a thin rain falling, seeing that light and rain and the eventual draw as symbols of a world in twilight. So often during those four and a half years I had been told, in the Press, from the pulpit, in political debate, that nothing could be the same again; it was strange to come back and find so little change upon the surface. I suppose that to Philip Trevor, my father and I can have looked little different. He looked the same to me.

PART 3

London 1919–26

I

Chapman & Hall

I joined the staff of Chapman & Hall in September 1919. And since so many of the situations to which I was exposed during the next ten years were conditioned by that association, I must here give some explanation of the structure of the house, which not only launched Dickens but published for Anthony Trollope, Charles Reade, Ouida, Edmund Yates, R. D. Blackmore, Charles Lever, Harrison Ainsworth, Elizabeth Arkell and Charles Kingsley, and which for over thirty years employed George Meredith as its reader.

It was through W. L. Courtney, at one time his tutor at New College, that my father became the managing director in 1904. When I met Courtney first, in 1914, he was on the verge of seventy, tall, benign, gracious, with a grey drooping cavalry moustache, but it was not difficult to recognize beneath the uncertain mask of age the dashing and impressive figure who had come up to London in the early 'nineties impatient with 'the drudgery of lecturing and the narrow interests of Senior Common Room to join the editorial staff of the *Daily Telegraph* and startle the more conservative of its crusted journalists by appearing at the office in a white shirt front, smoking a Corona while he was writing a leading article.'

In addition to being dramatic critic of the *Daily Telegraph*, Courtney edited the *Fortnightly Review* which was owned by Chapman & Hall. In that capacity he was invited to join its board. He soon found much there to disquiet him. The firm owned Dickens's copyrights, and as long as it alone could issue a complete edition of Dickens, the shareholders' dividends were secure, but the copyrights were running out, and provision had to be made at once for the day when Edwin Drood passed into public ownership. Courtney remembered his old pupil who for several years had been employed in a half-time capacity as literary adviser to Kegan Paul.

Ethridge, the secretary of the company, shrugged on hearing of my father's appointment. 'They may put him in, but within a year I'll have him out,' he said.

Ethridge was responsible, as much as anyone, for the firm's dubious position. I remember him as a kindly white-haired man who used to slip half-crowns into my pocket. He had a curious nervous twitch in his right side that would jerk his elbow and leg sideways, bringing it into violent and often painful collision with chairs and tables. The younger McKennas made a passive verb out of this idiosyncracy. 'I Ethridged myself as I went through the door,' they would say.

I saw him as ridiculous and kindly but he was a devious creature. I will not say that he was actually dishonest, but he was and knew himself to be lazy and incompetent. Afraid of having his deficiencies recognized and knowing that, through the Dickens copyrights, Chapman & Hall would last his time, he attempted to secure the resignation of any managing director the board might appoint, by passive sabotage. His chief contribution to the firm's policy was the assurance that there was 'no money in miscellaneous publishing'. By that he meant anything but Dickens.

My father was promised that Ethridge should be pensioned off before he took up his appointment, but at the last moment the board lacked courage, and my father was not the man to dismiss a member of his staff without definite complaint. He resolved to make a loyal servant of him. If he did not succeed in making Ethridge a useful member of the firm, he rendered him a harmless one.

My father's job was to reorganize the machinery of the firm and to create a general list that would maintain a profitable turnover when the Dickens copyrights ran out. During the decade before the war, he added to its list books by H. G. Wells, Arnold Bennett, Somerset Maugham, Sheila Kaye-Smith, W. H. Mallock, Colonel W. P. Drury, Keble Howard,

Temple Thurston, J. Johnston Abraham, R. J. Campbell, Desmond Coke, Ridgwell Cullum and P. F. Warner.

This is no place to tell how my father reorganized and revivified the business during those first twelve years; he has told the story himself in *One Man's Road*. But that book was published thirty years ago, and such changes have taken place during that time that there is a period-piece interest today in a description of the atmosphere of a London publishing house at the turn of the century. Chapman & Hall was not a large firm in the sense that Macmillans and Longmans were, but it had a declared capital of £68,000 so that, in view of the greater purchasing power of the pound at that time, it was not a small one.

The premises were in Henrietta Street, No. 11, and ran through a block into Maiden Lane. It was a four-storied building; the main offices were on the ground floor; the books were stored at the back and the packing department was in Maiden Lane. There was no waiting-room. The visitor who wanted to interview the production manager had to duck under the counter and edge his way down a dark narrow passage.

My father's office was on the first floor; it was also the board-room, and a large table occupied the half of it. It was airy and pleasant with a bust of Charles Dickens on the mantelpiece. The rest of the building was let off in flats and offices; my father's secretary, however, was perched on the fourth floor. Nobody seemed to consider this arrangement inconvenient. It was a nice bright room for her, she said.

There was no telephone girl to supervise a one-line telephone, in the counting-house. There was only one extension, to my father's office. He had a blower beside his fireplace. If he wanted to speak to his secretary, he would blow down the tube, place it against his ear, wait till someone from the counting-house replied, then switch the blower to his mouth and say, 'Send me Miss Silk.' Sometimes if he was in a hurry, he would trot up three flights of stairs to dictate a letter. I doubt if he initiated three outside calls a week. He preferred to write or telegraph. The postal service was very much more speedy then and when I was a schoolboy at Sherborne I could get an answer within twenty-four hours to a letter addressed to London.

An author calling for an interview with my father would be

confronted by a counter against which would be leaning two or three booksellers' collectors, and behind which was a surly moustached clerk who could remember the days when Anthony Trollope, in his pink coat, banging on the counter with his hunting crop, had demanded 'those damned manuscripts in a hurry'. The author would be invariably kept waiting while the clerk dealt tardily with the booksellers one by one. My father was aware of the clerk's bad manners. 'I hope he doesn't put authors off too much,' he would say.

It was not till 1920 that a central telephone with extensions was installed, at the same time as a waiting-room.

My father's routine was strenuous. He reached the office every morning at nine o'clock and opened the mail with the surly clerk. No general communication could come in to the firm without his seeing it. He was through with that in half an hour, when the counting-house opened and the day's work began. The entire editorial staff, with its attendant branches of publicity and sales promotion, was in my father's hands. He had no assistant. He examined every manuscript that was offered.

He had no publicity department. A publisher at that time did not so much advertise his books as announce his list. My father extracted the 'quotes' from the reviews and drew up the advertisement himself. He also wrote the 'blurbs' for the spring and autumn lists. There was no 'promotion' of a book; no biographical details about authors were sent out to the Press. If an author cared for that kind of thing, it was up to him to ask a friend to 'put something about him in his column'. It was not considered good form. Occasionally my father would send a complimentary copy of a book to somebody of consequence in the hope that he might 'talk about it'. But he did not do this often, only when he was quite sure of the book's quality. A book was issued and allowed to take its chance. If it appeared to be 'catching on', the publisher increased his advertising. But by and large a bestseller sold itself.

There were no story conferences. A manuscript for which the firm had an agreement would ordinarily be sent straight off to the printers and my father would not look at it till it was in proof. Occasionally an author would ask his advice on a point or two; if an author was inclined to go 'near the knuckle' my father would 'vet' the typescript, but there was no going over a manuscript with an author. If you had asked Arnold Bennett 'who his editor was' at Henrietta Street, he would not have known what you meant. In those days it was assumed that an author knew his business and delivered a completed manuscript.

My father had no 'expense account'. His authors called on him by appointment and the cordiality of their relations is indicated by the number of books that bear his name upon the dedication page, but the business lunch was no part of the pattern of my father's life.

The agent who placed the firm's advertising was one of the directors of the Norwich Press. He was also a shareholder in Chapman & Hall. About once a year he would invite my father to lunch. My father hated these occasions though he liked the man. 'I know what it'll be,' he would say. 'Over the coffee he'll tell me that the Norwich Press happens to be rather quiet at the moment; "If you have a manuscript on hand," he'll say "we could give it prompt attention."' The Norwich Press were good craftsmen, they were no more expensive than anybody else, there was no reason why part of the firm's printing should not have gone there. But my father did not like to think that he was being 'got at'.

He was extremely punctilious, he was in fact over-punctilious in refusing anything that could be construed as being a 'perquisite of office'; in 1919 when the board voted the staff a ten per cent Christmas bonus on their salaries as the result of an exceptionally good balance sheet, he took no bonus himself although he was as much in a salaried position as any member of the staff and had no share in profits. When he asked his secretary to type an article for him, he paid her at the current rate per thousand words. He did not feel justified in employing a member of the staff for his personal profit, although the work was done in Chapman & Hall's time on a Chapman & Hall machine and most men in his position would have argued that a secretary was employed primarily to relieve her boss of burdens.

Courtney was equally punctilious, though in a way that was less advantageous to the interests of Chapman & Hall. Anxious to appear impartial, he avoided the suggestion that his critical judgement was affected by his connexion with the firm; he was reluctant to review a Chapman & Hall publication in the *Daily Telegraph*; if a friend asked his advice about a manuscript, he would recommend it to Heinemann or Macmillan; during the First World War the *Daily Telegraph* charity books went, on Courtney's recommendation, to Hodder & Stoughton. Courtney had the Victorian view that business and friendship should be kept apart.

Temperamentally Courtney and my father had a great deal in common. They hated to cause pain and to give offence. In conversation Courtney, as befitted his years and his position, spoke with an air of authority, but he was non-committal. He rarely expressed a definite opinion. In his articles he would write, 'On the one hand it may be argued . . . but it should not be forgotten that there are others who will contend . . .' He was judicial. He summed up the case, but he left the verdict to the jury.

For over twenty years Courtney and my father met three times a week, at the Friday board meeting and on Mondays and Wednesdays when Courtney called in for a cup of tea on his way to the *Daily Telegraph*. For twenty-two of those years they ran the firm between them, but I doubt if they once in all that time solidly 'discussed the situation'. Courtney had made his decision when he chose my father for the directorship. He then left my father to run his own show.

That was exactly what my father wanted. He worked fast and thought fast. He disliked 'talking shop'; he disliked discussions; discussions became arguments and arguments became quarrels. He had a Dickensian delight in seeing people happy. The least suggestion of acrimony fussed him. To the agents who offered him manuscripts he would write, 'I will put your proposition before my board next Friday'; but in fact my father was the board. The votes taken on his recommendations were a formality. Douglas Goldring once referred to the board as 'that elegant abstraction'. To Evelyn Waugh's contemporaries at Oxford my father was known as 'Chapman & Hall' and the *Isis*, when Evelyn went down, referred with regret to the loss of their able editor who had joined in London his binomenal father.

There is a quality of rather touching comedy about the long relationship between Courtney and my father. The first basis of pupil and tutor was never wholly lost. They treated each other with the greatest tact and courtesy. If ever there was a point at issue my father preferred to write.

There often were such points. Courtney's reluctance to cause offence led him to accept articles for the *Fortnightly* for which he had no immediate use, and it was the rule of the house not to pay before publication. If an author began to remonstrate, Courtney to keep him quiet would have the article set up in type and a proof sent. The months went by and not only did the author become restive but the printer would demand rent for the type which was kept standing. The matter would be brought to the managing director who would write officially to Courtney. If the letter was posted on a Tuesday, Courtney's secretary would ring up on the Wednesday morning to say that Mr. Courtney was very sorry but that he would not be able to come in that afternoon. It would be difficult for them to meet until the letter had been acknowledged and the matter closed.

When I was at Sandhurst, I sent Courtney the manuscript of a poem on a Sunday afternoon. On the Monday morning Mr. Courtney's secretary rang up Henrietta Street to say that he would not come in that afternoon. My father wrote to me, 'I presume this means that Courtney has turned down your poem.' It did.

Once Courtney came into the room when my father was signing his letters. One of them was to Courtney. 'I've just been writing to you,' my father said, and handed him the letter. Courtney read it through. 'Thank you,' he said. 'A very interresting letter. I shall not answer it, but I shall take note of it.'

There was one other active member of the board, Roland Truslove, the son of the Bond Street bookseller. My father had secured his election some time before the war when he was Dean of Worcester College, Oxford, believing that a closer connexion with the book trade would be beneficial and that Truslove would attract young Oxonians to the list. My father's hopes on both counts were disappointed. But in an unexpected direction his advent did prove advantageous. Chapman & Hall acted as English agents for the technical publications of the

American house of Wiley. They also themselves published a few textbooks for engineers. Truslove suggested that this branch of the firm's activities should be increased and a special technical department was started which was to prove in time the mainstay of the house's fortunes.

Truslove was conscientious in his attendance at the Friday meetings, but it cannot be pretended that he contributed anything of value to the deliberations.

That was how the firm had been run for sixteen years, and very profitably too; the shareholders received their dividends and proved their content by never bothering to attend the annual meetings. There was no reason to believe that prosperity would not continue during the post-war boom which every pundit prophesied. It was felt, however, that new blood was needed. That was where I came in. I was to bring young authors to the list, I was to advise the board on contemporary trends. I had no fixed duties. I did not take over from anyone. I relieved my father of a certain amount of hackwork, but I had to create my own activities.

§

I occupied a small room on the fourth floor. I sorted out manuscripts and read them. I drew up advertisements and sent out paragraphs. I interviewed some of our authors and discussed their books with them. I worked from Monday to Friday, from 9.30 to 5.30. I had no expense account.

By and large there are not many periods of my life that I would not be glad to live again, but that of the next eight months is one of them. I was desperately bored. Hour after hour I sat in that small room reading tenth-rate novels. When it is considered how bad are many of the novels which are published, the reader is invited to reflect on the quality of those which are not. The layman may imagine that it is with an air of excited expectancy that a publisher's reader cuts the string round a manuscript; this package may conceal a Conrad or a Hardy. But in England it is extremely rare for a novel of any merit to be offered without a letter of introduction. During my seven years as a reader, I only recommended one novel that arrived anonymously—*The Granite Hills*, by C. E. Heanley. I thought it good, but we had no luck with it; as far as I know, its author never published another novel.

I once asked George Doran if he did not think a publisher would save time and trouble by returning unread any manuscript that came in unrecommended. 'Not in the long run,' he said. 'By reading what people want to write, you get an inkling as to what they want to read.' But he told me that after I had ceased to be a reader, and I had not that consolation as I waded through those bulky piles. In the summer it was not so bad, as I took the manuscripts to Lord's and read them as I watched the cricket, but the winter seemed very long, and the reading of manuscripts hour by hour deadened my enjoyment of reading.

I was not only bored but I was lonely. Perched on the fourth floor, I was cut off from the atmosphere of the office. My father's secretary was in the room next to me; when her blower sounded I would pray that it might be for me, a summons to my father's office or a telephone call to be answered in the counting-house; it rarely was.

Those were no doubt difficulties to which I might have adjusted myself in time. It was my first experience of office routine. No ex-serviceman found easy the return to civilian life, but I had an added problem—my father.

It is perhaps never easy for father and son to work together in business, and the very fact that in all other things we were so close made it the more difficult for us. It placed our relationship on a new basis. My father and I were very different; I was more like my mother. The attraction of opposites brought us the closer, emotionally, but in the conduct of business it made special difficulties. We each had our way of doing business. As I have already said, my father's mind worked fast. He liked to make quick decisions. He disliked discussions. Discussions seemed to him a brother to argument and cousin to a quarrel. I on the other hand like talking round a subject.

As we had walked round the slopes at Sherborne and over the heath at Hampstead, our talk had run from one subject to another. I soon found that we could not do that in an office, and because I felt that some subjects needed to be discussed I would wait to discuss them at home.

This was the last thing my father wanted. He liked very

naturally to put Henrietta Street aside when he was back at Underhill. Yet how else was I to get things said? This was particularly a problem when Barbara and I were living with my parents, but the essential difficulty remained later when we took a cottage in the country. I could not discuss certain matters in an office. 'I'll wait,' I'd think, 'till I spend the night at Underhill, then I'll bring it up.' This made my home less of a home to me, and it made my visits less congenial to my father.

In addition during my first months at Chapman & Hall, the atmosphere was aggravated through my marriage being a failure from the start.

II

Marriage

My marriage broke up in January 1922. It reached the divorce courts a year later and I was granted a decree of annulment. The marriage was never consummated. For this failure my inexperience was entirely to blame. Young people today can have no idea of the general ignorance at that time about the physiology of sex. Certain subjects were not discussed. Dr. Marie Stopes's *Married Love* which had been published in 1918 was a revolutionary book and by many was considered to be a shocking one. I had no idea of the amount of tact and skilful patience that is required to initiate an inexperienced girl into the intimacies of sex. I had imagined that a few casual encounters in the red light districts of Mainz and Nancy would be a sufficient training for me. Actually I should have been better off without it. It made me think that the whole thing was simple and straightforward. There is only one training that is of the least value to a young man—a love affair with an experienced woman.

Every unhappy marriage, so Tolstoy opened in *Anna Karenina*, is unhappy in its own way. Our particular brand of unhappiness was a special one; we never quarrelled, we stayed good friends, but the failure to establish physical relations created a barrier between us. We could not be outspoken with one another. One of the pleasantest things about marriage is the sense that it gives two people of being a team. Two lives become one life; you plan a joint future for yourselves. You share your troubles with another person. There need be no secrets. You can confide openly in a way that you cannot with your closest friend. That was impossible for Barbara and myself. We could not plan far ahead, because we knew at the backs of our minds, that unless a change took place in our relations, unless this issue was straightened out, a drastic crisis was inevitable.

After our honeymoon we did not have a single open talk. I do not know how Barbara felt during those months. She must have enjoyed the status of a married woman; she must have enjoyed the independence which that status conferred; she was only eighteen; she had so very recently been under strict parental control; she must have enjoyed going out to parties as a wife and such simple entertaining that we could afford. But she must have been fretted by a niggling knowledge that basically things were wrong. She must have been embarrassed and sometimes humiliated by the confidences that married women made to her and the questions that they asked her.

Myself, knowing that I was responsible for the situation, I had a deep sense of shame. I had prided myself on my dash as a footballer and cricketer; but I had failed in the primary, the most elemental test of manhood. I had been nicknamed Tank at Sandhurst, yet I could not make my wife a woman. I was too ashamed of myself to consult a doctor. By the time we did, in the following summer, it was too late. Mental inhibitions had been created.

For me one of the most difficult features of the situation was the contrast between what I was and what I seemed to be. I appeared to everyone to be an extremely fortunate young man, married to an attractive wife, with an exciting career opening before him. Actually I was nothing of the sort. Yet I could not confide my problems to anyone. I had the sense all the time of flying under false colours. When I look back on the thirty months that Barbara and I lived together, I cannot help thinking that we are lucky to have emerged from them so little scathed. My mother maintained a correspondence with Barbara until she died. Indeed, among the letters that arrived after my mother's death was one to her from Barbara. I have no doubt that Barbara has had a happy life and marriage.

§

Novels often falsify life by failing to indicate the variety of a man's interests and occupations. His life contains many separate compartments. For hours on end he can forget that he is the partner in an unsatisfactory marriage. In one of his novels, W. L. George[1] compared such a marriage to a cut on a fingertip of which you are only conscious when your finger brushes a rough surface; and though I would not care to relive that period it contained, as even the worst period can do, a number of good times.

It was good, for instance, to get back to Rugby football. I joined Rosslyn Park and turned out for their 'A' side every Saturday. One of my functions at Henrietta Street was to inveigle new talent to our list and I was encouraged to go to parties and clubs where I was likely to meet writers. That side of my work I thoroughly enjoyed; I am gregarious, I enjoy parties and the meeting of new people. I was a member of the Savage Club and lunched there most days, in good company, with men like C. S. Evans, A. P. Herbert, St. John Ervine, Norman Davey, C. E. Lawrence, J. Johnston Abraham.

The cocktail party was not yet in vogue. There were tea parties instead, and after-dinner parties. In the modest circles in which I moved it was unusual to be offered a cocktail before dinner, and when you were, it was a single cocktail that had to be drunk quickly. In most houses *le mauvais quart d'heure* persisted.

After-dinner parties were general. You arrived about nine and were offered coffee and cakes and wine and beer and sandwiches. You aimed—at least I did, living in Hampstead—at catching the last tube home. There might be dancing, somebody might sing. As often as not one wore a dinner jacket. It is the spread of the cocktail party as much as anything that has made dressing for dinner difficult. People come on to dinner from a cocktail party and cannot be bothered to go home to change.

Barbara and I could not afford to entertain elaborately, but we had Sunday tea parties and now and again my father invited some of our more special friends to dinner. A young couple is not expected to entertain and we had no lack of invitations. Barbara was pretty, friendly and quick-witted; everybody liked her. I felt proud walking into a room beside her. All that side of

[1] W. L. George died in 1926, in his early forties. The author of *A Bed of Roses* and a number of sociological novels, he was a prominent and forceful personality.

our marriage went very well. It was fun talking the parties over afterwards.

There was quite a number to talk over. Mrs. Belloc Lowndes gave lunch and tea parties. Violet Hunt gave dinner parties and once a year an elaborate white-tie evening party at which champagne was served. W. L. George gave dinner and after-dinner parties in Albion Street. J. D. Beresford was then Collins's adviser. He had a large house in St. John's Wood and presumably an expense account, for he gave parties there of considerable size. I have many pleasant memories of St. John Ervine's hospitality. Ernest Rhys was at home every Sunday; so was Mrs. Dawson-Scott, the founder in 1921 of the P.E.N. Club. She was in 1919 active with the Tomorrow Club which met once a week in a long narrow room in Long Acre, where a literary topic would be opened with a forty-minute talk by somebody of prominence. Sidney Dark spoke as an editor, Andrew Dakers as an agent, W. L. George as a novelist. There were gatherings of a hundred or so writers and embryo writers; after the talk there was an interval for coffee; then there was a general debate; the discussion was most animated when we were talking of royalties and which editors paid the most.

A sister novelist described Mrs. Dawson-Scott as a 'ramshackle woman'. I can see what she meant. Mrs. Dawson-Scott was shapeless and draped herself with shawls and beads. There was a certain physical resemblance between herself and Mrs. Belloc Lowndes, though Mrs. Belloc Lowndes aimed at being chic. There were other resemblances as well. Neither was a particularly good novelist, though Mrs. Belloc Lowndes made a niche for herself as a writer of crime stories—she chose her subjects shrewdly, particularly in *The Lodger* which she built on the Jack the Ripper case—and made a reasonable income, selling a serial every year to the *Chicago Daily Tribune*. Socially there was a great difference between the two. Mrs. Belloc Lowndes, the sister of Hilaire Belloc, was the wife of one of the chief editors of *The Times*, and moved in the big world. The resemblance lay in this, that both took an intense interest in the private lives of writers and the commercial side of writing; they were both, let me hasten to add, extremely good friends to writers.

Hugh Walpole drew a picture of Mrs. Belloc-Lowndes in *Fortitude*, which she resented but which was not unfair. The intrigues of publishing fascinated her. She knew what advance each author got and whether or not he earned it. She would whisper across a lunch-table, 'Are you happy with Heinemann?' as a seductress would have said, 'Does your wife really understand you?' She was useful to writers. She would bring them into touch with editors who could help them. Her kindness was uncalculated; by that I mean that she got nothing out of it for herself. Nor was she overflowingly maternal. She was a very nice woman.

As indeed was Mrs. Dawson-Scott who in her way did no less for writers. She could not afford lunches at the Ivy, but she brought writers together at her Sunday afternoons in Alexandra Road. In my first years in London I can remember many friendships that began or were cemented there, and, as the founder of the P.E.N. Club, her name will be always venerated.

§

1920 was a difficult year for me. I was worried at Underhill; I was worried at Henrietta Street, I was also finding it extremely hard to get myself started as a writer. While I was in the army, I had imagined that novels and short stories would flow from my pen the instant I was released from khaki. I could not have been more wrong.

It may seem that, isolated in a fourth-floor office, remote from scrutiny, I was admirably placed to write novels, articles and stories in Chapman & Hall's spare time. Did not my father write his reviews for the *Daily Telegraph* between his interviews with authors? Had not Maupassant made ample use of his leisure as a bureaucrat? And indeed when I had visualized my future in the preceding summer, I had seen myself getting most of my solid writing done in Henrietta Street. But I was soon to learn that I could not write novels as I could write letters, between one interview and the next. I needed leisure, freedom from interruption. I needed time to brood between the periods of actual writing. I was, in fact, up against one of the main problems of the novelist.

Some years ago Cyril Connolly conducted in *Horizon* a

symposium on the best way to deal with it. If his pen does not support him, and he has not a private income, how is a writer to supplement his earnings? Most of the contributors were agreed that the ancillary occupation should not be connected with authorship; should not be reviewing or lecturing or B.B.C. scripting. Preferably it should not be desk work. I endorse their views. When I was doing active soldiering in the First War, I wrote a lot. Writing was a relaxation, a relief after parades, exercises, lectures on military law. I came fresh to writing, at the beginning and end of the day. In the spring of 1921, I was, as a reservist, recalled to the Colours to meet the threat of a general strike. In the afternoons after training I wrote in three weeks 50,000 words of a novel that was eventually published. In September 1939 I was recalled to my regiment. I was half-way through a novel. Rising early and returning to my desk after parades, I finished it before I was posted to a staff appointment with the B.E.F. For the remainder of the war, I was a chair-borne warrior. Quite often, particularly in the Middle East, I had very little to do, but hard though I tried, I could not force myself to write after spending eight hours in an office. One must, at least I must, come to a desk with a feeling of excitement, antennae alert, nerves tense.

During my first year in Henrietta Street, when I went to the office five days a week, I wrote nothing except a few *causeries* for *John O'London's Weekly*; Byron's love affairs, the Browning courtship; that kind of thing; nothing worth putting between covers. Ideas for short stories did not come to me. This inability to write contributed to my dissatisfaction. I suspected that I was not getting ideas because the conditions under which I was living were inauspicious. I had to reorganize my life. Living at Underhill I was in the atmosphere of Chapman & Hall for twenty-four hours of the day. Perhaps this monotony of atmosphere was responsible for the stalemate of my marriage. Barbara and I were living under the same conditions after marriage as before. Perhaps if we had a home of our own it might be different. In the spring of 1920, with my savings from *The Loom*, I bought a half-acre strip of land at Ditchling, under the Sussex downs, and by means of a mortgage, built during the summer a small wooden bungalow. We christened it Half Acre and when I last drove through the village in the summer of 1939 I saw the same wooden placard on the gate.

Ditchling was two miles from the nearest station, Hassocks. The fast trains did not stop there. I had not a car. It was scarcely practical for me to go up to London and back each day; so I suggested to Chapman & Hall that I should undertake half-time employment, coming up to the office on Mondays and Fridays and taking back to the country manuscripts when necessary. The board suggested a rise of salary, to £300, if I continued to come to the office every day, but my mind was firm. If I was to do any real writing, I had to have three days clear in the middle of the week. So I fell into the pattern which I have followed with modifications all my life, dividing my time into two sections, periods in the country when I concentrate upon writing, periods in a city where I concentrate upon social and administrative activities.

It is a pattern which has worked well with me; a writer's mind has to be tended as soil has, carefully. Ideas must be given a chance to put down roots. Early waking in fresh air, quiet uneventful days, long solitary brooding walks and early evenings are a salutary treatment, provided that at other times the mind is given sufficient stimulus, enough variety of experience.

I have been asked by young writers of today whether it was easier to earn one's living by one's pen forty years ago. On the whole, I think it was. Then as now, very few English writers had a magazine market in the U.S.A.; and payment in England was very low. Two guineas a thousand words was the average rate for routine reviewing. I was glad to get three guineas a thousand for a featured article. For a short story I would get four guineas a thousand. But there were many more London newspapers then than now, six evening papers and eight dailies. There were a great many fiction magazines; there were six literary weeklies. There were also several glossy fashion papers that printed feature articles and stories. It was not difficult to pick up four or five pounds a week with journalism; and five pounds went a long way in 1920. Income tax was not high on a small income. In 1920 I earned about £400 with my pen. I had my Chapman & Hall salary. Barbara had about £50 a year. We did not manage badly. I did not drink spirits then, but we always served wine when we had guests. I played cricket regularly and cricket is not a cheap game. I was a member of the Sette of Odd Volumes—a dining-club where I could entertain my friends. We had a gardener once a week and a char who scoured the house every Friday. I was short of money, but I was not accutely worried by a lack of it.

I worked hard at Half Acre. A book of short stories was ready for the spring of 1921. A novel was finished by the early summer. During the autumn I wrote a book called *Public School Life*. I was full of projects. The two days in London gave me the mental stimulus I needed. During the football season I spent Friday nights at Underhill. Sometimes Barbara came up, but more often not. In the summer we usually had a week-end guest at Half Acre. As I said, Barbara and I never quarrelled. She was good company, but by the spring of 1921 we had come to realize that the situation could not continue; that something must happen soon.

I can see myself as clearly as though it was last week, walking down Bedford Street on a sunny morning in the summer of 1920. I can see the low-roofed buildings in the Strand that were soon to be torn down to house the Tivoli, that was in its turn to be replaced by Peter Robinson. My heart was heavy. For everybody else the world seemed a pleasant enough place. I tried to reassure myself. 'You're only twenty-two,' I thought. 'This can't go on for ever. Something is bound to happen soon to change it, for better or for worse. Don't they say that one's skin changes every seven years? In 1927 you'll be walking down this street wondering why you were so depressed today. You'll be only twenty-nine, younger than Maupassant when he wrote *Bel-Ami*.' August, 1927, I was to recall that morning as I waited on the waterfront of far Tahiti with a very different problem on my hands.

§

The end came at Christmas, 1921. I became involved with a young woman, shortly to leave for India to make a prudent marriage, who was giving herself a fling before she went. It was not a serious involvement, but it was a signpost to the road on which I knew myself to be set. I recognized the impossibility of the routine of evasion and deceit that was inevitable if a break was not made. We spent Christmas at Underhill. In January Barbara returned to Half Acre and I remained in London.

It was a surprise and a shock to both our families, especially to my aunts at Midsomer Norton. I was besieged by letters begging me to do nothing drastic, to 'give the thing time'. I was in my own mind convinced that a marriage that had once gone wrong could not be saved, but there was, I thought, no hurry. Time would produce its own solution.

The winter passed and then the spring. In July Barbara wrote that there was something she wanted to discuss with me. My spirits sank. I presumed it was to do with money. London was proving more expensive than I had expected. Half Acre was a drain. I was uncomfortably in debt. She called for me at Henrietta Street. 'Shall we go for a walk?' I said.

We walked into St. James's Park. It was a warm, sunny day. Barbara looked very pretty, very fresh; she was wearing an unfashionably cut cotton frock; 1922 was the year when women's waist lines ran below the hips. Even at the time I thought that fashion hideous. I was then deeply committed to a sultry tempestuous romance with a woman three years older than myself. It was one of those romances that come the way of most young men if they are lucky, that mould them, determine their taste, make men of them. I look back on it with warmth and gratitude, but I could not that morning help comparing her with Barbara. We sat on a seat looking across the lake. I looked at Barbara, interrogatively. She gave a little laugh. 'It's a funny thing to ask one's husband. But I want to be married again.'

I misunderstood her. I thought that she was suggesting we should resume our marriage. I hesitated, recalled on a wave of memory to the summer of 1917; she looked so very charming. Might it not go right now, with the experience, the confidence that had come my way? I played for time. 'Do you think it would work?' I asked. She laughed again, a dry, slightly contemptuous little laugh. 'That's my problem, isn't it?' she said. Then I understood; and a great wave of relief flooded me. I was free, free, free.

III

A London Bachelor

For four and a half years I lived the life of a London bachelor; and I can think of nothing better to be at the age of twenty-five if one has enough money to indulge modest tastes. For the first half of that time I stayed at Underhill. Then I took a flat in Kensington.

Of the many flats in which I have lived from time to time, that first flat at No. 22 Earl's Terrace, remains my favourite. Earl's Terrace lies back from the Kensington High Street, behind a screen of trees. It has a private drive. It backs upon Edwardes Square. Its rooms are high and airy, with tall French windows. I was on the first floor; the traditional L-shaped drawing-room had been divided, with a bathroom set in the corner. A ceiling-high pair of doors separated the bedroom from the sitting-room. I replaced the doors with a curtain, in the way that the Algonquin Hotel does in New York. I ran white bookshelves, four feet high round the walls of the sitting-room. I painted the ceilings primrose yellow and the walls pale blue. I had a number of black-framed etchings, by Nevinson and Wadsworth; I had in the sitting-room a black pile fitted carpet, with a grey one in the bedroom. The curtains were dark blue damask with silver shreds. I had a modernistic screen, painted by Roger Fry, of a Provençal landscape which I had bought at the Omega Workshop, and to which I was to detect a reference in *Brideshead Revisited*. I had a divan bed, so that the bedroom could become a sitting-room for parties. The bedroom opened on to a 'leads' on which I arranged flower-boxes in the summer.

It was a service flat, and a sound, economical housekeeper provided a good dinner at five shillings a head. A bachelor

could live well in London on £800 a year. I had about that and
was not uncomfortably in debt.

I have seen enough of other cities, New York in particular,
to have standards of comparison in assessing my love of London. I am never surprised to hear provincials and foreigners
decry it, complaining of its kill-joy restrictions, its lack of
hospitality, of the difficulties of getting from one place to
another, with its residential area scattered over so wide an area.
The visitor arriving by air and driving in by motor-coach must
be appalled by the drab monotony of its streets, one after another, indistinguishably undistinguished. Yet for the Londoner
and those who have the good fortune to become identified with
the city's life, not even New York and Paris possess a comparable magic.

It has a lived-in atmosphere. Its streets for nine hundred
years have been untrodden by foreign feet. There have been
riots and revolutions; kings have been deposed and a king has
been beheaded; but through that long succession of different
reigns and parliaments and changing loyalties, the life of the
individual Londoner has continued without basic interruption,
widening its boundaries, deepening its interests. I know of no
city that is more many-sided; it is the spiritual, cultural, social,
administrative, financial centre not only of a kingdom but of a
Commonwealth. The court is there, Parliament is there; so
are the law courts, the Archbishop's palace and Threadneedle
Street. Every Englishman, and most Scotsmen, have roots of
some kind there. New York, for all its drama and excitement,
has the immense deficiency of not being the administrative
centre of the country. At a London club or at a London dinner
party, you may sit at the same table as a Member of Parliament,
a diplomat, a banker, a theatrical producer. The Londoner does
not need to rely on the reports of special correspondents to learn
what is happening in his country. The means of self-informa-
tion are available. He can find out for himself from his acquaintances. Whenever I return to London, I have the sense of
returning to a hub. I no longer need to get my information at
third hand. I belong to five London clubs and three dining-
clubs—in addition to M.C.C.—and each one is a window opening on to a different area of thought and conduct.

The variety of London life makes it difficult to present a complete picture of a Londoner's routine. Novels for the most part present an incomplete picture of the city's life, except when they are subjective, when they are told through the eyes of a single character. *The Forsyte Saga* is, in my opinion, the finest novel of London, yet it is hard not to be surprised at the way in which the Forsytes spend their whole time entertaining one another. We are told of the fashionable legs that sat under James's dining-table in Green Street, but we are never shown any Forsyte engaged in an activity that did not concern another member of the family; and if old Jolyon walks into his son's club at nine o'clock at night he, of course, finds young Jolyon sitting there.

I have already referred to H. S. Mackintosh, who was my contemporary at Sherborne, who lived in Hampstead, and of whom I saw as much as I did of anyone before I began to travel. We both played football for Rosslyn Park and cricket for J. C. Squire's Invalids. We had several mutual friends. We dined together once or twice a month. We had similar tastes. We went to 'deb' dances and received our share of entertainment. An American visitor would have considered that we belonged to the same world. Yet when we were trying to fix a date between ourselves, we would usually find that the nearest date available for both of us was ten or twelve days ahead. A novelist writing about us would have assumed that in the course of those ten days we would meet each other somewhere. Yet actually we never once in all those months met accidentally. Not once did our circles intersect. That is, I think, typical of London life.

Londoners have occasionally protested when I have talked in this way about London. 'You must remember that you are not a typical Londoner. You are a writer. You are not tied to an office desk. You are mobile.' My answer to that is, 'There is no such thing as a typical Londoner. But all of us who are native to London, who adore London, are typical of London.'

The only way in which I can present the kind of life I led in London between 1922 and 1926 is through a series of snapshots of the various worlds in which I moved. J. C. Squire said of himself that he was a centipede with a foot in a hundred worlds. All Londoners are centipedes to some extent.

I said that there were few better things to be than a bachelor in London at the age of twenty-five with a modest income. I might have added that there was no time when it was better to be just that than in the early 'twenties. Recently the 1920s seen through the coloured mirage of the Scott Fitzgerald legend, have been accepted as a synonym for 'late nights and famishing morrows'. It may have been like that in Paris where expatriate Americans, on the crest of the Wall Street boom, with prohibition recharging every battery, stimulated but not exhausted by the war, were 'hitting it up, high, wide and handsome'. It was not like that in London, or at least it was not for me. England was exhausted and was also impoverished by the war. Income tax was modest in comparison with what it is today, but it did seem to us hard that we should have to work for three months of the year for nothing. We had to work hard to keep ourselves afloat. I could not afford to lead an existence of night clubs and late drinking. Moreover, I did not want to. I had to keep fit if I was to play Rugby football every Saturday during the winter and cricket two or three times a week during the summer. I was perhaps exceptional in that, but not extraordinary in view of the number of young men who were turning out every Saturday afternoon, in striped jerseys, as the representatives of Blackheath, Harlequins, Richmond, Rosslyn Park 'A' and 'B' XVs.

I played regularly for Rosslyn Park until April, 1926, nearly always for an 'A' XV. I was picked once or twice for the first XV, but as a forward I was too light and small for first-class football. In the very first match after the war, I played against the London Scottish. From the kick-off, the ball came straight at me. As I prepared to catch it, I realized that the ball and two burly Scottish forwards would reach me simultaneously. That is about all that I remember of that match.

'A' XVs play against public schools, minor provincial sides, and the 'A' XVs of other first-class clubs. On each Tuesday morning I would receive a card. 'You have been picked to play against East Wanstead. 1.12 train from Liverpool Street. Meet at barrier. Tickets taken.' Most of the side would have spent the morning in their offices. They would have time for a quick sandwich and a cup of coffee. The train would be crowded with city workers returning to their suburban homes. We should be unlikely to get seats. The ground would be quarter of an hour's walk from the station. Pavilions were scarce after the war. We should probably find ourselves changing in an ill-lit, draughty converted army hut. There would be no spectators for our match, except when we were playing against a school. Nothing was at stake. We were playing for the game's sake, as hard as we knew how. I can remember every single school and house match in which I played at Sherborne. But I can only remember occasional incidents out of my seven seasons with the Park; those usually were in matches against schools when our opponents were desperately anxious to win, when individual honours were to be won or lost. But I enjoyed my football for the Park more than I had done at Sherborne.

After the match, bruised and dirty, we would change back in the ill-lit hut, wash indifferently in tepid water, mislaying socks and ties. There would be a heavy tea, thick-cut slices of buttered bread with jam and anchovy paste, and slabs of cake. Then in the grey, damp dusk we would trudge back to the station. Our bruises had not begun to stiffen. We were languid, relaxed, at peace. The train would not be crowded now. We would all get seats. We would talk over the match, and about the next week's game; at Liverpool Street we would buy evening papers to learn how the first XV had done, how Chelsea and the Spurs had fared. The team would now divide. Half would return to their homes, the remainder would go on to supper. Each football side had its own rendezvous. Ours was at Dehem's Oyster Bar, where we would drain pints of lukewarm beer and at a certain point consume 'a cut off the joint, two veg. and cheese'. We would be feeling very gay by closing-time when we waved each other good-bye and separated to our separate homes.

We were good friends, all of us. In a sense we knew each other very well. We knew our natures by the way we played; the one who was brilliant in attack, but half-hearted in defence; the one who was modest, the one who was boastful, the ones who avoided the 'dirty work'. We knew our essential selves better than our best friends did. At the same time we knew very little about each other. We knew which schools we had been at; but we knew nothing of each other's homes. We did not know how well off our parents were, where we worked, with what measure of success. We did not know who was married, who was engaged. The early and middle twenties are a crucial period in a young man's life; he is coming to terms with himself and his potentialities; he is laying the basis for his career; he is falling in and out of love. It is a very wholesome release for him to be able for a few hours a week to escape from his professional, social, amatory problems, into the healthy anonymity of Rugby football. I can wish nothing better for a young man in London.

Often on Sunday mornings when I lay in bed with stiffened limbs, knowing that I had set myself right for an entire week, and that Tuesday morning would bring the card with its mandatory summons, I would remember ruefully that in a few years' time the régime would be discontinued. Hardly anybody plays football over the age of thirty; very few last that long. I had already seen several team-mates drop out of the game. A minor injury made them miss a couple of games. On their return they were out of training; then they caught, or fancied that they had caught, a cold. They received a tempting week-end invitation, and that was that. Football is not a game to which you can return after the age of twenty-four, as you can to cricket. I wondered how my end would come. I prayed that it would be delayed as long as possible. What should I do with my week-ends without football? I did not know then that the issue would be solved, as were so many others, by travel.

For two consecutive winters I was abroad; then in the autumn of 1928, on the eve of starting for a trip to the West Indies, I thought I would like to make one last appearance for the Park, knowing that it would be my last one. I turned out for a 'B' XV. It was a mild autumnal afternoon at the old Deer Park. We won without a great deal of difficulty. It was not a very strenuous game, but once when I came down hard I was shaken for several minutes and realized that I was too old for football. I managed, however, to score two tries, one in the last minute of the game. So I left the field with the consoling knowledge that I had scored with the last football that I touched.

§

Cricket is in a different category; there is no reason why one should not go on playing till one is seventy. I should have gone on playing it much longer if I had spent less time abroad and if the Hampshire village of Silchester, whose team I captained after the Second War, had possessed a prettier ground and a less rustic wicket. As it was, I had practically given up the game when in the summer of 1955, shortly before my daughter's wedding, I thought it would be pleasant if her fiancé—Christopher Keeling—and myself turned out for M.C.C. together. I suggested that we should put our names down for the game against Douai College, since the captain, R. H. D. Buckston, was an old friend of mine. Unfortunately there was not a vacancy for my future son-in-law, so I took the field alone.

We won the toss and I was put in No. 9. It was a warm sunny day, the wicket dry, and Douai has always been a lucky ground for me. But as I sat in my pads, I almost hoped that the captain would be able to declare before it was my turn to bat. It was a long way out there to the wicket. I was definitely relieved when I did not have to bat. This was no spirit to play cricket in, I told myself.

The Douai XI was not strong and wickets went down steadily. I was fielding at third man and deep long-on. Not much came my way until, late in the afternoon, a tail-ender got a half-volley in the very centre of his bat. It came to my right side about a yard away, slightly below my knees. It was hit so hard that it bruised my hand right through, but I saw it all the way. There are few moments comparable to the mingling of excitement and relief with which one feels and sees a ball within one's hands. I can remember a dozen or so catches in my life, and this was one of them. When we got back to the pavilion, Buckston said, 'Well, Alec, it was nice of you to come along and show these young fellows how to make a difficult catch look easy.'

'This is where you check out,' I told myself. 'Don't spoil the memory of this.'

In the 'twenties I had no prescience of such a moment. I fancied that I would want to go on playing cricket until

stumps were drawn. I played three or four times a week, mostly
for touring sides, for the Stoics, the Thespids, a side that was
closely connected with the stage, for Richmond's mid-week side,
for the Chiltern Ramblers, a side founded in 1923, consisting
basically of young barristers and doctors recently down from
Oxford. Its standard was the highest that I was privileged to
meet; it usually fielded one or two first-class players, R. H.
Bettington, G. T. S. Stevens, G. M. Louden, G. A. Lowndes,
the Doggarts and the Prices; and it included men who were
later to achieve high distinction—Frank Evershed, Walter
Monckton and Miles Dempsey. In 1929 and 1930 I played my
qualification matches for M.C.C. and was elected to membership in the following year. During the 'thirties I played most of
my more serious cricket for M.C.C., captaining their Sussex
College tour. I also played for two amusing semi-literary sides,
J. C. Squire's Invalids and Clifford Bax's Old Broughtonians.

In *Cakes and Ale* Somerset Maugham referred to the period
when men of letters, to show their manliness, drank beer and
played cricket; he was presumably thinking of those two sides.
They were very different sides, captained by very different men,
though many of the same men played under both flags. Clifford
Bax was a natural batsman, tall, with a long reach. He was on a
fast wicket a dangerous opponent. He played a number of fine
innings in good company. Had he gone to a public school and
undergone routine coaching he would have been a county
player. He was sound in the field. Before the First War, he had
a house at Broughton Gifford, to which he invited a number of
his friends every August for a cricket week against neighbouring
villages. During the war he sold his house, but continued to
organize a series of cricket weeks, first at Newbury, afterwards
at Bath. He continued to run these teams until 1933, when he
gave up the game and his side was captained by A. D. Peters,
until the outbreak of the war.

On the fixture lists of our opponents we were often billed as
Authors XI, but Bax's name for us was 'The Old Brough-
tonians' and we were very far from being an Authors XI,
though the team usually contained a number of writers—
Edward Thomas, Harold Monro, J. C. Snaith, J. C. Squire,
Ralph Straus, A. G. Macdonell, Eric Gillett. Music was

represented by Sir Arnold Bax, Armstrong Gibbs, R. O. Morris and Keith Falkner. As the tour wore on, an excess of conviviality diminished our performances in the field, but during the first days we held our own against and on occasions beat sides like Melksham, Landsowne, Trowbridge.

The Invalids was a very different side. It was based on London and fielded a side every Saturday. J. C. Squire had been to a public school, Blundell's, and to Cambridge. He had had the advantage of professional coaching, but had no aptitude for the game. He was very short-sighted, his hands could propel a Buick but they were not shaped for the catching of a cricket ball. He had faith in his capacity as a bowler to diddle a batsman out; and it is true that a long partnership is more likely to be broken by a ball that bounces twice than one of regulation length. The score book shows that he did quite often get a good batsman out; it also shows that after breaking a partnership he went on bowling, to the benefit of the batting side. Clifford Bax, as a captain, was a student of the game who had watched a great deal of good cricket. J. C. Squire was not and had not. Yet in the field the Invalids were as effective as the Old Broughtonians. Their victims included the Lords and Commons at the Oval and the R.A.O.C. at Aldershot.

In 1925 J. C. Squire published privately a brochure in which he described the genesis of the side, in a military hospital, when he and two or three others agreed that when peace came they would make the most of it by organizing a weekly cricket side. Though Squire is alive no longer, the team is still in existence. Like the Old Broughtonians, the Invalids were frequently billed as Authors XI, but it was no more an Authors XI than the O.B.'s. Squire, when asked what the qualifications were for membership, would reply, 'To be a friend of mine.' There was in fact no membership; no committee, no election and no subscription. Anyone who had played for the side was entitled to wear its colours, orange and hospital blue in broad stripes, with crossed crutches on the pocket and the stripes on the cap running from crown to forehead in the Harrovian style. The colours suited one or two players with sallow complexions.

The Invalids have been immortalized in the village cricket match in A. G. Macdonell's *England, Their England*. A few years ago in Fiji I was interviewed on the radio by a cricket addict. 'I suppose,' he began, 'that your chief claim to fame is having been Bobby Southcote in *England, Their England*.' With such modesty as I could assume, I said that I had myself written a few books. 'Of course,' he said, 'but *England, Their England* must come first.' I let it pass. It is better to be known for something than for nothing, though indeed Bobby Southcote is less a caricature than a composite portrait, in the same way that the match itself is a composite account of many matches. I have heard several people say, 'I remember that match so well, it was at——' To my clear recollection incidents in it were taken from matches at Ditchling, Bridge and Fordcombe, and I did not play in the game in which the American guest, on hitting the ball, flung away his bat and ran for point; other players will no doubt recall other incidents. I can recognize the fat publisher as Cecil Palmer, the fierce major as Reginald Berkeley. J. B. Morton was the journalist browsing in the grass, and J. C. Squire was the poet Hodge.

There was no match quite like that; but the atmosphere of an Invalid match is faithfully reproduced, with Squire writing his *Observer* article against time, with the team arriving late in driblets, with the earlier arrivals getting lost in bars, with the tenth man, having missed his train, driving all the way down by taxi, with the last man failing to appear at all, having been sent to the wrong ground, and the taxi-man being requisitioned to take his place. More than once in a match against a school, where punctuality was required, the five first arrivals have elected a leader in the absence of their captain, tossed and gone in to bat, desperately uncertain of their capacity to hold out till lunch.

Usually they did; for that was one of the surprising features of the Invalids; Squire's men, when occasion required, played above their form.

Squire was a much loved man; the loyalty of his friends was great, but as the editor of the *London Mercury* I do not believe that he ever got the best work out of his friends. As the anthology of *Mercury* pieces shows, he published a number of fine things, but he adopted, in matters concerning writing, an offhand, slightly arrogant air of condescension that made a writer of my age think, when he had produced something that he thought above his standard, 'Why bother to send it to Jack? He'll only patronize it.' On the cricket field, we knew both that he knew nothing about the game and did not know that he did not. We were resolved to spare him the fate of an earlier Sir John; he must not make an exhibition of himself in Coventry. We must do something special for his sake. How else are to be explained those many victories against better sides?

§

The atmosphere of the cricket field is very different from that of football. A few years ago I wrote a piece on cricket for the American *Sports Illustrated*. The last line was, 'That is the secret of its charm, the people that you play it with.' When my daughter announced her engagement to me, my second question was, 'Does he play cricket?' Before you play cricket, you have to get twenty-one other players and two umpires to agree to play with you. No one can stop a man who is not a cheat from playing golf and lawn tennis, but the cricketer who is anti-social, no matter how well he plays, is not asked to play again. I have not known one cricketer who was not basically likeable. Cricket would be impossible if one did not like the people with whom one played it. So much of a match is given up to conversation. Right through the day, nine of the twenty-two players are doing nothing. They are sitting in deck-chairs in the shade, watching the game. In addition to that, there is the forty-minute interval for lunch, the twenty minutes' interval for tea; there is the changing period in the pavilion, the drinks after the game; and it must not be forgotten that for a fifth of the time it will be raining, so that both of the XI's will be sitting in the pavilion listening to the pattern of rain on corrugated iron.

On the cricket field I have made the friendships that have lasted me through life. In football, you play with practically the same side every Saturday. It takes a little while to get to know the individual members of your side, particularly if they do not stay on for supper; as I myself did not during my married period. You never see your opponents at all. Football lasts a very short time; five, six, seven years and it is over. When you

give up playing football, you drop out of football. Cricket lasts
thirty to forty years and when you stop playing you still belong
to the world of cricket. There is the Lord's test match every
June. There are late summer afternoons when stockbrokers
knock off early to spend an hour or so at Lord's. There is the
Forty Club annual dinner. Of the men that I played football
with I occasionally see my former captain Eric Atkinson, now
settled in the U.S.A., while Noel King, one time Governor of
Penang and now Brother Proconsul to the Sette of the Odd
Volumes, is one of my closer friends, but that is all. On the
other hand, I see my old cricket friends regularly; they are
indeed the one group of friends with which I find it easy to keep
in touch. Now that I am committed to a scattered way of life,
I sometimes wonder whether I should not be as grateful to my
father for having introduced me to cricket, as for having read me
Shakespeare in the nursery.

§

Until 1926 I devoted my entire summer to cricket, watching
and playing it, apart from the two days, Mondays and Fridays,
that I spent in Henrietta Street. I did a little casual journalism,
but I left my solid writing for the autumn and the winter; and
before long I found that I had to reimpose the routine that I had
started in Ditchling, of spending the middle of the week in the
country. I could not concentrate sufficiently upon my writing
with a telephone beside me, and the manifold distractions of
London a few yards away. I needed to carry on the sequence
of my ideas, to live with my plots and characters for hours
on end. So every Monday evening I would catch a train from
King's Cross to Radlett station, and walk for a couple of
miles to the village of Shenley where I had a room at the White
Horse Inn in which I was fed and boarded for eight shillings a
day.

I have not been to Shenley for over thirty years. I presume
that it has been overwhelmed by post-war development. It is
close to the film studios at Elstree, and when I drove out to see
the filming of *The Trial of Oscar Wilde* I could scarcely recognize the countryside with which my boyhood was familiar. In
the early 'twenties Shenley, on the edge of Metroland, was

surprisingly rural for a village so close to London. There I had complete peace of mind. I wrote for three hours every morning; took a five- to six-mile walk; lunched frugally, wrote until I had finished my daily quota of three thousand words, then took another walk. It was dusk by then. I would read over the fire for a little; then bath and change my clothes; spend an hour or so in the taproom, sometimes playing darts with the villagers, dining at eight o'clock and returning after my meal to the taproom, listening to local gossip, arguing amiably as to the respective merits of the Spurs and Arsenal, of the Yorkshire and Middlesex XIs. After closing-time, I would go into the owner's sitting-room for a final gossip. It was a Benskin's house that sold a very powerful bottled beer, Colne Spring. I had first encountered it at Watford after a football match against West Herts. It was a hot September afternoon. We came off the field, thirsty and exhausted. We poured the beer down our throats without realizing how strong it was. We could barely walk to the changing room. At Shenley I mixed it half and half with bitter; even then it was a strong brew. But at the age of twenty-five, playing football every Saturday and walking eight to ten miles a day, I did not need to worry about my weight and wind.

The village pub is one of the institutions that the American troops in Britain during the war found most congenial. It is a club, without a committee, but with unwritten laws; if you obey those laws you very soon find that you are a welcomed member. I made several friends at Shenley, particularly the landlord and his family. Their company was precisely what I needed after a long day's work; friendly, unexacting, unstimulating. Writing is a solitary occupation; after sitting at one's desk alone for a whole day or trudging over the fields, wrestling with one's ideas, one does not want to spend the evening with a book. One needs company; but one does not want the company to be so stimulating that it will disturb the steady flow of thoughts below the surface.

Sometimes I returned to London late on the Thursday evening, if I had been invited to or had arranged an amusing party. But as often as not I did not come back till the Friday morning; I dined at Underhill and very often stayed the night there, though a 28 bus ran straight from Golders Green station to Earl's Terrace. My social life was concentrated on the week-ends and the summer months. I have kept my engagement diaries, and the pages of these years are black with dates; I scarcely had an unoccupied London evening; in my two and a half years in Earl's Terrace, I do not suppose that I had a single meal alone. I had a wide acquaintance, and every year increased it. I did not belong to any one world. I have never been a member of any set or group. The life of Underhill did not launch me socially in any particular direction. I am not sure if I am not exceptional in that. I rather think I am. Most men, through their families, through their home, through their school and university, start adult life with a definite background which they accept or from which they break away. I started from scratch in 1919; as an advancing army lives off the land, I made friends as I went along.

Max Beerbohm wrote an essay on 'Hosts and Guests', in which he said that everyone was by nature either the one or the other, and I very definitely am happier as a host than as a guest. When I meet at a party people whom I like, my instinct is to invite them to a meal. I make the first move in friendship. There is no time to waste and first impressions are seldom wrong. I enjoy entertaining. This is a Waugh characteristic. My father loved having his friends around him. Evelyn is at his warmest and most expansive in his own house, at his own table. Whenever I visited my aunts at Midsomer Norton, I found the house full of people, dropping in for tea or for games after dinner. I always look forward to my own parties. I am certain then of being with the people I really like, and—which is important to me—of drinking the wines that I prefer. The role of host is also more congenial to one who prefers listening to talking. If one has paid for a supper one does not have to sing for it. As a host I consider I have done my duty when I have assembled people who, I think, will like each other, have provided as good a meal as I can afford, have rescued the con-versation when a lull seemed imminent, and drawn into the conversation any guest who seemed ill at ease. A host should not overdress, nor should he dominate the conversation.

In my flat in Earl's Terrace I had a succession of lunch- and dinner-parties, and I think I can claim to have sponsored one of the first cocktail parties in London. In the spring of 1924 I was discussing with C. R. W. Nevinson and his wife the difficulty of finding anything to do between half past five and seven. Why, we agreed, should we not have a party at that time? As a result of this discussion, they issued an announcement to their friends that the Nevinsons were emerging from their hibernation and would be at home from 5.30 onwards on a certain Saturday in April. The Nevinsons touched life at a great many different levels and their evening parties at Steeles Studios were a feature of the 1920s. But so astonished were their friends by this unusual form of entertainment that when I arrived shortly before six it was to find an array of glasses, two pitchers of iced punch and one other guest. I profited by this experience, and some while later, when my turn came to be a host, invited my friends to a late tea which was followed by daiquiris stirred by a member of the American Embassy. My friends were so unprepared for this form of cherishment that they fancied they were were being offered a kind of sherbert. Sheila Kaye-Smith did not make her dinner date.

§

I wish that I had kept a list of the people I met between 1919 and 1926. It was, as I have said, part of my job at Henrietta Street to be in touch with writers, and though I had few links with Bloomsbury I met at one gathering or another most of the literary figures of the hour. One day I hope to write a book about them. But when I try to reconstruct my life during those four bachelor years, I find that it was centred upon two or three houses, two or three people; or rather that it was enlarged and broadened by those few houses and those few people.

Of these, Clifford Bax was by a long way the most important. In the early summer of 1920 I received an invitation from him to join his cricket tour at Newbury. My acceptance was followed by an invitation to dine with him at a restaurant in Kensington. He was then in his middle thirties. He was tall, clean-shaven, shabbily dressed in loose-fitting tweeds; he had a gentle manner. After dinner we went back to his studio in Edwardes Square, a large, untidy room on the top floor, with a

An O.B. cricket dinner. Left to right: Clifford Bax, John Chisholm, Eric Gillett, Kenneth Lindsay, the Author, A. D. Peters, Clem Hurn, P. Knox-Shaw, A. G. Macdonell, Keith Falkner, Alec Hurn

The author and P. Knox-Shaw on an O.B. tour

Ruth

stove, an immense divan, and a fine Queen Anne bookcase; it had a small bedroom, austere as a monk's cell. He had had printed the scores of the matches that his team had played at Broughton Gifford. I turned the pages with awe, reading names that had been long familiar, Stacy Aumonier,[1] J. C. Snaith,[2] Herbert Farjeon;[3] these men were to become my friends. I felt I was entering a new world.

And indeed I was; in a wider, deeper sense than I had guessed. Clifford Bax was exactly the friend I needed. Through missing Oxford, I had missed the chance of having my ideas developed in tutorials. Bax was fifteen years older than myself. He was both a mentor and a friend; a very human friend. The circumstances of his life gave him glamour. He had a considerable private income and was the first man with whom I was on intimate terms who did not have to worry about small sums. This gave him a patrician air. His private life had been erratic. He had married a woman several years older than himself, had become the father of a daughter, then run off with a young woman. His wife had refused him a divorce. After a while the young woman left him for someone who was free; she was followed by a succession of consorts. He was very attractive to women; his gentle caressing manner masked the vivid masculinity that was exemplified on the cricket field. He lived as, I felt, a poet should.

He was a dedicated person; he had studied Eastern philosophy, the cast of his mind was metaphysical. He professed to be a Buddhist, yet he enjoyed fully the pleasures of the world. The key to his nature lay in the contrast between the anchorite austerity of his bedroom and the vast divan, an altar spread for sacrifice, beside the stove.

Our talk moved from one subject to another, easily. Cricket, poetry, love. I could be myself completely with him. He gave me a great, great deal. But I do not think it was a one-sided friendship. He was, when I met him, in a despondent mood. He had been failed for the army on medical grounds and had

---

[1] One of the most successful English short-story writers of the 1920s.

[2] Author of *Broke of Covenden* and *Willow, the King*, among many other novels.

[3] A dramatic critic, author of *Advertising April* and *The Nine o' Clock Review*.

worked in censorship. Non-combatants tend to drift together, and it was not a healthy atmosphere for Bax, who had been already set apart from his fellows by his financial independence and an unusual upbringing; he had had private tutors and studied at Heidelberg instead of an English university. His father, in my opinion, made a mistake in not sending him to Eton, where he would have been brought up with young men of birth and fortune, and where he would have established contact with his intellectual equals. As it was he lacked a common multiple with his contemporaries. His plays and poems had at this point enjoyed little success, in large part for that reason. In his most successful play *A Rose without a Thorn* he was dealing with material—Henry VIII's marriage to Catherine Howard—with which the audience was familiar. But the audiences of *The Venetian* were puzzled by their ignorance of the characters, interests and period involved. This lack of a common multiple delayed the public recognition of his quality. Magazine editors talk about 'reader identification'. For a story to be effective, the reader must be able to think, 'This might have happened to me.' Bax's problems as a young man were not general ones. His lack of public success and his failure to pass the medical tests had led him to pass the war years in the company of misfits, invalids and conscientious objectors. They were, for the most part, disgruntled, disappointed people; many of them sponged on him. I was the first young, healthy, normal friend that he had made for several years. I fancy he found himself rejuvenated by me and by my appreciation of his work, particularly of his poetry. For over forty years our friendship has been close and constant.

§

The other chief figure in my life was a very different person. In October 1917 I had read in the *Saturday Review* the notice of a novel by Douglas Goldring called *The Fortune*, which it described as being 'difficult to forgive'. I ordered a copy and was much impressed. Books, like wines, lose and acquire qualities, and today *The Fortune* might not seem exceptional. But in 1917 it was an exciting book. It was one of the first novels—it may well have been the first—to debunk the 'old-men-in-their-clubs' attitude to war. I was delighted when I met its author in the summer of 1919 at a party of Harold Monro's at the Poetry Book Shop.

That autumn I wrote to ask Goldring whether there was any chance of my luring him on to Chapman & Hall's list. For several weeks I received no answer. Then, late one November evening, he arrived without writing or ringing first, hatless, in a thin and rather threadbare coat, carrying a large pile of manuscripts. He had been in Germany, he said, investigating post-war conditions, as secretary of Clarté, an international movement started by Henri Barbusse to ensure the avoidance of war through the brotherhood of man.

The pile of manuscripts contained a complete wartime novel that had not found a publisher—and never did—a collection of essays, and the opening chapters of a new novel that we published in the following spring under the title of *The Black Curtain*. He talked of the manuscripts, which he agreed to leave with me, then about conditions in Germany. He was a good talker, with that capacity for evoking a place and character with a phrase which enriched his travel books. Time passed quickly. Five o'clock became six; I had to be getting home. Goldring lived on the edge of Regent's Park in St. James's Terrace. 'I'll drop you at Camden Town,' he said, and waved a taxi. It astonished me, who never took a taxi unless I had luggage or was in feminine company, that the hatless possessor on a cold evening of a threadbare coat and much dog-eared manuscript should be so extravagant. But it was a gesture, I came to recognize, that was typical of Goldring's character and career, a symbol of contradictoriness and strength.

During the next seven years, I was to see as much of Goldring as of anyone and the fact that we later drifted apart was the result of geography, not of disharmony of outlook. Goldring was then in his early thirties. He had come down after a year at Oxford not through conflict with authority but because of a legacy that allowed him to lead in London the life of a young man of fashion in the Balzac manner. He was slim, light-haired, of medium height. He was a good dancer and gregarious. I asked W. L. George what he had been like before the war. 'He had a very well-cut evening coat,' was George's answer.

Goldring's money did not last him long, but he had fun with it, and for a writer the squandering of capital is not the serious matter that it is for the solid citizen. A writer's capital is his experience of the world and Goldring amassed plenty of that in return for his 'blue chips'. Some of his money he invested in a publishing house which failed to prosper but set its imprint on a number of good books, including Flecker's *Golden Journey to Samarkand*; he also acted as sub-editor of the *English Review* under Ford Madox Ford. In the intervals of these editorial activities, he travelled on and off the map, wrote several novels, a book of travel sketches and a volume of charming London verses, *Streets*.

His obituary notice in *The Times* in 1960 was headed *A Propaganda Novelist*, which was the sub-title of his autobiography *Odd Man Out*. He chose that title because circumstance, so he felt, had stranded him on a lonely atoll. This belief was the result, I fancy, of his war experiences. He volunteered in August 1914 but was discharged for medical reasons three months later. This was a great misfortune for him. It forced him into the company of *embusqués* and smug civilians whose prattling of the good that the war was doing made him a pacifist.

I had Goldring in mind when I made a conscientious objector one of the characters in a novel. I took a man who, rejected on medical grounds, became so exasperated by the warmongers and war profiteers that when conscription came, rather than re-offer himself for medical examination, he sought exemption on conscientious grounds.

This situation in Goldring's case produced *The Fortune*. He spent a part of the war in Ireland, marrying an Irish girl, Betty Duncan, and Ireland increased his irritation with official Britain. There were those who described Goldring as embittered and there are in his books streaks of bitterness, or perhaps it would be more accurate to say outbursts of irritation. But in himself I saw few signs of it, any more than I have seen signs of it in Richard Aldington, who vented his spleen in books like *The Colonel's Daughter* but kept his friendships and his poetry clear of it. He was a delightful companion.

Chapman & Hall published four of Goldring's novels. There were excellent passages in all of them but not one quite came off; I think because through financial pressure he never devoted a solid consecutive period of time to their composition. He would put them aside for three or four months while he worked on articles, and when he returned to them he was in a different mood. A novel needs to be the outcome of a single integrated process of creation, in the way that a book of travel or memoirs does not. On the other hand his travel books, *Gone Abroad*, *Northern Lights and Southern Shade* and his book of critical essays, *Reputations*, re-read very well.

§

Each new friendship when one is young, and often, for that matter, when one is middle aged, is a window opening on a landscape. Through Douglas Goldring I met the 1917 Club set.

The club was founded as a rallying-point for left-wing opinion at the time when the anti-war spirit was becoming turbulent and Ramsay Macdonald, in token of its past, lunched there on his first day as Prime Minister.

It was housed in No. 4 Gerard Street, opposite the '43', that curious night club which figured in so many memoirs of the period and in *A Handful of Dust*, and which kept its doors open, in spite of police hostility, into the middle 'thirties.

In its beginnings the club was a refuge for those in political conflict with authority, but it soon became a refuge for those who were in personal conflict with domestic tyranny. It represented everything that most alarmed W. W. Jacobs. Psycho-analysis was new and fashionable. Not many people had read Freud in the original but his theories were widely interpreted as an encouragement to rid oneself of inhibitions, and the 1917 Club was well stocked with male intellectuals in their middle thirties ready to assist the rebel daughters of country rectories in a pursuit so advantageous to themselves. Most of those rebels are now venerable grandmothers, but the flinging of many bonnets over windmills owed their geneses to meetings in No. 4 Gerard Street.

Douglas Goldring's novels *Cuckoo* and *Nobody Knows* give a good impression of its atmosphere. Contemporary films and novels take Noël Coward's *Poor Little Rich Girl* as a typical example of the period, but for me the 1917 Club girl is more typical. Intolerant and valiant, she came up to London in a mood of revolt and idealism, resolved to exorcise the kind of living and of thinking that had made war possible. Retrospect pictures her in a top-story converted flatlet with plain wood furniture from Heal's, a divan bed piled high with coloured cushions, the walls lined with sagging bookshelves, the table littered with pamphlets from the Bomb Shop; her hair is bobbed, she wears a jibbah, the smoke of incessant cigarettes drifts into her eyes; with a glass of Russian tea beside her, she debates the destiny of man far into the night; in the morning, stretched on her stomach before her popping gas-fire, propped up on her elbows, she turns the pages of the first blue-bound volume of *Ulysses*.

The 1917 Club was untidy. Its members forgot to pay their subscriptions and those who did, entered themselves as country members, though they lived in the King's Road, Chelsea. But it was friendly. You could get wholesome food there and, with Goldring on the wine committee, sound claret far more cheaply than you could get sour Chianti in Soho. I had many convivial evenings there and meetings in the 1917 Club led to conviviality elsewhere, particularly in the Caves of Harmony, the dance club run by Harold Scott and Elsa Lanchester, which is described in *Antic Hay*. Situated on the ground floor of No. 107 Charlotte Street, above a negro night club called the Wonderful Minutes, on Saturdays from ten o'clock to dawn it offered dancing and a cabaret. It looked ordinary enough, rather like a village hall, with a stage at one end and benches round the wall. Off the hall was a small room with tables and a canteen bar where you could get soft drinks and sandwiches. It had no licence. A few people brought flasks, but the majority did not. One of the chief features of the 1917 Club group was, in fact, a lack of spirit drinking. They were wine drinkers, when they drank, but they were temperate. Some people came in fancy dress, some in evening clothes, others in tweeds.

Harold Scott and Elsa Lanchester were mainly responsible for the cabaret. They also acted one-act plays, the Anatole dialogues, for instance, and *La Ronde*. During 1922 and 1923 I went there nearly every Saturday.

It was the kind of place that depended for its success upon the personalities of those who ran it and performers of the quality of Elsa Lanchester and Harold Scott could not be long limited within such a narrow sphere. In the summer of 1923 I went there with a party of Nigel Playfair's. It was, I think, one of his first visits and his interest was the beginning of its end. He recognized Elsa's individual talent, and transported her to the Lyric, Hammersmith; from there the road has run straight for her to many successes on stage and screen. She has been as a wife an ornament but not an appendage to Charles Laughton's career. She has cut her individual road. In 1950, in New York, Evelyn and I went to see her starred performance in the Plaza's Persian Room. She had altered little in appearance. Though her technique was surer, she had the same *gamine* charm that had delighted us a quarter of a century before in Charlotte Street.

§

I was to fight many battles on Goldring's behalf with Chapman & Hall's board. He was always short of money. He would deliver a novel on a Wednesday afternoon, insisting that the cheque for it be signed by Friday, so that by calling round on us at half-past five, he could get it to his bank by the morning's post to meet the cheque that he was proposing to issue now to a travel agent. It was absolutely essential, he would assure me, that he crossed to France that week-end. His whole personal life depended on it.

My father would raise his hands in a histrionic gesture. How did he know what might not be in the book? Only thirty-six hours in which to read it. There might be libel. There might be a scene 'too near the knuckle'. There were limits to the demands which authors made of publishers. I would wheedle and cajole, and as I brought forward each new argument I would wonder how long it could go on. Douglas was in the middle thirties. He had been writing for thirteen years. He had never caught the public's favour; was he likely to, if he continued to put this strain upon himself?

But I need not have worried about his future. For thirty-five years his career was to follow the switchback course that is the lot of authors. He wrote several honest novels, some travel books, a series of reminiscences that have a permanent library value as period pieces; no one for instance should attempt to recreate the London of Ford Madox Ford and the *English Review* without reference to *South Lodge*. As secretary of the Georgian Society, he did much to preserve London's architectural charms from the house breakers. No book of his reached the bestseller list; he never made much money, but he never forfeited the respect of his peers. And in his second marriage he had the good fortune to find the personal happiness that he was missing when I met him.

When I wangled his cheques out of the board at Henrietta Street, I did not realize the immense resilience of the born man of letters. Most of the men who say they want to write do not really want to write at all but to have written; the prestige of the author's life appeals to them. But just as there are certain men for whom a life without horses is no life at all, so there are men for whom there is no alternative to a life with pen in hand. Douglas Goldring was one, my New York friend Charles Norman is another. Such men have a deep and sincere love of letters, a deep and sincere impulse to self-expression. Nothing gets them down. They finish one book and begin the next. It is a question of faith, in the last analysis. The believing are rewarded. In major issues it does not pay to hedge your bets. If you put all your eggs into one basket, the fibre holds. At the end of *Odd Man Out* Douglas Goldring wrote, 'I am able to say now once again and from the heart, that—hang it all—I've had on the whole a happy life.'

My first meeting with him was symptomatic not only of his own character and career, but of the intrinsic attitude of the born man of letters—the man with a large pile of manuscript, a whole batch of it unsaleable, but a new book begun confidently; a man who is in desperate need of twenty pounds, but gives a friend a lift in an unnecessary taxi.

§

A few doors down Henrietta Street were the offices of the agent Curtis Brown. I had frequent occasions to call there. One of its junior employees was Luke Hansard, a descendant of the parliamentary Hansards. He was a little older than myself. He had had a leg badly damaged in the war, and walked with a limp. He was a noisy, ebullient, warm-hearted man. He was as bored at No. 6 Henrietta Street as I was at No. 11. 'If you complain about having to read manuscripts that aren't worth publishing, think of me, reading manuscripts that aren't even good enough for an agent to send out to a publisher.' He said that Curtis Brown ought to hang up a door sign, *Aux bonnes tripes*. It was very certain that he would not be employed there long; and within a few months he had moved to the south of France, to a small Provençal cottage a mile from Mougins, with his wife Rene Juta, the sister of Jan Juta.

In the late summer of 1922, I went to stay with them. This was my introduction to the enchanted coast that has never lost its magic for me.

How different it was then! The passion for sun-bathing had not begun. The Riviera was considered intolerable after Easter. It was a winter resort, and the big shops and hotels were shuttered after the first of May. The Luke Hansards were one of the earlier English couples to find London too expensive after the war, who felt themselves, at first, victims of circumstance at being forced, for reasons of finance, to linger on after the season's close; but soon discovered that the heat was by no means excessive. Seated on their shaded porches, drinking the light wines of the Var, looking out over the blue Mediterranean, reading in the continental *Daily Mail* of how another test match had been drawn through rain, they congratulated themselves on their good fortune. For me the summer is wasted in which I have not spent a few weeks in the south of France. It was through Luke Hansard that I came to love it.

I also, through him, enlarged my knowledge of London. His mother lived in Cadogan Square, and she kept open house every Sunday in a large L-shaped drawing-room that was so filled with antiques that you would have likened it to a museum if it were not obviously a personal collection amassed with loving care. Luke's mother was then in her later sixties, handsome, tall, white-haired, and very much the *grande dame*, in the manner of Queen Mary. Whenever in a novel I introduce the character of such a woman, I write out of my memories of her.

She would have twenty or so guests every Sunday. They would be mainly men, of all ages. Her husband was a retired army officer, a gunner who occupied his leisure with wood carving of genuine quality. Among the guests would be a sprinkling of the brother officers who had paid court to his wife when they were dashing subalterns, and now as prosaic bachelors with enlarged or withered figures, in striped trousers and black morning coats, sipped their tea, munched hot buttered scones, and lamented the trouble they were having with a housekeeper, or their difficulty in getting a butcher to supply them with the proper cuts, while Mrs. Hansard smiled as indulgently as she had thirty years ago when they had brought very different confidences of their exploits in the lists of love. To me, they were charming and pathetic; sixty then seemed to me an age astronomically remote.

But the elderly courtiers were very far from being in the majority. There were many young people there who had come originally as friends of Luke and his sister Arrdyn de Lembcke, but soon became conscious of a deep affection for their mother. Mrs. Hansard had a young heart; it was easy to confide in her. She had led a strict and formal life, in terms of the proprieties, but she had an indulgence for the frailties of the young. A visit to Cadogan Square was an essential feature of my Sunday routine.

Arrdyn de Lembcke soon became as good a friend of mine as her brother. Her husband was in business, in Lima; she spent the winters with him, but was in London alone in the summer. She was and is a popular and sociable woman. She needed an escort to dances and parties, and she often took me with her. Cleveland Amory has written a book entitled *Who Killed Society?* I have never known how to define 'society', but I suppose that the big houses to which Arrdyn took me were 'society'. It was both a highly pleasant experience for me as a man and important for me as a novelist. I saw how the 'big world' lived. I also mixed with men and women who were not connected with literary Bohemia; thus I became able to include in my novels men of administration and finance. My canvas was widened. The novelist has to describe the business of his characters, and the reader soon wearies of meeting in book after book, publishers, advertising agents and theatrical producers. He longs for a change, to be meeting the kind of people whom he himself is meeting—underwriters, stockbrokers chartered accountants.

§

Arrdyn de Lembcke gave me a social education. It was a very different education that I received at the hands of the woman to whom I have referred in an earlier chapter as the object of a sultry tempestuous romance in 1922.

I met her at the Caves of Harmony at the end of March. She was about my height; dark, hazel-eyed. Her hair, cut in a fringe, was coiled round her ears. She had a full, trim figure. She was wearing a plain black dress; the bodice fitted tightly; from the hips swung a kind of fringe, of thin black silk streamers. She looked about twenty-seven.

I noticed her the moment I came into the room. I had gone there with Stacy Aumonier, Cecil Palmer and Mrs. Cecil Chesterton. She waved at Aumonier as she danced past. 'Who's that?' I asked.

'A wild, attractive lady.' He told me her story, in synopsis. She was kept by a rich stockbroker, considerably older than herself. She was exceedingly unfaithful to him. No, she was not promiscuous, but she was never for long without a lover. She drank more than she should. One of her haunts was the buffet bar of the Marlborough Road Underground. That was where he had met her. It was a few yards from the St. John's Wood Art Club, and he went there when the club was empty. 'Will you introduce me?' I said.

'There isn't any need.'

She had a basement flat near the Edgware Road tube station, in Oxford and Cambridge Mansions. The first time I went there, she checked me when I was about to shut the sitting-room door. 'Don't shut it,' she said. 'The door presses on the telephone wire and makes a singing sound.'

I looked up and saw that the telephone wire had been run inside the framework. It would have been very easy to cut away a half-inch of the woodwork so that the wire was not touched. I pointed this out to her. 'I know,' she said. 'I'm always meaning to.'

That unshut door was typical of her life. Most people would find it impossible to live in a sitting-room whose door was never shut. But for Phyllis a sitting-room was not a place where you sat quietly reading a book before a fire. When she wanted to read, and she read a lot, she read in bed. For her a sitting-room was a place you rushed through, to change clothes, to play a gramophone, to fix a drink. She had a large acquaintance. She was always on her way out to somewhere, on her way back from somewhere. Her protector occupied very little of her time. The thing had been running for three years and he was, I suspected, anxious to be rid of it. She was quarrelsome and jealous, and an elderly man has need of a new stimulus.

It was a pleasant, four-roomed flat with a neat compact dining-room, but she rarely cooked a meal. Reggiori's was round the corner. It was simpler to go out for a steak. Wireless did not exist in those days. I do not think that gramophones had self-changing attachments; at any rate, hers had not; we were always moving the gramophone from one room to another; the records were always running down; our life went to an accompaniment of fox-trots and running bath-water.

It was a happy time, an immeasurably immense relief after the two and a half years' strain of a marriage that was not a marriage; a voyage of self-discovery. I now realized what novelists meant when they talked about the endlessly re-newed delights of love. It was a miracle that surpassed my dreams of it. We were together as often as we could be. I did scarcely any writing during that year. I was living at Under-hill. I had my two days a week at Henrietta Street. I played cricket three or four times a week. We met most evenings. All Sundays we spent together. I would get there about eleven, to find her reading. The long day wore on, with the beam of sun-light slowly travelling across the ceiling. If we felt hungry, she would make a sandwich. It was too much trouble to go out to Reggiori's. We would dance to the gramophone. We would doze and chatter. In the early evening we would make for the Café Royal, for the red banquette seats of the Domino room, to dine off a sole *bonne femme*, our favourite dish, and sit there afterwards, hand in hand, sipping at a glass of port; languid with loving, utterly at peace.

We did not look ahead. We made no plans. Our different positions, disparity of age, my lack of money precluded that; we accepted the situation and did not discuss it. In the late autumn she told me that her protector had suggested her making a trip to Australia. It was, I fancy, his generous way of breaking off the entanglement. She went with a return ticket, but he knew that she would not use it. Making a fresh start in a new country, she was almost sure to marry; as she did.

'Do you want to go?' I asked her.

She shrugged. 'I think so. It'll be something new. I could do with a change.'

'And you'll be back in June?'

'I imagine so.'

'My divorce will be through by then. Things should be easier.'

During the last weeks, we had exercised a certain degree of caution, out of concern for the King's Proctor.

'Everything will be better then,' she said.

We talked as though it were a six-month separation; but I think that we were both secretly relieved that our romance was to end so smoothly, before it had cooled, with no regrets, with nothing but gratitude on either side. *Coupé net en pleine ardeur*, in terms of Maupassant.

When one is young one is confident that there is something better round the corner. Actually many years were to pass before I found a comparable happiness; then it was very different. I was a different person.

It was not only in terms of love-making that those nine months were an education for me. Phyllis was the first woman of the world that I had met. As her escort I absorbed a knowledge of the kinds of attention that a woman expects from a man; the technique of dealing with waiters, porters, taxis, so that a woman feels she is taken care of, that everything has been decided for her in advance, that she has no concern except her own enjoyment. A woman once said to me of a friend of ours, 'When he takes you out, you don't feel that you are being taken out.' It is not a question of money, of how much is being spent upon her; on the contrary a bunch of violets presented with a gesture can be more endearing than a corsage of gardenias proffered automatically. The smallest excursion can appear as an occasion, if a man shows that he regards it as an occasion, that to him it is of supreme importance that a particular woman should accord him the privilege of a leisure hour.

There are things that cannot be learnt from a pamphlet on etiquette. You can only acquire them from being in the company of a woman who is dear to you, whom you are resolved to learn how to please.

§

I had, I said, few links with Bloomsbury, but through my connexion with the Poetry Bookshop I met the majority of the younger poets. I went to the Poetry Bookshop for the first time in the autumn of 1915 when I was on sick leave from the Inns of Court with a sprained ankle. *Georgian Poetry 1913–1915* had just appeared, and a reading was being given of Gordon Bottomley's play *King Lear's Wife*. Harold Monro, in the uniform of a private soldier, read the part of Lear. From then on, I constantly visited the Bookshop.

It was in Devonshire Street; a charming eighteenth-century house with panelled walls. It was a publishing house, a bookshop and a club, Harold Monro living above the shop. It published Georgian Poetry. Before the war it had published *The Poetry Review*, in which Rupert Brooke's *Grantchester* first appeared. It also issued small volumes of poetry, Robert Graves's *Over the Brazier*, for example.

During my visits there I got to know the editress, Alida Klementaski, who later became Harold Monro's wife. After the war I met Monro himself, and being at a loose end after my transfer to the Reserve I undertook some half-time employment with him as a salesman and librarian, attempting a catalogue of modern poets. I greatly valued my friendship with Monro. He was a cricketer out of practice, whom I persuaded to play in one or two of the matches that I organized, and through my offices he joined one of Clifford Bax's tours. During the winter we played squash rackets at the R.A.C. He spent a week-end at Half Acre.

His evening parties were exclusively masculine. He served sandwiches and table wines. There were no spirits. They began at nine o'clock and continued long after the tubes had ceased to run. I met the Sitwells there and T. S. Eliot, Ford Madox Ford, Edward Shanks, Humbert Wolfe, Richard Aldington, F. S. Flint and John Gould Fletcher. There would be thirty or forty guests. It seems in retrospect that he had three or four of these parties every year. Harold Monro's own reputation as a poet slumped during the 1930s, but the younger poets of today are conscious of his quality. His poems appear more often in anthologies than do those of poets whose stock stood higher in the 1930s.

§

The three chief hostesses for men of letters in the 1920s were Lady Ottoline Morrell, Lady Cunard and Lady Colefax. I barely met the first two, and I did not meet Lady Colefax until the 1930s. I wish I had known her earlier. She had charm and warmth and a genius for creating an atmosphere in which artists could be at their ease and at their best.

The equivalent in my life was a somewhat different person, Gwen Otter, who kept open house in Chelsea, in Ralston Street.

The peak of her life came, I suppose, in the Edwardian era; certainly her brother Frank was one of the characters of Edwardian London, a man who lived high and well, who gambled away his health and wealth, who was a legendary figure when I was young. Gwen Otter had an eccentric appearance, she claimed descent from Pocahontas and she dressed dramatically in turbans and trousers. Before the war she had had a cook of remarkable attainments; and even in the 'twenties when taxation and extravagance had reduced her income, her *cuisine* had the kind of quality you find in certain small Soho restaurants; it was distinctive, though one had to be on one's guard against an excessive use of garlic.

Her sitting-room had been decorated by Marcel Boulestin. It had a violent blue ceiling and silver walls and alabaster lamps. She had some valuable books, Burton's *Arabian Nights* and the limited editions of the 'nineties. She had Beardsley pictures and a pen-and-ink drawing of Aleistair Crowley by Augustus John. She entertained incessantly. She was very deaf and preferred being a hostess to being a guest. I think she only went to parties to collect new guests. She enjoyed shocking the bourgeoisie. Before the war, when homosexuals had been looked at askance, she had not considered a party of hers complete that did not include one. Later, when perversion was accepted and while the colour bar was operative, she entertained negroes. When a friend invited her to an after-dinner party, she replied that she would love to, but she had a guest.

'Bring him along too.'

'I'm not sure that you'd approve of him.'

'Why?'

'He's a dentist.'

The prospective hostess assured her that she had nothing against dentists, but she was discountenanced when Gwen Otter arrived with a coal-black African.

On Sunday at lunch her cook made a special effort. Gwen never knew how many guests she would have, and she did not always remember their names. She would usually arrive late and I suspect that this was subsconsciously due to a wish to be relieved of exposing her ignorance of her guests' identities. By leaving us to introduce ourselves to one another, she did not embarrass a guest by revealing that she did not know who he was.

I met Gwen Otter in the summer of 1923. She soon became a very dear friend of mine. I lunched at her house most Sundays and dined there once or twice a week. I made a number of friends there; and often I found that someone who had seemed stand-offish and superior in a more formal setting was in fact a very friendly person. No. 1 Ralston Street was a kind of club and some of us would arrange between ourselves to dine there on the same evenings. We did not invite ourselves. Gwen Otter would have resented that. We were tactful. Audrey Lucas, for instance, would let me know that she was dining there on Thursday. I would then ring up and say, 'I was wondering, Gwen, whether, if you weren't doing anything on Thursday evening, you would like to come to me. I'll have one or two people round.'

There would be a pause. Then Gwen would say, 'No,

dearie, I don't think I can do that. But why don't you come here and dine with me?'

Rebecca West, James Laver, Marda Vanne, Berta Ruck, Ernest Thesiger, William Gerhardi, John Rothenstein—how many acquaintanceships did not become there transmuted into friendships!

§

In most ways I was leading a very carefree existence at this time, but I did have two constantly niggling causes of disquiet; one of these may seem infantile to the reader. I began to lose my hair, rapidly, on the front of my head. We are all, I suppose, self-conscious about some aspect of our personal appearance. I have never been worried about my height. I could hit a cricket ball harder and farther than most men, and on the football field I was one of the toughest forwards in the Park. I had no illusions about my looks, but I had been proud of my hair; it was dark and thick; it had a natural wave; I parted it in the centre. It was a great grief to me when it began to thin. I took elaborate precautions to arrest the tide. I subjected myself to a glass comb that emitted violet sparks; my scalp was scraped with an ivory knife. I bought expensive toilet preparations. Hairdresser after hairdresser assured me that though he could not bring back my hair he could save what I had. Their attentions availed nothing. My brother's friends at Oxford nicknamed me the Baldhead. I did not like it, but I accepted it, I hope with grace. Week by week, the ravages became more marked. Finally a female hairdresser, inspecting the tuft of hair upon my crown, inquired on a note of some contempt, 'Do you part this thing?'

Film stars presumably know what they look like, but for the most part we only see ourselves before a mirror, shaving, or, in a woman's case, making up. We do not know how we look when we are amused, depressed, excited. We do not know what are the expressions that antagonize or endear us to our acquaintances; and I, looking at my reflection in the mirror with a horror that mounted monthly, felt that I presented a ridiculous appearance, with my young complexion and

o

balding pate. I thought I looked an overgrown baby. Perhaps I did.

I attribute the relative chastity of my existence between 1923 and 1926 to my belief that no girl could possibly fall in love with anyone so unattractive. I conducted my campaigns with a lamentable lack of confidence, and my creative energies were sublimated in my writing.

With my other cause of disquiet, the reader will be, I hope, in greater sympathy—the course of events in Henrietta Street.

IV

Troubles in Henrietta Street

My father's autobiography, *One Man's Road*, received a large and welcoming Press and sold well for that kind of book, but when the question of republishing it was recently raised, it was felt that though the early chapters evoked a vanished world with charm, and as such had a permanent reference value, the second half was dull. 'I suppose,' an editor commented, 'that those years were undramatic—his asthma preventing his going out, I mean.'

But that is not the explanation. The second half of my father's life was not dull but he could not write about those parts of it that were dramatic.

You can write freely about the dead, but you have to be circumspect about the living. No family man can tell the truth about his home; and a man such as my father could not have written fully about the various problems, and they were many, with which Evelyn and I presented him. From the age of twenty-seven he could only write honestly of the things that had happened to him professionally, and he could not always write of them. While he was chairman of Chapman & Hall he could not tell of the firm's stormy history between 1924 and 1934, when it passed under the genial and effective dictatorship of Philip Inman.

In an earlier chapter I described how the firm was organized when my father joined it in 1904, but I did not explain its financial basis. Beginning in the 1830s as a small family business, its capital in the course of ninety years became dispersed by legacies and bequests among a number of small shareholders.

During the early years of my father's stewardship the preference and the ordinary shareholders both received their dividends. Everything went so well that no one realized how immense a burden was placed upon a small business by the claims of 2,001 cumulative preference shares, since a few lean years could place the ordinary shareholders in a hopeless position, nor what an additional burden was created by the fact that no one employed by the business held more than few nominal shares; no one, that is to say, could regard his salary as a return for invested capital. This was a great, great handicap.

Publishing is a pleasant trade for three or four men who invest a portion of their capital in a business which will provide them with the type of work which they enjoy, and from which they can draw a salary in lieu of dividends. Publishing is the most fascinating profession in the world for a man who cares for books, who is interested in human beings and who has varied interests. He can make his business as wide as are those interests. He can indulge his hobbies. If he is interested in fishing, porcelain or stamps he can, by publishing the appropriate books, keep in touch with the most prominent figures in those fields in a way that as an unconnected amateur he could never do.

But the scattered shareholders of Chapman & Hall were getting no fun out of their money. They had a risky investment; their shares could not stand as collateral for an overdraft; and at that time they could have received a five per cent return from War Loan. The moment they ceased to be paid a substantial dividend by Chapman & Hall they would start to grumble. That moment was soon to come.

§

It is surprising how quickly an economic typhoon blows up. We blame politicians for their lack of prescience, but in our own affairs we are no more farseeing. Everything seemed to be going well in Henrietta Street. New blood had come into the business. New authors gave the list prestige. The young man who before the war had been in charge of the technical department, J. L. Bale, returned from war service confident and adult, and considerably enlarged that side of the firm's activities. The turnover increased; there was no lack of cash in the bank.

The future seemed bright, but the balance sheet for 1921 showed a diminished profit. In 1922 the profit was even smaller. There was no dividend for the ordinary shareholders. 1923 saw the dividend due to preference shareholders reduced to four per cent—it was the first time the preference shareholders had not been paid in full since my father had been in control. As the dividends were cumulative, this meant that the prospects for the ordinary shareholders were poor. Trouble could be expected at the next meeting.

The crisis was unexpected, and the first inevitable question was, 'Why has it happened?' Bale suggested that an analysis be taken of the profit and loss of the separate sections of the firm's activities. My father looked glum when he told me of this request. 'I suppose he thinks that he is responsible for most of the firm's profits.'

Bale was at that time in the thirties. He had not been to a public school. He had not been an officer in the war. He had had to fight his way. He was alert, witty, intelligent. He had a perky face; he wore spectacles, he was balding, his hair was red and he wore it long, letting it curl at the nape of his neck. He was ambitious and not the man to give away points.

When the profit was split up into the various departments it was found that the technical books had earned practically the entire profit and on a much smaller outlay of capital, the general books including Dickens doing little more than pay their way. This was not an unusual situation or indeed an unhealthy one in the average privately owned firm. Directors owning their own business are content to cover costs on the kind of book which they are proud to publish and rely for their bread and butter on bibles, diaries and annuals. But Chapman & Hall was not owned by directors who enjoyed the prestige of their imprint upon good books, but by a group of scattered shareholders who were only concerned with their dividend warrants. Bale was in a strong position.

Careerism was alien to my father's nature; this was a lovable and admirable trait in him, but it created complications because he did not recognize careerism in others. If he had faced the predicament, he would have realized that the success of the technical department entitled Bale to a seat on the board;

he should equally have realized that with Bale as a director his own son would have been superseded. And I do not think that anyone questioned my value to the firm. His prudent course would have been to reorganize the board in view of the existing crisis, placing the two representatives of the younger generation on it. Bale was very loyal, and if he had been met half-way he would have been disarmed; but my father did nothing and Bale, moving first, requested a directorship. It cannot have been easy for him to do so, and it confirmed him in his belief that 'you don't get anything in this world unless you ask for it'.

'I'll have to give him what he wants,' my father said to me. Even then he did not realize that Bale's promotion would alter my own position. But of course I did. I was not yet sure of my own future plans but I definitely did not want to have Bale's seniority in the succession confirmed. So the suggestion had to come from me, that the board should be further enlarged. I proposed, in addition to myself, W. L. George, one of our most effective and publicity-minded authors.

I resented having to make this suggestion myself, as much as Bale had done. We both, in fact, had a sense of grievance.

§

The shareholders' meeting that followed the announcement of these changes was not harmonious. Among the shareholders was Bale's brother-in-law, an engineer called Clapham, one of those clever, aggressive fellows who cannot argue calmly and in consequence wake irritation on the other side. He held a very small number of shares which he had bought on Bale's recommendation. When the adoption of the balance sheet was moved, he rose in a fighting mood. Things were not good enough, he said. Was the board taking its position seriously? He quoted from one of Courtney's previous speeches. 'We are here to publish books and we have published them.' Clapham was scathing. 'You are not here, gentlemen, simply to publish books, but to publish them in such a way that you make profits for us, the shareholders.' He read us an angry lecture and sat down.

He put our backs up very definitely, but his virulence had a salutary effect, like a shot of hormones. 'The fellow must be made to eat his words.'

This was in April 1924, and the next twelve months were the happiest, or perhaps I should say the least unsatisfactory, that I spent in Henrietta Street. I enjoyed the importance of being a director. I enjoyed the drama of the meetings, the interplay of personalities. On the suggestion of the secretary, Gatfield, staff conferences were held after the board meeting to discuss points of management and policy. George always stayed behind, though Truslove and Courtney left. For George it was an adventure and his presence revivified the air. But when the next balance sheet was cast, the profits were found to be no higher than the previous year's, and the prospects of the ordinary shareholders were rendered worse by a further addition to the firm's indebtedness to its preference shareholders. We expected trouble at the Annual Meeting and we got it.

Clapham arrived in company with Bale and two other gentlemen whom I was seeing for the first time. The balance sheet was read and my father offered as encouraging a speech as he could under the circumstances. It was too early yet to judge what effect had been produced by the various measures that the new board was taking. He was certain that there would be an improvement next year.

Clapham was on his feet. He hoped, he could only say he hoped, that the managing director's prophecies would be fulfilled. In the meantime there was a point he would like to make. He noticed that two of the directors, Mr. W. L. Courtney and Mr. Alec Waugh, had published books under another imprint. He deplored this. How could we induce our friends to bring their books to Chapman & Hall when we were ourselves publishing elsewhere? Myself, I was working off an agreement with Grant Richards signed thirty months before I had joined Chapman & Hall, but Courtney was in a different position. Hutchinson had offered him for his *Memoirs* a larger sum than we would have cared to pay. We were glad to have had him accept that offer, but that was a tricky point to explain to shareholders. Courtney said something about 'a certain delicacy' having prevented him from discussing terms with friends. Clapham snorted. It was a shorter and less violent speech than he had made last time although he had more provocation. I suspected that he was holding his fire. He was.

My father next announced that two of the directors, Bale and Truslove, had retired in rotation and offered themselves for re-election. Would any shareholder propose their re-election? Clapham was on his feet. Could the names be taken separately? It was obvious what was coming now. Bale's name came first. Clapham proposed his re-election and flung a bouquet to his brother-in-law's skill and industry.

Then it was Truslove's turn. Clapham was again on his feet. What good, he asked, was Mr. Truslove doing? What was his connexion with publishing? His father might be a bookseller, but he was at Oxford, helping undergraduates. What were his qualifications as a publisher?

My father reminded the shareholders that it was Mr. Truslove's initiative that had led to the enlargement of the technical business. Maybe, retorted Clapham, but that was fifteen years ago. What had Mr. Truslove done since? What prospect was there of his doing anything effective in the future? The firm needed someone who understood engineering from the inside, who could advise on technical books and bring technical books. Such a man was sitting beside him now in the person of R. E. Neale; the shareholders should elect him instead of Mr. Truslove.

It was the first time that any of us, except my father, had heard of Neale. Clapham proceeded to expatiate upon his merits. His qualifications were considerable, and Mr. Neale, Clapham concluded, would not be deterred by 'feelings of a certain delicacy' from persuading his friends to be published by Chapman & Hall. He underlined 'a certain delicacy' with a sneer.

The proposal took the board completely by surprise and Courtney was not the man to deal with an emergency. I imagine that it was quite illegal for a shareholders' meeting to elect a director without warning the other shareholders; if it were not, a small group of shareholders could vote themselves on to any board. But this did not occur to us at the time and in the heat of the moment.

It was a stormy meeting. Clapham's face got whiter every

time he spoke, and his tone grew more aggressively insolent. 'Money, that's all we want, money,' he declaimed.

Eventually both Truslove and Neale were elected to the board.

§

Neale was to prove an asset to the firm. He was conscientious and hard-working. He was also a pleasant fellow, and a genuine friendship grew up between my father and himself. But the manner of his election was unfortunate, and it set a precedent. Bale must have known that Clapham was to propose his election. He had, that is to say, plotted against the board in general and Truslove in particular. But his own experience had warned him that you had to fight for what you wanted. He was justified in thinking that there was no other way of getting Neale elected, and he considered that he was acting in the firm's best interests. The future endorsed that belief. Neale did a great deal for the firm. But by one of those anomalies of chance that makes publishing a fascinating trade, his most valuable single service was not in connexion with Bale's department.

In 1928 my brother was having difficulties with his publishers. Tom Balston, Duckworth's partner, had taken a chance on him a year or two before, paying him an advance of £50 for a book on Rossetti before a line of it was written. The book had done well and received a number of good reviews. Evelyn naturally offered to Duckworth his first novel *Decline and Fall*. They liked the book, but on moral grounds they wanted alterations. Evelyn would, I think, have been prepared to make minor deletions, but their demands were ridiculous. I saw the marked manuscript which they returned and can vouch for this. In the opening chapter, for instance, where Pennyfeather was 'debagged', they objected to the description of him running round the courts without his trousers.

The manuscript was next offered to Chapman & Hall. My father, though he admired the book, was hyper-sensitive where the interests of any member of his family were concerned. Bale was not enthusiastic. Ralph Straus who was then on the board did not particularly like Evelyn and was not too anxious to have him as one of the authors with whom he would have to deal. It was Neale who insisted that the book be published. It was a coincidental reversal of Truslove's case. Truslove had been brought on to the board in the hope that he would introduce the young idea from Oxford; instead he was responsible for the enlargement of the technical department. Neale was elected to strengthen the technical side, and championed an *avant-garde* intellectual who was to become the firm's most valuable asset, in terms both of prestige and profit.

V

Good-bye to London

'Money, that's all we want. Money.' The prospect of facing every year Clapham's white face and rasping voice was not a pleasant one, but at the moment there seemed no alternative. Authorship is a precarious profession and my stock did not stand high on the literary bourse.

I imagine, indeed, that by April 1925 most of my friends had written me off as a one-book man. I had published two novels since the war; neither sold over 2,500 copies; the second had sold worse than the first. I had published four general books, none of which sold over two thousand copies. I wrote articles for the newspapers, but pay was low. My short stories did not appeal to the glossy magazines. I had had no luck in America. I was not making more than £500 a year by my pen.

That same month, however, I published a novel entitled *Kept*. It sold six thousand copies in England and as many in America. It was far from being a bestseller, but a sale of five thousand copies was by no means negligible then.

Kept exploited a new technique for me. I have specialized in two kinds of novel—the chronicle novel, a type fashionable at that time, a modification of the 'cradle-to-grave' novel popularized by *Jean Christophe*, in which a character or group of characters are taken through a series of crises covering a number of years against the social and political background of the time; stories with a theme rather than a plot, which attempt to reach a conclusive climax, but very often appear to stop rather than to finish. In 1934 I published a chronicle novel in this style about a family called *The Balliols*, which did reasonably well on both sides of the Atlantic.

My other type of novel was described by the *New York Times* as a symphonic novel. Here I have a definite plot, a theme, an action concentrated into a short space of time, with a crowded canvas, with each minor plot woven into the main plot. *Island in the Sun* and *Fuel for the Flame* were symphonic novels. So was *Kept*, to which I gave the subtitle *A Story of Post-War London*.

I stumbled on the technique by chance. Most novels are the outcrop of personal experience. I do not mean that one transcribes a personal experience directly, that one 'puts one's friends into books', but that by brooding over a personal experience one recreates it in another shape; and I wanted to relive my romance of 1922 in print. I planned to call it *A Kept Woman*.

One of the things I like doing best in fiction is the re-tracing, step by step, of the road that has led a character or a group of characters into a dishonourable situation. At each step they have felt themselves to be doing the best, the natural, the inevitable thing; yet the road has led into a morass. In *A Kept Woman* I planned to show how a war widow, supported by a man whom she believed would soon be free to marry her, drifted, on finding that he was not, into a romance with an idle man-about-town.

As I planned the story, I felt that my chief difficulty lay, I will not say in justifying, but in making appear human the conduct of the hero. He was a man who could have afforded to marry or take the woman under his protection. Was it not basically base of him to accept a sharing of her? It was a position that a Maupassant hero would have accepted with a shrug, but I was writing of an Anglo-Saxon. To make the man's conduct pardonable, I would have to show that though he could have afforded to marry her—if she had wanted him—marriage on his income would have forced on them a limiting and depressed way of life. I wondered how big an income I could allow him. I had given him the symbolic name of Ransom Heritage, presenting him as a man who had lost ambition during the war, who wanted no stake in the future, had resigned his commission in the army and was proposing to spend the rest of his life selfishly and indulgently, cutting into capital when he needed it. He was a man who had never pictured himself in terms of marriage. Yes, but even so, I thought, how large an income could I allow him? Fifteen hundred a year, twelve hundred? I needed to present him as a young man of fashion. He must not be too poor.

I took my problems to W. L. George. After a board meeting at Henrietta Street we walked across the park to his house in Hyde Park Terrace. 'Would fifteen hundred be too much?' I asked.

'It is more than most Civil Servants earn. How much did you marry on?'

'Five hundred.'

'Exactly. Suppose you double it?'

'A thousand sounds terribly little.'

George laughed. 'We're like two Arab traders bargaining in a bazaar.'

In the end I did not specify the actual sum, but I need not have caused myself concern. Novels are mainly read by women, and none of the women to whom I mentioned it were in the least shocked by Ransom's conduct. Men were like that, they said. But they were shocked by the woman's conduct. She should have been loyal to the man who was looking after her. It had never occurred to me that she needed any particular advocacy. I came to the conclusion that men and women apply a higher standard to their own sex than to the other.

I started the story as the study of a triangle. For a month it progressed well; then it died on me. This, I have since discovered, is normal procedure for me. I need a rest, then I begin again, usually from a different angle. I did not know this then. I was worried, I mentioned it to a very good friend of mine, Sylvia Beaufort-Palmer. 'What's it called?' she asked.

'*A Kept Woman.*'

She pouted. 'I don't like that. Why not call it *Kept*?'

That gave me an entirely new slant. I visualized a group of post-war characters all of whom were kept in a different way, living on the past, on capital, on a title, on a reputation won during the war; with the figure of England herself in the background living on her triumphs of the eighteenth and nineteenth centuries. At the very end I would have one of the characters say, 'We're all kept, aren't we, in one way or another?' Ransom

Heritage's romance would be a symbol of London in 1925. At a second attempt the writing of the book went quickly.

§

Kept made a great difference to me financially. F. E. Baily, the editor of the *Royal Magazine*, invited me to write some stories for him. He asked me what I usually got paid for 'that kind of merchandise'. I had been getting four guineas a thousand from the *Blue Magazine*. I chanced my arm and told Baily eight. He pouted. 'Well, if they're good enough I shan't grumble.' He did not grumble. Then a friend of the cricket field, A. D. Peters, set up as a literary agent. He suggested that I should write a serial for a newspaper. I was shocked by the suggestion. I thought myself 'above that kind of thing'. But I listened to his exposition.

'A serial is 80,000 words,' he said. 'You write a five-thousand word first instalment, setting out the situation; the hero must meet the heroine in the course of it; it must have a punch in the last line. Then you write a second instalment of three thousand words; that must have a punch line too. The editor will commission it on the first two instalments. The rest of the serial is straightforward, in two-thousand word instalments. It doesn't matter about punch lines, once the reader's attention has been caught. You'll get £350 for it. You can make the serial the framework for a novel later.'

I let myself be tempted. The eventual result was a quite poor novel, *Love in These Days*, which earned me quite a little money. A good deal of fun is involved in the launching of a serial. It is exciting to see one's name placarded all over London; there was a bigger space for posters in the front of buses then. Bus after bus announced my story. I saw them first on a snowy morning. I had emerged from the tube station at Hyde Park Corner. I was crossing the circus on the way to the Savile Club when I saw a fleet of them, sweeping up Piccadilly. I stood transfixed and was nearly run over in the snow.

The publicity involved brought me a number of commissions to write articles in the women's magazines. Peters exploited the new situation adroitly. I have heard authors say that they do not need an agent, that they can do the work themselves at a saving of ten per cent. Personally, I do not know how I could have managed without Peters in London and the Brandt office in New York.

For more than forty years Peters has been one of my closest friends. We have played a great deal of cricket together, for the O.B.s, the Invalids, Hampstead and M.C.C. We meet constantly at the Savile, we have travelled together in France and in Morocco. We have arranged for our visits to New York to coincide. We were together in London during the blitz of '40–'41. When I showed him the first draft of this book he said, 'I am not the right person to judge it. I know you so well myself that I cannot tell what impression it will make on somebody who does not. I'm handing it over to my young men.' As Peachum said to Lockitt, 'We know enough about each other to hang each other.' I know him too well to write about him, other than objectively.

Of medium height, thick-set, blonde-haired, fresh-complexioned with a broken nose—his background is Scandinavian—he has an air of surly apathetic indolence. No one is livelier company among tested friends, but he can make a disconcerting first impression, particularly on Americans. 'There he sits like a great Buddha,' I have heard one say. 'I don't know how to get at him.'

This manner is a great asset to him as an agent. Publishers and editors stand in awe of him, so do his authors. No author would dare to make an extravagant demand, and when he says to a publisher, 'Take it or leave it,' it is recognized that he is not bluffing. He is on the surface unenthusiastic; this too is a valuable trait. A writer very easily loses his head, when things are going well. He imagines that, because he has sold in a month a couple of short stories to the *Saturday Evening Post*, he can rely on a five-figure income for the next five years. Peters brings him down to earth. His judgment is nearly always sound. He may seem discouraging when an author hurries round breathlessly with an idea for 'an entirely different kind of book'. But he knows that a cobbler should stick to his last and that there is no point in flying off at a tangent because one book has sold disappointingly. A Peters author hesitates to suggest a re-orientation unless he is absolutely sure that he is right. That is as it should be. Writers have a daemon, an inner voice that guides them. They should never oppose that voice. Only three times in nearly forty years have I ventured to disagree with Peters. Each time I knew that I was right.

'On the surface unenthusiastic'; that needs qualifying. In his office, when your manuscript lies open on his desk, he will confine himself to the business immediately in hand; the size of the advance, the rates of royalty, but he has a most encouragway of saying something nice about one's work, when one least expects it. You are on your way to watch a cricket match, or standing in a queue outside a cinema, and he will casually remark, 'I was re-reading that last novel of yours over the week-end. You really are going from strength to strength.' That builds one up far more than a routine compliment by return of post.

In adversity, Peters is a bastion. Every writer has periods when everything goes wrong, just wrong, like a golfer whose putts won't drop. More than once, I have rung Peters in despair 'I must have a long, long talk. Can you give me half an hour?' He has sat impassive at his desk, while I have unfolded the garment of my distress. His expression does not change. He makes no response. I slowly realize that though I have asked for half an hour I have hardly anything to say. I have been in this kind of mess before; sooner or later my putts have begun to drop again. Four minutes and I am silent. Then Peters speaks. 'I don't think you need to worry. I saw Newman the other day. He's really very satisfied with the way things are going. You're bound to break through soon, he thinks; if not with this book, then with the next. Oh, by the way, Priestley was talking about Tangier. It wasn't his kind of place, he said, but it might be yours. Why not go down there for a month? I could raise some money if you're short of it.'

How often have I not walked out into Buckingham Street, my self-confidence restored by his massive presence, his impervious indifference to bad luck. Having had Peters as my agent has been for me as a writer the greatest piece of luck that has come my way. When he took over my affairs in 1925, he trebled my income within six months.

Indeed, during that winter I must have seemed a fate-favoured mortal. I was twenty-seven years old. I had no entanglements. I was on the board of a publishing house with long and proud traditions. An early success can be a handicap, but I had shaken clear of that. I was gregarious. I enjoyed parties. London was the best city in the world for a bachelor with enough money to indulge his fancies. I had work that I enjoyed. My prospects could not have been brighter, and yet within a few weeks I was to walk out on it all, with a round-the-world ticket in my pocket, my flat sold up, and my post in Henrietta Street, as a literary editor, resigned. My friends thought me crazy. Peters shook his head. 'You have had this little success. Your job is to follow it up and consolidate yourself.' But I had no doubt that I was right.

In a travel book *Hot Countries*, published in 1930, I gave the following explanation for my eccentricity. One of my chief duties at Henrietta Street, I said, was to keep in touch with Chapman & Hall authors. One of our authors was G. B. Stern. She had a villa on the Italian Riviera, and I made my editorial duties an excuse for visiting her as often as I could. On one of these visits we discussed a story by Somerset Maugham, *The Fall of Edward Barnard*, in which a young Chicagoan sails for the South Seas resolved to earn sufficient money to support his American fiancée, only to be seduced by the lazy charms of those enchanted islands and linger on by the lagoons with a Tahitian damsel, raising coconuts. We wondered, G. B. Stern and I, whether an author would not be wise to follow his example. We were producing, then, a novel a year, five or six short stories and a number of newspaper articles. Were we not setting ourselves too hard a pace? Could we not live in Tahiti on 30,000 words a year? Might we not produce better work, under more congenial conditions? Why not quit the rat race? We discussed the problem for an evening and then forgot the matter. Her husband, however, wrote an account of it to S. P. B. Mais who then ran a gossip column in the *Daily Graphic*. Next day his readers were informed that Mr. Alec Waugh was shortly to leave for the South Seas. That settled it.

The gossip column, I explained in my foreword, was the only part of the newspaper that is really read. A new novel might be reviewed at the most flattering length in the Sunday supplements,

P

but your friends will ask when you propose to break your silence. If, however, at the foot of a column in an obscure provincial paper you are listed among the guests at a raided night club, everybody sees it. For the next month every Press paragraph about me referred to 'Alec Waugh, who is shortly leaving for Tahiti'. Friends in the Savile proferred their advice on the best way to go there, and offered letters of introduction to acquaintances at ports of call. As the weeks went by and I was still around, I noticed a look of disapproval on their faces. 'What, still here?' I began to feel like a gate-crasher at a party. In self-defence I bought a round-the-world ticket through the Messageries Maritimes.

That is the story as I told it in *Hot Countries*. It made a bright first chapter and later, when I went on a lecture tour in the U.S.A., it furnished me with an amusing opening. And it was true up to a point, but only up to a point. The 'twenties are supposed to have been a frivolous period, but even in a frivolous period a young, ambitious man does not throw up his prospects for the sake of a gossip paragraph. There were many and better reasons.

Firstly, though I was making money with articles and stories, I was worried about my writing. The *Daily Mirror* serial, which I was enlarging into a full-length novel, was unsatisfactory. It was a watered-down version of *Kept*—a description of dances, parties, night clubs, country-house week-ends, a reflection of the life that I was leading, that I enjoyed, that I had every intention of continuing to lead while I was in London, but which had ceased to provide me with any fresh material for my books. I had exhausted my material. I was discovering, in fact, that while certain novelists can remain in the same locality all their lives, their material remaining fresh because they are digging deeper into themselves, storytellers like myself can only arrive at novelty by lengthening their radius; since they cannot deepen they must broaden their experience. I needed to renew myself.

I was stifled, too, by the political climate of the moment. It is hard to explain exactly why without indulging in high falutin. Were I to say that I was suffering from loss of faith, the retort of anyone who knew me then would be, 'I never heard such nonsense. Your health was good, your books were selling, you had plenty of friends, you had no responsibilities, you were doing the kinds of thing you enjoyed. You always looked as though you were having the best of times in the best of all possible worlds. Loss of faith, indeed; come off it.'

Perhaps 'loss of faith' is too big a phrase. I had best come off it. But if it was not loss of faith it was something near to it— a niggling persistent sense of everything's ultimate unimportance. There seemed no point to anything. It was a post-war reaction. During the war everyone had, according to his separate lights, kept his spirits high in the belief that everything would be better afterwards, that the world would have learnt its lesson, that social injustices would be removed, that there would be an end to secret treaties, that a League of Nations would ensure that the crime of war would never again be perpetrated. Had I not on the waste land of Passchendaele, at Van Diemen's farm, seen myself and my pen dedicated to the creation of a different world?

Yet now, eight years later, it was abundantly clear that the world had not learnt its lesson. The League of Nations was ineffective. Countries were split by suicidal party strife. The men of my generation had been impotent. What had we done? nothing. Where was the torch of revolutionary freedom that we had vowed to light? How had it happened? Why had it happened? Where had we gone wrong? Events had followed too swiftly on each other. The old men were in the saddle. We had been caught up into the confusion of our private lives, harassed by the demands of livelihood. We had found ourselves with a part of ourselves out of sympathy with the left-wing movement with whose interests we had thought ourselves allied. They had been so smug, so self-righteous, those non-combatants exchanging anecdotes about their C.O. gaol experiences on Dartmoor; and with a part of ourselves we had found ourselves in sympathy with the conservative elements to whom we had fancied ourselves implacably opposed; they were stubborn and reactionary, with closed minds, but they were honest men and they had fought in Flanders. We had hesitated—the young men of my generation—wondering at what altar we should vow our loyalty; before we had made up our minds it was too late.

'The world it was the old world yet', and if the war, with its prodigious expenditure of life and capital had achieved nothing, what else could? We could not have the faith that our fathers had had in the basic importance of careers, in saving money and founding a family. What was it, what could it be, when the very fabric of Western existence was unstable, but the pouring of water through a sieve? It was easy to wonder, in such a mood, whether the Polynesians had not built on more sound foundations. They lived, by all accounts, without wars and jealousies, without class distinctions, careless of their possessions, lovers of the sun. Surely it was worth going there to see?

I might also find there a solution to another very pressing problem. Every generation of males believes that the young woman of its day presents a problem radically different from and more exacting than those which she presented to its parents. Certainly my sons today assure me that she does. But I am inclined to believe that the young woman of the early 1920s presented very special difficulties. The war had telescoped events. The young woman of 1912 was a sheltered creature. She was chaperoned. She had no vote. Very few careers were open to her. She was dependent upon masculine patronage. The double standard was in effective operation. Eight years later she had a vote; chaperones had been discarded; she had a latchkey, a bank account, an unsupervised correspondence. She met men on equal terms in every walk of life. The double standard was ceasing to exist. A French novel, *La Garçonne* (*The Bachelor Girl*), had given a label to a new post-war phenomenon.

This was precisely what *avant-garde* intellectuals like Ibsen, Shaw, H. G. Wells had been demanding for twenty years; and today the equation has been satifactorily resolved; but in 1924 it was apparent that this freedom had come too quickly. The ex-debutante was demanding at the same time the right to lead her own life according to her own lights and the chivalrous solicitude for her welfare which had been bestowed on Victorian damsels like Dora Copperfield.

You would take a young person to an evening party; as midnight approached you would feel that it was time you were going home; you would tell her this and she would laugh lightheartedly. 'Fine, if you're tired. But I'm enjoying myself. I'll stay on a bit; don't worry about me, I can find my way back.' Which she had, of course, a perfect right to say. She was the bachelor girl of 1924. One did, however, feel resentful ten days later when she would round on one with a 'You are no good to me. I need a strong man who'll make up my mind for me.' She was trying to get the thing both ways and she was succeeding.

At about this time there was a law case which has become a *cause célèbre*, concerning a race-track racket run by a husband and wife, in which telegrams were sent to a bookmaker from a small country post office after the race had been run, with the time altered on the form. When the trick was discovered, the husband was sent to prison but the wife was acquitted on the grounds that as a woman she was a helpless creature, without a will of her own, subservient to her lord and master. Masculine indignation was at fever point, and the victim of the bachelor girl's emotional intransigence listened readily to the wooing whispers that were coming from the palm-fringed lagoons of the Pacific, in the poems of Rupert Brooke, Maugham's *The Trembling of a Leaf*, Frederick O'Brien's *White Shadows in the South Seas*, Robert Keable's *Numerous Treasure*. The dark ladies of Polynesia with their wreaths of flowers around their necks and the white tiare blossoms behind their ears might well provide the antidote to the capricious tyranny of the ex-debutantes of Mayfair.

§

Events follow fast when one has made up one's mind. I resigned my salaried post but not my directorship at Henrietta Street. The board granted me a year of absence. I found a purchaser for my flat. Carpets and curtains went. My financial position was basically sound; I was in debt and overdrawn; but Peters, though he had opposed my going, was extremely co-operative once he realized I was inflexible, and guaranteed a loan of £500 with my bank. By the time I had paid off my over-draft and bought a ticket, my letter of credit only totalled £225, but I was confident that the stories and articles I wrote during the journey would soon settle my indebtedness to my bank.

I had no qualms about the future. The great thing was to get away. I had my ticket in my pocket.

De Quincey said that one never does anything consciously for the last time without regret; but I cannot say that I felt sentimental when I closed the files on which I had been engaged for six and a half years. I was not, after all, saying good-bye to Henrietta Street. I was a director still, and though my room and desk would be handed to another, I should often walk up the curving staircase to my father's office. I did, however, on that April evening take a valedictory backward glance at my six and a half years' traffic. What had I to show for it? What had I done for the firm? What had I done for literature? What mistakes had I made? Which manuscripts had I missed?

I had introduced to the firm a number of good writers; Norman Douglas, W. L. George, Oliver Onions, Ralph Straus, Douglas Goldring, Ford Madox Ford. Through my intervention C. K. Scott-Moncrieff's translations of *The Song of Roland* and *Beowulf* had appeared under our imprint. I had failed to spot the commercial possibilities of a book about Byron called *Glorious Apollo*, but it was not, let us face it, very good. I acquit myself on that score. I had failed to recognize the quality of T. F. Powys and that was a sin against the powers above. The manuscript arrived in handwriting, recommended by an agent whom I despised, but even so, *mea culpa, mea maxima culpa*; I had tried in vain to persuade the firm to publish James Branch Cabell's *Jurgen*, but they refused. I had read, with high excitement, the first novel of a friend—Norman Davey's *The Pilgrim of a Smile*. Davey came to nothing, but he did show promise. In April 1926 I thought, 'Well, anyhow, I spotted Norman Davey.' I did not realize, then, that I had done something which entitled me to much more regard.

In 1921 Arnold Lunn had brought to Chapman & Hall the scheme of publishing an anthology of Georgian Stories. He edited two numbers, then lost interest, and since the series was profitable I took it over and edited, anonymously, the 1926 volume. In it I included a long story by my brother called *The Balance*. It was an *avant-garde* piece; he has not thought it worthy of inclusion in his collections of short stories, but it was the one story in the book that aroused curiosity and conjecture.

It recorded the sound of a new voice, and on the strength of it Michael Sadleir invited its author to contribute to his annual compilation *The New Decameron*.

The Balance was the first contribution to appear in print under the signature Evelyn Waugh. I can claim therefore to have introduced the public to his work.

The reader of this book may be surprised at finding so little in it about Evelyn Waugh. If I were not myself and if I were to pick up the autobiography of Alec Waugh, the first name that I should look for in the index would be Evelyn Waugh. I am sorry to disappoint that curiosity.

In a sense Evelyn and I have never been very close. He is more than five years my junior and that gap was made to seem greater when we were young by the war and by the publication of *The Loom of Youth*. When he was a fag at Lancing, I was in the public eye. He thought of me as an uncle rather than as a brother. We have different tastes, in many ways. He does not care for ball games and three-quarters of my English men friends are cricketers. We belong to several London clubs, but we no longer have one in common. I should doubt if we have met twenty times in the last twenty years. But we have always kept in touch and been good friends.

During his early years I was seeing him every holidays and my father's letters were full of news of him. Childhood contains significant clues to the eventual man. I naturally know things about him which no one else does. But it is a responsibility as well as a privilege to be the brother of as important a writer as Evelyn Waugh. He is in my opinion incomparably the finest novelist of our period. I constantly re-read his books with delight and admiration, and if by writing about his early days I could interpret him to his readers, if by explaining certain things about him I could increase the pleasure which they take in his work, I should want to do so. But I am afraid that I might get the picture out of focus. I might lay the wrong emphasis on certain episodes, and mislead rather than guide those readers.

Eric Linklater recounted in one of his books an incident during the war when Evelyn was examined by a psychiatrist, as part of the military routine, to decide if he was fit for commando work. After a lengthy cross-examinaton there was a pause. Evelyn said, 'You have been asking me a great many questions, do you mind if I ask you one?' The psychiatrist looked surprised but said, no, he didn't mind. 'Then why,' Evelyn said, 'have you asked me nothing about the most important thing in a man's life, his religion?'

That is where I lack the key to Evelyn. I cannot enter imaginatively into the mind of a person for whom religion is the dominant force in his life, for whom religion is a crusade, as it is with Evelyn. You cannot appraise a stained-glass window if you look at it from the outside, and not possessing the key to Evelyn's nature I might give, in a full-length essay, written though it would be with affection and esteem, a misleading picture of him.

So I will confine myself reluctantly to this brief fraternal tribute of gratitude for the great pleasure that his books have given me and for the high honour they have conferred upon the the name of Waugh.

PART 4

World Tour

I

East of Suez

I bought a round-the-world ticket from the Messageries Maritimes. It began with an eighteen-day cruise round the Mediterranean, from Marseilles to Alexandria, stopping at Naples, Athens, Constantinople, Smyrna, Jaffa, Beirut, Rhodes and Cyprus. From Port Said I was booked through the Red Sea to Djibouti, Ceylon and Singapore. At Singapore I was to take one of the Burne Phillips boats that plied along the coast of Java to the northern Australian ports, then Sydney. At Sydney I would tranship to a Messageries steamer running to New Caledonia. Thence a French intermediate-class liner sailed to Marseilles via the New Hebrides, Tahiti, Panama and the French West Indies. Travel was first-class throughout. I could break my journey as often as I liked. The actual time I had to spend on board was about four months. The ticket cost £166. When people used to ask me how I could afford to do so much travelling, I replied that I spent far less abroad than in a London flat. Travel, by ocean liner, was indeed in those days one of the cheapest ways of living, certainly for a freelance writer who carried his office with him and could work in his cabin or in a saloon.

I left England if not at a moment's notice, certainly at short notice. My finances were restricted, since Grant Richards was in liquidation, and not only my English but my American royalties on *Kept* were frozen, but I had a commission from Hutchinson's group of magazines to write them six short stories; and I also had an agreement for a *Daily Mirror* serial. For the last three years I had been contributing to the *Evening Standard* short essay-type articles for which I had recently had my price raised from five to eight guineas. I presumed that my trip would provide ample material for such articles. I did not doubt my ability to keep myself in funds.

Rarely have I known a greater peace of mind than on the morning when I boarded the *Amboise* at Marseilles. It was a peace comparable to that of a Turkish bath; you have surrendered your possessions at the door; you have left your clothes in a cubicle; nothing can disturb you; no telephone can reach you. Wrapped in the anonymity of a towel, you let the mantle of dry heat enfold you.

It was June, a Mediterranean June; out of a pale blue sky the sun shone ceaselessly. The nights were warm and starlit. The sea was calm. The ship was not crowded. The food was excellent and varied. Table wines were on the house. Every second or third day there was a fresh port of call. Among the ruins of Smyrna, I had my first glimpse of the Arab world, in a small café in a shaded square, where I sipped thick black coffee and watched fat Syrians, puffing their vast glass-bowled pipes, while beggars moved from group to group, and shoe-shine boys importuned me with their brass-bound caskets. At every port there was a change of passengers; new faces at my table, new accents and new points of view. I wrote a couple of articles for the *Evening Standard* and sketched out a synopsis for my *Daily Mirror* serial. There was a cartoon in *Le Sourire* of a Frenchman asking another why he kept a dog. 'To recognize my wife's lovers,' he replied. I devised a story in which a colonel would discover that his wife had had an affair during his absence, because of the warmth with which his dog greeted a newly joined officer. That would do for one of my six Hutchinson short stories. I would call it *Guard of Honour*.

At night, after dinner, on deck under the stars with the sound of music borne faintly from the saloon, I would let my book fall forward on my knees, my mind abroad. The past with its problems lay behind me, the present was delightful and the future stretched ahead of me, rich with possibilities. My plans were vague and imprecise. I had no fixed date for my return. An old school friend, Arthur Hogg, lived in Alexandria, in a family cotton business; on his mother's side he was a Peel. I was to stay with him three weeks. I had letters of introduction

in Colombo. I planned to stay a week there, but Malaya was
the main target of the first part of my journey. I had there two
excellent friends—one a man many years older than myself, one
of the chief lawyers of Penang and a close family friend for
many years, the other my contemporary, Noel King, who had
played in my side at Rosslyn Park and was now a magistrate in
the Dindings. I would see how things worked with them
before I made any further plans, and all the time there would be
that ticket in my pocket, the ticket that bore the magic name
'Tahiti'.

Tahiti. There I would resolve every problem; everything
until I reached there would be a prelude, a preparation; Egypt
and Malaya would be introductory, a stepping-stone; they
would acclimatize me to the tropics, so that when eventually I
saw Tahiti, I should have a standard of comparison. That was
what made those eighteen Mediterranean days so blissful, the
knowledge that Tahiti waited.

§

I approached the Far East with caution and distrust. The
Kipling legend was in disrepute. My generation was impatient
with the narrow, uncompromising attitude of the retired *pukka
Sahib*. Was not that talk about the White Man's Burden in
part responsible for the war? Had not our Empire inflamed
Germany's jealousy? What right had we in India anyhow?
These tiresome old Tories lived luxurious, self-important lives,
surrounded by a staff of servants, then expected to be treated
like nabobs on their retirement in Bath and Cheltenham. While
I was staying in Diano Marina, G. B. Stern had pointed out to
me a retired colonel who had been indignant because an
English girl had danced with an Italian officer in the kursaal at
Alassio. 'Anyhow we should keep the kursaal white,' he
grumbled. That kind of thing could be amusing, but it was
irritating too. I imagined that I should have to be on my guard
constantly against snapping back, that I should feel my blood
mounting at seeing Asians treated as though they were slaves.

But it was not in the least like that.

I stayed at the Club when I was in Penang. Penang was not a
large place then. There was a disproportionate number of men

to women. Men were not encouraged to marry young. Indeed, when I returned to Malaya in 1955, one of the chief differences I noticed was the comparative unimportance of the Club. Men married younger; and because of air travel and air-conditioning, wives, when their children had reached school age, were not faced with the alternative of abandoning their husbands or their children—a choice which they resented, feeling that either way they would choose wrong. In 1926, a number of the men who sat in the Club every evening were in the later forties, their wives having gone back to England to be with their children. Most evenings they would assemble with the young bachelors in the Club. Night after night the routine was similar. Offices closed at four o'clock. The sun set at six. That allowed two hours for golf or tennis at the Country Club. By quarter to seven the card-room and the smoking-room of the town Club would be in session. Five to six men would form a group, each ordering a round in turn; each round would be prefaced by a shout of, 'Boy!' The orders were usually for *pahits* (pink gin) or *stengahs* (whisky and soda). They would drink for two or two and a half hours; then they would move into the dining-room; they would eat quickly a five-course, tasteless meal, washed down with a tankard of beer. Very soon after dinner they would go to bed.

Sitting night after night with one group or another, listening to their talk, I absorbed the essence of their lives. It was very different from what I had expected. Here were sound, solid men, very like those with whom I had played football for Rosslyn Park and cricket for the Stoics. They had come out to do a job, as expeditiously as possible. They had no sense of mission; they had eventual retirement in mind. They were anxious to get on as well as possible with the Malays and with the Chinese traders. They did not think that they were grooming Malaya for independence. They did not foresee a day when the Union Jack would cease to fly over the Residence at Kuala Lumpur. They knew that the better the country was run, the easier it would be for them to do their job. They built roads, drained marshes, established schools and hospitals, sent back the most promising pupils to England for further study. That was the British colonial way of doing things. I think it was a good one, and I think the men who carried it out were honest and efficient men. Malaya was, as I saw it, a happy place. I do not think I was mistaken. The eventual take-over by the Malays was smooth and harmonious, without rancour upon either side.

I spent three weeks in Penang, then I visited Siam. Siam as an independent country was in a very different position from Malaya; yet the Siam that I saw was not so very different from Malaya. On later visits to Siam, I have spent most of my time in Bangkok, where I have been enchanted by the unique quality of a way of life based on royal custom and tradition. But in 1926, I spent only a few hours in Bangkok, before going north to the forests beyond Chiengmai, where a number of British companies held teak concessions. In many ways that territory was an extension of the British Raj. A British forestry officer, the technical adviser to the Siamese government, took me with him on a tour of inspection.

I spent a month upon that tour. We travelled with an establishment of nine elephants and forty coolies. I was woken at a quarter to six each morning, by a cup of tea, to the sound of packing. While we dressed and breakfasted at our leisure the camp was struck. Our bedding and our food were stacked on elephants and coolies' shoulders. A head boy supervised it. By half-past seven our ponies were waiting for us and the procession was half an hour's march away. Elephants move slowly. Two miles an hour is the maximum. Fourteen miles is a long day's march. Not that you can picture jungle miles in terms of English miles. Along the majority of roads you could not drag a bullock cart. For the most part you are piloting yourself with the aid of a heavy staff along steep, stony paths, or slithering over slippery rice-fields. The streams through which you wade are high above your knees. The average village road is a narrow isthmus of caked mud running between bogs into which you are likely to slide every seven steps. You are muddy, you are drenched with sweat.

I made the trip in September. The mornings are few in the autumn when you are not drenched with a heavy downpour. You are very weary by the time you reach, after a seven-hour march, the compound or the stream by which you are to spend the night. You sit forward on a log, limp and motionless, while the coolies cut away a clearing in the bush, while your boy runs up your tent and your cook prepares your tiffin. You are too tired to talk over your meal; the moment it is over you fling yourself upon your bed. In a couple of minutes you are asleep.

It was a varied countryside through which I travelled. The word 'jungle' evokes a picture of tangled undergrowth, of scarlet macaws, of monkeys screaming to each other from every bough, of large, many-coloured butterflies, of snakes and bears, and natives shooting at you from behind trees with blow-pipes. It may be like that on the Amazon, but Siam's is a very friendly landscape. There are cobra, it is true, but you rarely meet them. I only saw a couple of small snakes, which may not have been poisonous. You will hear the screech of monkeys, but they remain invisible. Though you may come upon the tracks of a bear, the bear is an animal that must be hunted. Though the foliage is in places overpoweringly luxuriant, the country is for the most part open. The flat land is planted with rice and the undergrowth is inconsiderable in the actual forests.

The Laos of the northern states are quiet, simple, decently-lived people. The railroad linking Chiengmai with Bangkok had only been built a few years before my visit. Most of the Britons whom I met there had come up, in earlier days, by water; a five weeks' journey. The Laos of the north had more in common with the Burmese of the Shan states than with their compatriots in the south. They spoke a different language and sometimes employed a different currency. Remote though they might be from the country's administrative centre, they were centuries remote from savagery. They grew their rice, carried their produce to the markets, tended their animals and chewed their betel nut. If you were to ask them how far a certain place might be away, you would be answered by some such practical method of reckoning as, 'Half a bullock's march,' or, 'As far as you can hear a dog bark.' But otherwise it was impossible to realize that you were two hundred miles away from anything that could be called a road.

Each assistant in a timber company had a central compound where he kept his clothes and files, but his work consisted mainly in long marches to supervise the work in the various

sections of his district. His district covered a wide area. Sometimes there was a rest house for him. More often he cleared
himself a camp near a stream, where his elephants could
water.

For me, my month north of Chiengmai was a prolonged
picnic; we were welcomed everywhere we went; we provided a
break in the monotonous week-to-week routine. But I could
picture the life of an assistant during ordinary periods. For
weeks on end, through a succession of rain-drenched days, he
would never see a white man. There was no congenial com-
panionship at the end of a long day's march; no antidote to the
maladies of jungle life; the discomfort, the itch of prickly heat,
the leeches, the mosquitoes and the mud sores; the sandflies that
no netting can keep out; the red ants that night after night make
sleep impossible; the long depression of the September rains,
when bedding and kit are soaked and it is impossible to wear
dry clothing; the fever that takes its toll, slowly, spasm by
spasm, of his vitality and courage.

Men like this brought increased amenities and increased
prosperity to a vast territory whose possibilities its own nationals
had ignored. My gorge rises when I hear such men dismissed
by untravelled bureaucrats as 'colonial exploiters'.

After my month in the jungle, I spent four days at Chiengmai. Chiengmai, when I returned there in 1958, was unrecog-
nizable, apart from its scarlet and gold temples and its broad
brown river. It was a very quiet place in 1926, with its rest
house by the railway and the Gymkhana Club where the white
residents congregated every evening after work. It was a small
community. There was the bank manager and the British
consul. There were the forest managers and an occasional
assistant who had come in from the jungle for a rest. There was
an American Mission which was responsible for schools and
hospitals and ran a leper sanatorium. The Gymkhana Club
occupied a large field a mile or so out of town. It had a polo
ground, a golf course and a tennis court. By five o'clock, when
the heat of the day had lessened, the white community was
scattered about the field. There was a period of strenuous
exercise, then, when the light failed, there would be a gathering
round a large table on which had been set out drinks and glasses

and a little lamp. There were rarely more than a dozen people there, not often less than ten. It was very peaceful; in the swift-fallen dusk the large field, with its wide branched trees rising from a hedge, looked heart-breakingly like an English meadow. Mosquitoes buzzed about our ankles and the women slipped their legs into sarongs, sewn up at one end in the shape of bags. This was the hour that made amends for the heat and dust of the long sun-soaked day, and this is how it was, night after night, throughout the year, except for a week at Christmas, when the assistants came in from the jungle for 'the Christmas meet'.

The talk was subdued and intimate. Listening to it, evening after evening, I absorbed the atmosphere of the life of the young timber man. Here, I felt, was the kind of material that I needed for my novels.

One story in particular affected me. A few months earlier a young assistant went off his head; he imagined that he had con-tracted syphilis, and that the villages were placarded with notices warning the local girls against him. Not only had he not contracted syphilis, but he had led a life of blameless chastity. 'Why did it happen?' I asked. Shoulders were shrugged. Queer things happened to people in the jungle; the loneliness, the discomfort, the malaria; men began to brood, and then . . . Nervous breakdowns were frequent, I was told. The incident was not considered particularly remarkable. But I, as a novelist, saw there the germ of a short story. Was not his chastity the clue—or one of the clues?

I pictured him as a young man who had come out half-engaged to be married. He had vowed to keep himself 'pure for her'. But when he had seen the life that she would be called upon to lead as an assistant's wife, he had wondered whether he had the right to impose such a life on a young, gay, sophisti-cated woman, used to the bright lights and varied entertainments of a big city. He would think of himself as a man unfit to marry. As a young man, living alone, sexual repression would simul-taneously corrode his thoughts. A man might easily catch syphilis in Bangkok. A man who had syphilis was not fit to marry. He himself was not fit to marry. Might not the two ideas have got confused in his nerve-racked brain; so that he had come to think of himself as a man with syphilis? Was that too fanciful an explanation? I did not think it was. A nervous breakdown was a form of lunacy, the outcrop of delusions.

I wondered how I could tell the story in such a way that my hero would not be identified with a real character. I have usually found that you can put a real situation into a book without offence if you change the circumstances. I found my solution when the head of the American Mission took me round the leper colony. The bungalows were arranged like a garden city, neat and trim and flowered. Men and women were housed in different sections. 'At the start,' he said, 'we allowed married couples to live together; but we found it did not work, for many reasons.' Ah, I thought, this was it. Why should not my timber man imagine he had leprosy? The same confusion could arise. A leper was not fit to marry. He came to think himself a leper.

§

From Chiengmai I went south to Lumut, where Noel King was in charge of the Dindings. Lumut was a night's sail from Penang by one of the pleasant steamers that then worked up and down the coast. They were elegant like a yacht, with clean, compact cabins and a spacious dining-lounge. There would be usually a dozen first-class passengers aboard. It would be a calm passage except on the rare occasions when what was known locally as 'a Sumatra' blew. You embarked at five o'clock; by the time you were settled into your cabin, the sun was 'below the yard-arm' and it was time for the first *pahit* or *stengah*. Introductions are not necessary east of Suez; and Malays, Chinese and Europeans met on equal terms. There was much common ground for talk. An hour, an hour and a half passed pleasantly; then there was the traditional five-course dinner. By half-past nine I was asleep.

We docked next morning at six o'clock. Noel King was on the landing-stage. Lumut lay within the curve of a river; hills rose on either side of it; the district officer's house was half-way up the slope. There was an idyllic peace about the village, with its attar huts built on stilts over the water, its one main shopping street and two or three solid official buildings, the court house, the prison and the guest house. King was then close on thirty; he was in charge of a large district; he administered its finances and its laws; his decisions in court were subject to reversal in Penang; he had to account to higher authority for his conduct and expenditure, but to the Malays and Chinese of the Dindings and to the British who were stationed there he represented the British Raj; and this I thought, might well have been my life, if chance had not made a writer of me.

It was a hard life, but it had many recompenses. We would wake every morning, Noel King and I, as day was breaking, at about six o'clock. I had not slept well. I never found it easy to sleep in that damp, heavy heat. I would soak my pyjamas, and then the sheets; I can never sleep unless I have some weight upon my shoulders. Finally, naked between blankets, I would fall about four o'clock into a heavy sleep. I would wake half-refreshed. Bathrooms in Malaya consisted then of a vast stone jar from which you scooped water with a dipper to splash yourself. I felt better after that. I went on to the veranda in my dressing-gown; a pot of tea was set beside a dish of fruit. The air was cool. The village wore a clean, fresh look, as though it had been washed during the night. Small boats with high wide sails were drifting up the broad brown river. It was a lovely hour, calm and peaceful; a preparative for the long hot day. I thought of my father, six thousand miles away in Hampstead, hurrying his breakfast, hurrying down the hill, coughing on the exposed, windswept station; very likely not finding a seat in the tube, having to swing from a strap.

For an hour or so Noel King and I would sit gossiping on the veranda, then we would shave and breakfast. By half-past eight he would be in his office, dealing with the routine duties of administration. There would probably be a case to hear in court. One morning I went down to listen. The case was conducted in Malay; I could not follow it, but I was acutely conscious of the dignity he assumed, sitting in his chair of office. By half-past twelve he would be back in his house, for a gin *pahit* before lunch. Afterwards he would take a quarter of an hour's sleep, but he would be back in his office by two o'clock. He worked a six and a half hours' day in the heavy heat; and even then his day's work was not finished. After an hour of tennis, he would go to the local club, of which not only Europeans but Chinese and Malays were members, and where his attendance gave him a clue to what was happening in his district. Sometimes he would go farther afield, to Sitiawan. He dined late, usually after nine, and was in bed by half-past ten.

That is how it was, day after day; doing the same kinds of thing, seeing the same people, discussing the same subjects, with newspapers and mail arriving once a week. It was a monotonous life, with its special temptations, of which alcohol was the chief. If you are seeing the same people day after day, discussing the same subjects, through drink alone can you create a keener atmosphere, since for most of the men who were bachelors or unattached males there was not the emotional stimulus of women. But it had the very ingredient that I had missed in London, in my own life and in my friends' lives; a sense of purpose.

And this, I kept reminding myself, might have been my life. That knowledge gave me a basic kinship with the men whom I was meeting. They were my type of man, raised in the same stable. Here, surely, was the material for which, as a novelist I had been looking. I could identify myself with the life here and the people. I could write its story and their story. I had already found two plots in Siam, I had only to stay here to find more.

On my last afternoon in Singapore, however, I bought Somerset Maugham's new book *The Casuarina Tree*. It contained six long short stories about Malaya. I took it on board with me. I have seldom enjoyed more the reading of a book. Some of his finest stories are there—*The Letter, P. and O., The Outstation.* At the same time, I was disconcerted by it. It did exactly what I had planned to do, far better than I could hope to do. It presented and interpreted the life of the white man in the Far East; it showed how quite ordinary people could become of absorbing interest because they led extraordinary lives. Everything was there; the life on the plantations, the officials in Kuala Lumpur, the district officers, the proud and sensitive Malays, the devious Chinese. What was the point of my returning to Malaya; what could a minor writer accomplish in a territory that a master had made his province? I must plough some other field.

This may seem a ridiculous decision. Every year nineteen

novels may be published about London, Paris and New York, but that does not deter the twentieth Londoner, Parisian, New Yorker from attempting to present his own view of his city. But the parallel does not hold good. There was only one Malaya about which I could have written and that was Maugham's Malaya. Only certain types of Briton went at that time to Malaya; there were only certain kinds of life that they could lead there. I should be describing the same scenery, the same characters, the same way of life. I should be echoing Maugham. When I left the Dindings, I had promised myself that my first objective when I got back to England would be the planning of a return visit. I had abandoned that project before I docked at Sydney. I did not go back to Malaya for nearly thirty years. By then it was a different place.

Tahiti

It was not only by *The Casuarina Tree* that my plans were altered for me at Singapore. At the Messageries office a cable from Peters brought the uncomfortable news that my royalties on *Kept* were still frozen, and that the *Daily Mirror* did not like the first two instalments of my serial. I studied my letter of credit with disquiet. I had made the mistake that most travel writers do, of under-estimating the cost of the side trips that I had taken and over-estimating the moneys that would accrue from the stories and articles that I was posting home. Unless good news awaited me in Sydney, I should be in a difficult position. Sydney was three weeks away. There was nothing to be done until I got there. I made the most of the amenities and amusements of the *Marella*, and during the mornings wrote two short stories.

In Sydney in hope and in anxiety I hurried round to the Messageries office. A large mail awaited me, but there was no cablegram from Peters. No news is bad news for a writer. I again studied my letter of credit. There was no alternative to an immediate return to London. When, I asked, was the next sailing. In eight days' time. 'Then I'll be on it.'

Six weeks later, in a ship that was due to dock in Marseilles in two months' time, I read myself a lecture. Tahiti was forty-eight hours away and I had £11 in my pocket. The whole point of this trip had been to see Tahiti and now through my own improvidence I should have to leave after a bare five days. I had travelled 15,000 miles for the sake of a five-day visit. Could folly travel further? What an ass, what a pitiable ass I was. Why had I spent all that time in Colombo and in Penang? Why for that matter hadn't I gone to Tahiti first? Why, why, why? Never had I abused myself more roundly.

I tried to draw such nourishment as I could from sour grapes. I had been away from England for seven months. I was homesick and I was tired. My powers of reception were exhausted. Perhaps Tahiti was not so wonderful, after all. Perhaps I had come to it too late. Had not Melville warned me that it would soon be spoilt? And when had he written *Typee*—eighty years ago? Hadn't Brooke, Frederick O'Brien, Keable echoed him? Perhaps I was lucky in having my visit limited to five days. Anyhow, five days was a long time; long enough to find background material for short stories; long enough to learn whether Melville had prophesied correctly; long enough to decide whether Tahiti was worth returning to; for after all, I always could come back. There was no angel with a drawn sword forbidding me this Eden.

So I debated with myself as the *Louqsor* rolled slowly eastward. And then, on a January afternoon, I saw Tahiti, with its towering mountains, its flame trees ablaze along the harbour, its yachts awash against their moorings, with its dock lined with laughing, chattering brown-skinned Polynesians. All my questions were resolved.

You can fall in love at first sight with a place as with a person, and I fell in love with Tahiti before I set foot on it.

§

I walked in a tranced state past the trading schooners. It was five o'clock and the waterfront was crowded. There were the Frenchmen, smart and dapper in their sun helmets and white suits; the Tahitian boys with narrow-brimmed straw hats; the island girls, bare-footed, in long print dresses that reached halfway down their calves, their black hair flung loose about their shoulders or gathered high with a comb upon their heads. Most of them wore behind their ear the white flower of the *tiare*. They walked with a strong, swinging, upright stride, while beside them and among them, dainty in frocks that had been copied from a Californian fashion plate, were the *blondes* and *demi-blondes*, some of them pushing bicycles, others loitering in the shadow of a parasol.

It was a variegated crowd, a mingling of every nationality and race, yet they gave the impression of belonging to one family, for that is one of Tahiti's miracles; it cancels all differences of race and caste. In the old days, when it was the custom among the Polynesians to exchange their babies or to present them to their friends, there grew up a saying that they were all brothers and sisters on the island, since no one knew for a surety who was the child of whom. The custom was by then a dying one, but even so, its influence persisted in the feeling of kinship that bound together this variously blended, variously conditioned race.

I took a seat on the veranda of the Mariposa Café; at the next table, some half-dozen young women were chattering merrily and noisily together. When I ordered a dry Martini they burst into a roar of laughter.

'Martini,' cried one of them. 'So that's your middle name. Mine's rum.'

For a moment I was puzzled, wondering into what menagerie I had stumbled, but before we had exchanged two sentences I had realized that their greeting implied no more than friendliness, that introductions were an unnecessary complication on the island.

'When we like the look of anyone, we speak,' they said. 'What's your phrase, Pauma?'

'A feeling is a feeling.'

They all burst into a roar of laughter.

They were always laughing, out of sheer light-heartedness. I moved my chair over to their table, and we chattered away in a rapid mixture of French, English and Tahitian, with French predominating since it was the one language in which we all were fluent.

'And you are leaving us on the *Louqsor*?' they inquired.

I supposed I was.

Ah, but I mustn't, they protested. We could have such fun. They would take me to Arue and Papara, and we would eat *feis*, which is the wild banana, and no one who had eaten *feis* could leave Tahiti. And as I sat among these laughing people, while the sun sank in a mist of golden lilac behind the crested outline of Moorea, I felt that my life would be half-lived were I to sail five days later. But I had only £11 in my wallet.

Next morning I went to the post office. How long would I need to get an answer from London to a cable? Shoulders were shrugged. It was hard, very hard, to say. Cable communications were intermittent. The line was only open for an hour, twice a day. I was to sail at 9 a.m. on Friday. I should have therefore to receive my answer by 3 p.m. on Thursday. London time was eleven hours ahead of Tahitian time. That was an added complication. It was possible, just possible for an answer to reach me on a Thursday afternoon, but only if London acted with great expedition, and only if the line was not crowded, if there was no atmospheric intervention. Was the betting a thousand to one against? The post office clerk nodded. That was about what it was. And the betting against my receiving a favourable answer was another thousand to one. I had left Australia in mid-November. Christmas had intervened. I had sent back no manuscripts that could be expected to do more than diminish my indebtedness to my bank. A thousand times a thousand. Wasn't that a million? Yet I could not risk leaving anything to chance. I should never forgive myself if I had not done everything I could to stay. So I cabled Peters, 'Will finances permit prolonged stay Tahiti?' There was no more that I could do. One day I would come back surely. In the meantime I did what I could; I packed a suitcase and booked a room at the hotel. For four days anyhow I could see the life here as a resident, as far as my slender resources would allow. I did not mind if I went back on the *Louqsor* penniless; the *Louqsor* would take me to Marseilles; and there, if the worst came to the worst, the British Consul would have to fend for me, even if he had to return me to London as a D.B.S. Anyhow, that was six weeks ahead. I was not going to worry about that now. I was going to have as much fun as Tahiti offered within the radius of £11. At that time you could get board and hotel lodging for 10s. a day. I thought of myself as a prisoner on the *Louqsor* with a four-day reprieve. I made the most of that reprieve.

In the light of it, I went round to the post office on the Thursday afternoon in a daze of anxiety and hope. To my astonishment, I was handed a green envelope; I paused before I dared to open it. I slit the flap. Then I closed my eyes. I spread the paper out; then opened them. Hilaire Belloc has written of that dream of all of us, 'The return of lost loves and great wads of unexpected wealth.' Writers more than most men are subject to sudden reversals of fortune, good and bad. At least four times I have been the recipient of unbanked-on manna. This was the first time. It was a quite long cable. The serial rights of *Love in These Days* had been bought by an American magazine for £500. My bank had been repaid. £300 stood to my credit. Tahiti and £300! I could do the conventional thing and let my ship sail on without me.

The million to one chance had turned up heads. But it was in fact more than a million to one chance. American magazine editors normally insist on having the first serial rights in anything they purchase. *Love in These Days* had not only appeared as a serial in the *Daily Mirror* but had been published in England as a novel. Never have I had since a similar experience, nor has any writer of my acquaintance. Was not the million to one chance a two-million chance?

If the coin had turned up tails and I had sailed by the *Louqsor*, how different my life would have been. I cannot begin to guess what would have happened.

III

Tania

I had done the conventional Tahitian thing and let my ship sail on without me. A little later I drifted into the conventional Tahitian romance, the kind of romance that has been described by Robert Keable, Robert Gibbings, S. L. Powell and how many others. I gave my own version of it in *Hot Countries*, in a chapter that I partially reprinted in a collection of short stories called *My Place in the Bazaar*. But I told it there in the third person, as a piece of fiction, as an adventure that befell a young English tourist. It is not easy to describe in the first person events that lie close to one in time.

I met her in a bus, on my way to Tautira where I planned to spend three days. It was in the afternoon. I had lunched well, the day was hot and I grew drowsy; I woke to the sound of laughter, the scent of coconut, and a soft warmth beneath my cheek. I had fallen asleep on the shoulder of a comely Tahitian damsel, and she was laughing at my predicament. I moved away, but she drew me back. 'No, no. You tired. You sleep.'

I was staying with the chief. That evening I went to the beach to watch the hauling in of the fishing nets. A large group of women had assembled, laughing, clapping, shouting as the fish were poured, a leaping, throbbing mass, into the large flat-bottomed boats. She was one of them. I went across to her. Nothing could have been more natural. I took her back with me to Papeete and established her in my hotel.

She was tall and very dark. She came from the Paumotus Islands and she cannot have had a drop of white blood in her. She was gay and friendly and affectionate; she bounded about

238

the place like a Newfoundland puppy. She was warm and sensual. It was the greatest fun making love to her. Polynesians, as hula dancers, acquire an astonishing mobility between the knees and navel. In that respect I have had no comparable experience. This was what I had come across the world to find; and it had come, as such things do in novels but so rarely in real life, spontaneously, without planning, unpremeditated. Here was my antidote to Mayfair, to *La Garçonne*; a light-hearted romance without complications, without responsibilities, in this Pacific pleasure-loving Eden, where life ran easily, without contention. I remembered that talk in Diano Marina eighteen months before. Why not live in Tahiti on thirty thousand words a year? Why not indeed? Life in Papeete was cheap enough, but it was cheaper in the districts. A bungalow on the edge of a lagoon; a couple of hours' writing in the morning, when the sun was low in the sky and the air was cool; with the daytime given up to fishing, swimming, picnicking in the hills off fresh-speared fish, and fruit pulled from the boughs; idling on a veranda in the heavy heat; then the long warm scented nights, the dancing and the singing and the final swim. So I brooded, sitting on the veranda of the Mariposa, looking out across the bay to the incredible outline of Moorea, for a week, two weeks, three weeks. . . .

Then, I began to realize that I was getting bored. The trouble may have been that Tania spoke hardly any French while I spoke no Polynesian and the succession of meals at which conversation was conducted mainly in signs became monotonous; or it may be that I was making Jurgen's discovery that 'to pass life gallantly was not enough'. At any rate, I found that time was hanging heavily. My conscience began to fret me. Even in mid-Pacific I had retained a sense of chivalry. How was I to get out of this? Then to my relief I learnt that Tania was as bored as I was.

One morning, I found her busily scrubbing floors and making beds with the hotel maids. I was indignant. I went in search of the proprietor.

This was outrageous, I expostulated. Tania was a hotel guest, her room and her meals paid for, yet here she was slaving like a skivvy. He nodded; he shrugged. Yes, he agreed. But then, what would you? These girls were Tania's friends. Tahitians did not look on work as work. Everything was a game to them. She was much happier scrubbing floors with her friends, than sitting at the end of a veranda, darning socks. If I insisted he would, of course, give orders that Tania should stay in her own room, on her own veranda. But would I be wise to insist? She was out of mischief with the other girls. In the corner of his left eye there was the suspicion of a wink.

'O.K.,' I said. 'O.K.' So time was hanging heavily on Tania's hands too. This let me out, I thought.

Once one has decided on a move it is well to make it quickly. I made inquiries at the Messageries office. One of their ships had had trouble with its engines. It would have to be over-hauled in Sydney. There might not be another sailing for ten weeks. There would be, however, a New Zealand ship sailing for San Francisco on Tuesday week. I made a quick calculation. Yes, I could afford it.

On my return to the hotel, I showed Tania the cable I had received a month earlier from Peters. '*Mère malade, retourner Angleterre*,' I told her. She pouted. '*Allons Chinois Pantalon*,' I said. By the time she had equipped her wardrobe, her high spirits were restored.

§

My ship sailed for San Francisco on a Tuesday morning; on the Saturday morning the west-bound ship docked, bringing its quota of passengers from London. Robert Keable was one of them. That night he gave a large party in the Diadem Hotel, the hotel once run by the Lovaina of whom Maugham wrote in *The Moon and Sixpence*. Next day he drove me out into the country to his house.

Nothing dates faster than the bestseller that seems 'shocking' on its first appearance and *Simon Called Peter*, which was nearly suppressed in 1921, would seem tame today; but Keable had a gift of narrative; he wrote with feeling and sincerity, out of his main personal problem—a conflict between religion and sex. A Church of England parson who had partially lost faith, he had left his wife and had subsequently fallen in love with a young Australian whom he brought with him to Tahiti, where she had died. He was now living in a common-law marriage with a Tahitian of good family.

He had built a house for Betty, the Australian, at Taravao, the narrow isthmus that joins the two chunks of land that comprise Tahiti. Most visitors to the island wish to face Moorea, the sister isle that lies across twelve miles of water. When I look from Cannes towards the Esterels, their last two peaks remind me of Moorea; but the Esterels never assume the incredible effects of colour that Moorea does, right through the day and night. Moorea is a constant miracle. Keable maintained that the outline of the *presqu'île* of Tautira is nearly as beautiful as Moorea, and that the countryside, because it is wilder, is more attractive. He was right in preferring his own countryside, but for me nothing in Tahiti could compensate for the loss of Moorea, as a perpetual back-cloth to one's day. Anywhere else, however, I would have agreed that Keable's house could not have been better sited. Low and long and white, it stood high on a narrow spur of land with water on three sides of it and the majestic mountains of the *presqu'île* across the bay. Its walls were decorated with Norman Lindsay etchings; he had rows of books; and a pleasant courtyard with a pool whose fountain would play intermittently. His pre-war English congregation would have been astounded could they have seen him reclined among cushions, clad only in a *pareo*, while his Tahitian princess, bare-shouldered and bare-footed, her black hair falling to her waist and a white flower behind her ear, glided negligently about the house. Yet when he said, 'And now how about some tea?' his voice had the parsonic intonation with which fifteen years earlier he had summoned the parish children to a Sunday-school treat.

I had not met him before, but we had friends in common, and it is easy to be confidential with someone whom you do not expect to see again. 'Tahiti is a long way off.' I did not imagine that I should return. Keable was a sick man—he died within the year—and did not intend to risk the return to a cold climate. He talked very openly about himself and about Betty and how you had to go on living, even if you were broken-hearted; that you had to adjust yourself to the second best.

He talked about his new novel *Lighten our Darkness*, which

was in the press. It was the story of a man who recovered his lost faith. After the title page he had a quotation from Keyserling—'We are here at the root of the truth that divine love lives within everyone and that it depends upon externals whether it manifests itself or not. These externals may be inclination to a woman, the influence of appropriate surroundings or a hard fate which cause the soul to change—the problem is always that the instrument 'man' shall be attuned in such a way that God may play upon it.'

Betty had done that for him, he said.

I made no comment, but it struck me as a sentimental and false thesis of the kind that was acceptable to the readers of glossy magazines. I could see the sub-title under the illustration, 'Broken Man Finds Soul Through Woman's Love.' That was why Keable was not a better writer. He saw life in terms of magazine psychology.

It was ironic that I should have thought that then, that I should have had those conversations then. Two weeks later I was to wave good-bye to a taxi from the steps of the St. Francis Hotel in San Francisco knowing myself to be the target of a similar experience.

§

Boat days in the 1920s were the big event in the island's life. The Union Steamship Company of New Zealand ran a monthly service between Sydney and San Francisco. Every fourth Saturday a ship arrived from San Francisco at 6 a.m. It sailed at 6 p.m. The Saturday was the occasion of long cocktail sessions at the Cercle Bougainville and elaborate lunch-parties. But the evening was ordinarily quiet. The ship had brought down the American and English mail; the residents wanted to read their letters. Sunday, too, was a quiet day. The residents were answering their letters, to catch the sister ship that arrived on the Monday afternoon and sailed early on the Tuesday morning. Monday night was the big night in the island's month. Papeete knew little sleep. I returned from Taravao in time for lunch and prepared myself for a last Tahitian evening. I was utterly exhausted when I finally walked up the gangplank. A wreath of pandanus was around my neck. I sat on deck in a hammock chair, looking down upon the harbour through half-closed eyes.

At that time there was an anti-climactic quality about departures from Tahiti. In 1914 a French ship, the *Zélie*, had been sunk there by the *Emden* and careful steering was required between the wharf and the gap in the reef. During the necessary three-quarters of an hour's manœuvring, the friends who had waved to one from the shore as the ship first drew away, went back to their homes and offices. It was curious watching the life of the town resuming its customary routine, indifferent to one's nearness. It seemed a symbol of something; but I did not know what. I was simultaneously tired and exhilarated and a little wistful.

Once again I read myself a lecture. I had made my experiment and it had not worked out. I was twenty-eight and a half. It was time I was making sense; Free love—*j'en avais soupé*— it might be fine for some people but not for me. My roots had gone too deep into a conventional upbringing of Hampstead, Somerset, Sherborne, Sandhurst. I must return to my base, make my peace with Chapman & Hall, resume the family tradition, write Galsworthian novels and in the fullness of time make a sound Galsworthian marriage, produce a family of Empire-builders and of the wives and mothers of Empire-builders. I felt very smug as I gave myself that lecture. It was nine o'clock. My eyes were tired after a night of little sleep. Tania was with the Chinois now, filling the gaps in her wardrobe; I was too tired to feel sentimental. The *Manganui* swung towards the reef; better go below and sleep, and wake to a new world at cocktail time.

That is usually how it is when one leaves Tahiti, but in 1927 Tahiti was not ten jet hours' flight from San Francisco. It was ten days' sail, or rather I should say ten moonlit nights'.

IV

Ruth

The *coup de foudre* has always seemed to me an axiom; whenever I have met anyone who has later come to mean a great deal to me, there has been on my side an instant recognition, the sudden impact of a new personality; always except this, the most important time. I cannot remember when I saw Ruth first; I cannot remember our first meetings in the casual give and take of shipboard life. Indeed she became aware of me before I was aware of her. I was drawn against her in the ship's bridge competition. She made a number of careless discards. She could not, she told me afterwards, concentrate upon her cards. That seems incredible to me. I could never see what she saw in me, she who had so much, who had access to so much, who was in herself so much.

§

She was an American, a few years older than myself. She was small and trim; her hair was brown with a glint of red in it. I do not think that she was pretty, but she had the most beautiful voice that I have ever heard. She was the most vivid, the most alive person I have ever met. She could light up a party, not by 'stealing the show', but by making the others more alive, so that they talked better, laughed more readily, contributed more to the general fund of gaiety.

She was a dramatic person and she had led a dramatic life. She was one of the first Americans to fly an aeroplane, and one of the seven or eight American women to be given an army commission in the First War, in her case to train pilots. She had driven racing-cars professionally. She had written scripts for motion pictures. In Spain she had remarked unguardedly that bull-fighting did not look so difficult. Someone retorted, 'You try to do it!' She took up the challenge, trained, learnt the technique and having killed her bull went to fashionable parties in Madrid in her matador costume.

She was wild, very wild; with an at times ungovernable temper. But she was capable of an extreme sweetness. She could make you feel as though you were living in an enchanted country, where the air was softer, the scent of the flowers richer, the plumage of the birds more bright. It is very hard to describe anyone so that the reader has a clear picture of that person. Someone once said to me, 'When you talk about Ruth, your voice takes on a different tone.' Perhaps something of what I felt and feel for her will be conveyed to the reader by telepathy.

It is rare after early youth for two people who feel themselves destined for one another to be free when they first meet, and she was married, to a man of fifty. They lived in California. They were on their way home from a fishing trip in New Zealand. During their twenty hours' stay in Tahiti, they had been so fascinated by the island that they planned to return in August. He was a highly paid short-story writer, a man of substance; he was also one of the finest New England types; he bore an honoured name; a direct ancestor is remembered still for the part that he played in the founding of the Constitution. By an earlier marriage he had had two daughters who were nearly grown up and who lived with their mother. His whole life was now built round Ruth. He was known to his friends as Govie.

§

The ship was crowded. It was one of the gayest trips that I have ever made; there were cricket matches between the passengers and the crew; there were deck quoits and deck-tennis competitions; there was a concert, there was a fancy-dress dance; it was very social and convivial. I cannot remember how, in that cosy atmosphere, Ruth and I got to know each other. I cannot even remember how it was that we came to take our first walk together round the upper deck; whether we were in the bar and felt the need for air, or whether after the concert or after bingo we had found ourselves there together. The only thing of which I am certain is that we did not make a date to meet there. It is incredible that I should have forgotten the details of that meeting. I recall so vividly every other detail of our next forty months. And I can recall so clearly every subsequent second of that evening, when we leant against the taffrail while a waning moon three-quarter full rose into the sky.

It was a warm, still equatorial night, with the ship rocking slowly in the trough of the long Pacific rollers, and silver coins of phosphorus washed against its sides. She talked to me about herself, about a young ship's officer—a Welshman—whom she nicknamed 'the lad', with whom she had fallen in love during a long trip from London to San Francisco in an R.S.M.P. cargo ship; how the captain had forbidden them to meet and they had sent each other notes by the cabin steward; how wild and reckless he had been; how he had begged her in San Francisco to run away with him. 'And I might have done,' she said, 'if I had had a passport of my own. My name was on Govie's passport;' of how he had threatened to have it out with Govie. 'He hired a car and started to drive down to Monterey. I had to race him. I had to go twenty miles before I caught him;' of how, finally, after they had said good-bye, she had driven down to the heights above San Francisco and watched his ship sail southwards through the Golden Gate.

'How long ago was this?' I asked.

'Fifteen months.'

'And have you seen him since?'

She shook her head. 'He's on the high seas nearly all the time. I've never been in San Francisco when he has.' It sounded a romantic story. I had no idea what seeds of jealousy were being sown that night.

We made no plans for the next meeting. We knew we should be often meeting during the day; I was certain that she would be on the upper deck when the bar was closed.

It was a night such as the last had been, with the moon smaller and rising later, seeming to lay its strip of ruffled silver across the ocean specially for us. Her voice had a new and deeper tone. I went down to my cabin in a daze. I had not believed that it was possible for anyone to be so adorable. It could not come to anything; I knew that. How could it? We lived six thousand miles apart, she was rich, she was married. If she had not broken up her marriage for 'the lad', why should she for me? I knew all that, but even so, my heart was flooded with a tenderness that I had not known before.

All next day I counted the hours until eleven o'clock. Without actually avoiding her, I kept out of her way. I did not want to make casual conversation, not after the last night. I drank very little at dinner. I was on the upper deck by half-past ten. I heard the music cease in the saloon, and the bar close. A quarter of an hour passed, half an hour, three-quarters. At midnight I went below.

Next day I made a point of sitting beside her on the upper deck, where she was watching the deck-tennis competition. We made polite conversation; she put on party manners, she seemed off-hand. Not only were my feelings hurt, but I was angry. How could she behave like this, after that? That evening there was the captain's dinner; after it there was a prize-giving for the various sports events. Ruth gave away the prizes. The passengers had beaten the officers at cricket. Chester Wilmot's father and myself received a testimonial at her hands. She smiled like a Lady Bountiful. She and Govie were good friends of the captain. The evening would end up inevitably in his cabin. There would be no chance of seeing her tonight. I went below at once.

I came on deck next morning in an angry mood. My vanity was hurt. I felt I had been played with. It was my turn now to be off-hand; if she went on the upper deck tonight, she would not find me there. Throughout the morning I savoured the prospect of revenge; but by the middle of the afternoon I realized that that would be denied me. We had run out of the tropics, the officers had changed into blue tunics, and the weather broke. Gales of rain slashed across the ship. So this is that, I thought.

It was still raining next morning; it was cold and the ship was not only rolling but pitching too. There were not many passengers at breakfast. I tried to walk round the deck, but I kept slipping. I started to feel queasy. Ten o'clock was early for alcohol, but a subsequent hangover was better than feeling seasick. I went into the bar. Ruth was sitting there, alone. She looked up, smiled and patted the seat beside her. She was wearing a pink scarf round her head that exactly matched her nail polish; I forgot my hurt feelings, and my resentment. 'What are your plans in America?' she asked.

'To go straight through to New York.'

'Oh, no, you are not,' she said. She looked at me, thoughtfully. 'Are you booked on a ship for England?'

'The *Aquitania*, tomorrow week.'

She calculated. We were docking on a Friday. 'That will give you two days in San Francisco.' She picked up the novel that I had put down on the table. *Masterson*, by Gilbert Frankau. She turned a page or two, then laid it down. 'Three days ago I sat in a cold bath,' she said, 'and read myself a lecture about you. I was Govie's wife, I told myself. I mustn't forget that. The effect of the lecture is wearing off.'

I had the sense of being taken over; it was an exciting feeling, that anyone should care enough to take me over. She smiled, with reassurance, as though there had been something settled.

'I'm glad that San Francisco will be your first city here,' she said. 'I was born in Upper New York State, but I think of San Francisco as my city. It has such glamour. Do you know George Sterling's lines:

At the ends of your streets are spars,
At the ends of your streets are stars.

It isn't what it was, of course, but what place is? Jack London's ranch before the war.'

She had known the London ranch, along with George Sterling and Ambrose Bierce. Rupert Brooke had stayed there in 1914. I told her that in Tautira a spruce little old Frenchman in a straw hat had come up to me with what I had thought to be an inquiry as to whether I knew a certain street in Paris—Rue Berbrouk. It had taken me a little time to realize that he was the Frenchman referred to in E. M.'s memoir, who had travelled up with Rupert Brooke to San Francisco, who had married a Tahitian and had adopted several children. 'It's only thirteen years ago,' I said. 'I don't suppose he's altered in that time. He's kept his hair and figure. He must have looked to me exactly as he did to Brooke.' I had had another curious feeling in Tahiti; that I was now an older man than Brooke.

Our talk moved easily from one subject to another, from books to personalities, from one country to another. I was utterly at peace, my destiny decided.

Presently Govie joined us. 'Alec's spending two days in San Francisco,' Ruth informed him. 'He'd better stay at the St. Francis, hadn't he?'

'He'll be done well there certainly, in every way.'

It was the first time that I had talked to him. He was a big, athletic man, clean-shaven, who had not put on weight. He was many-sided. He was an excellent raconteur, he did not monopolize but he dominated the conversation. He was witty; at any table at which he sat there was constant laughter.

Govie stayed with us for about an hour. I had not met many Americans in England; those that I had, had been connected with the book trade; agents, publishers and authors. This was the first time that I had been part of an American conversation, that I had sat with Americans while they talked of their own lives, their own friends and interests. Govie was an impressive personality, and extremely likeable. But he was at least twenty-five years older than Ruth. In the ignorance and arrogance of youth I imagined that what is known as 'that side of things' had been over for a long time between them.

The weather worsened as we approached California. Experienced travellers remarked ominously that it would be tough going in 'the potato patch' next morning. Only a couple of tables were occupied in the bar that evening. I sat across the table from Ruth. Round followed round in quick succession. It was for Americans the last chance of a legal drink. They were resolved to make the most of it. Most of the talk turned round the eighteenth amendment. 'Prohibition is better than no drink at all,' said Govie. I could take little part in the conversation. It was no evening for a walk along the decks. I excused myself, and went below.

I was reading in my bunk, just about to turn off the light, when there was a tap upon my door. A fellow passenger; a lady wanted to say good night to me, he said. I dressed and hurried up. There was a sound of altercation in the bar. Govie's voice was raised. There was a seat in the gangway and I waited. The door swung open. Govie came through it first, Ruth following. 'Leave me alone,' he shouted. 'I know when I've had enough and when I haven't, without your telling me.'

'Please, Govie, please.' She tried to block his way, but he pushed past her.

'Leave me alone,' he said.

She stood watching him go down the passage, then turning, saw me. 'I had to say good night to you,' she said. 'Tomorrow; it'll all start again tomorrow.'

She sat beside me. 'We've had such a little time. We've decided nothing. You are coming back to Tahiti in the summer, aren't you?'

It was the first time that she had mentioned it. 'Yes, I'll be coming back,' I said.

She sighed. 'I must have something to look forward to. You'll see how it is tomorrow.'

§

I soon saw how it was. Ruth and Govie had a suite at the St. Francis. A case of bootleg gin was delivered within an hour of their arrival. They had been away three months. The evening papers had reported their return. One telephone call after another, one visitor after another, with room service sending up fresh consignments of ginger ale. Every time the telephone went, Ruth's voice would be warm with welcome. 'But of course, how wonderful; yes, right away. I can't wait to see you.' Each time she would turn from the telephone with a helpless shrug. 'You see the way it is.' But she thoroughly enjoyed holding court.

For two and a half days that was how it went; always fresh visitors, always a fresh consignment of ginger ale. Once we went out to a Chinese restaurant to dinner; but it was much simpler during Prohibition to have food sent up when you were hungry. On the Saturday morning Ruth and I went shopping; she took me to Newmegen's book-store, and to Gump's to see the jade collection. The Gumps were close friends of hers.

Marcella, the daughter, had been with her in Spain and was to join them shortly in Monterey. From Gump's she drove me to the Stevenson statue. She read the inscription out loud. 'Delicacy and fortitude,' she repeated. 'That's been my motto. That's how I'd like to live my life.'

Those two brief excursions, but for the rest of the time there was the stream of visitors in the St. Francis suite and the rattle of ice against tall glasses. 'You see what it's like; you see what my life's like. Never a minute to myself. It will be just the same in Monterey. Are you surprised that I want to go to Tahiti, to an island where I may find peace?'

She said that to me the one brief time that we were alone together; on the Saturday afternoon when we had tea—a meal that ordinarily neither of us took—in the St. Francis coffee-shop. It was one of the loveliest hours of my life. I cannot remember what we talked about; except that there was no serious discussion of our plans. The time had not yet come for that. We would meet in Tahiti, to see 'what it was all about'. Till then we could let our talk drift from one subject to another, exchanging intimacies, building up the basis for whatever life might have to offer us. I have sometimes thought that we were closer to each other then, that we knew each other better then when we knew so little about each other, than ever we did later when we knew so much.

§

I was to learn quite a little of their life together, Ruth and Govie's, during those two days. He had been brought up in the East; connected by birth with the sea-board aristocracy, he had been at Yale, had married a Waterbury, had a house in West-chester. He had been reasonably well off. His short stories had sold in the high-paying magazines. Then his marriage had broken up. His wife went off with another man. It was then that he had come to California, to work in motion pictures, just after the war. It was there that he met Ruth. Chaplin brought them together. 'Govie's one of the finest men in the world,' he told her. 'But he's in a mess. He's drinking himself into a crack-up. He needs someone to pull him out of it.' She had gone round to see him. She had stayed there for five days. At the end of the five days they had decided to throw in their lots together.

That was how it had begun, and drink had always been an issue with them. She herself drank a good deal too much, and because she did, was liable to start a scene. But it was his drinking, not hers, that was the cause of friction. She was always watching to see that he did not take too much. Actually he never seemed to, and his friends felt that it was ridiculous of her to be so cautious. But she may have been right. He may have been one of those men who behave badly when they are drunk, who do stupid irresponsible things. She may have been able to recognize the warning signals when the rest of us could not. There were frequent scenes between them. Another took place that Saturday late at night.

Earlier in the day, over the tea-table, I had said, 'Wouldn't it be nice if we went to early service tomorrow morning?'

She hesitated. 'I would like to, but . . . I'm a Catholic. I don't think I told you.'

'We would go to church, though, all the same.'

'We could.'

But it would not be the same. I wanted to kneel beside her at an altar, invoking the clemency of 'whatever gods might be'. We left it at that, making no definite plans. Later, when that fierce quarrel broke—I do not know how it began, a discussion became an argument, an argument became a dispute—I realized as their voices rose that Ruth would be in no temper for an early service on the following morning.

§

Her train left in the early afternoon. Mine an hour later. I waved her farewell from the steps of the St. Francis. She was due in Tahiti on August 20. Six months away. A lot could happen in six months. My heart was heavy as I crossed in the ferry boat to Oakland. And is there, in the whole world, a sound more melancholy than the long slow wail of an American train as it sets out across a continent?

It was my first experience of an American train. I went down to the club car, picked up the current issue of *Harper's Bazaar*. Turning the pages, I read at the head of a column, among the advertisements, 'Alec Waugh's short story (continued from page 47).' I turned quickly to page 47 and saw there, proudly presented, with an elegant illustration, *Guard of Honour*; the story I had written in the Mediterranean, about the colonel's dog who betrayed a wife's infidelities. It was one of the more pleasant surprises that I have had. I had no idea the story had been accepted, and it was the first short story that I had sold in America. I saw it as a happy omen. I settled to my long wineless train journey with a lighter heart.

A visit to the U.S.A. had been no part of my programme when I had left England. One day I knew that I should go there. As a writer, I had thought of America as a country that would rain showers of gold on me, through its book clubs, its magazines, its lecture tours, through Hollywood. I saw myself as a seventeenth-century buccaneer returning to Plymouth laden with plunder from the Spanish Main. When I thought of America, I saw it as a market. I did not see it as a country; as a vast stretch of territory that had given a particular character to the men and women who had settled there. I was lucky to have sailed through the Golden Gate instead of, as do most Europeans, docking at Manhattan. It is hard for the visitor to New York not to be dazzled by the first sight of that tall-towered city, to mistake it for America. I was lucky, too, to see it through the eyes not of gain but of love. I was not thinking, as so many English writers do and as I had indeed pictured myself as doing, 'Now I can cash in.' It was at Ruth's side that I first saw America; I saw it as her background, I loved it because it was her background. She was to me unique and wonderful. Only America could have produced her; therefore America herself must be unique and wonderful. My instinctive reasoning was as simple as all that. I had fallen in love with America before I had put foot upon its soil. I have stayed in love with it.

During that long four-day journey to New York by train, my heart desolate with loss, I had time to realize how immense a continent I was traversing. So many miles between us. But as that sense of loss grew deeper hour by hour, there also grew, deepening beside it, a sense of wonder at and admiration for the faith and courage of the men and women who had made out of these vast tracts of land, and at the same time out of themselves, a single nation.

That sense has never left me. At each new visit I grow more conscious of a greatness there not only of territory but of heart.

Ten years later many English writers, alarmed by the Fascist menace, by what was happening in Germany and Italy, appalled by the apathy with which Britain and France stood as spectators of the war in Spain, remembering the economic crisis, seeing the seeds of decay in the social construction of their country, looked towards Russia for salvation. Russia, so it seemed to them, had built out of revolution a new form of society that did not need to prey upon its neighbours and impose its will upon them, since by the elimination of the profit motive it was independent of the hysteria of recurring booms and slumps. It was easy in those years for any Englishman whose telescope was focused upon Europe to become a fellow traveller if not a Communist.

In the spring of 1935 I made a trip to Russia. I saw only what I was meant to see, but I saw much. I saw a blueprint of the system. I saw how it was meant to work. And we have only to compare the conduct of the war under the Soviet regime with the blundering, selfish incompetence of the Tsarist generals to recognize that the new system is more efficient than the old. The three weeks I spent in Moscow explained much, but Russia, as a system, as a creed, said nothing to me who had seen another country that had been created by a revolution, a country that had been built out of that revolution, a nation whose citizens had not had to be bullied and coerced, but had developed the resources of their own soil through their own enterprise and had evolved their own form of government to protect the liberties they had won.

§

Most Englishmen love in addition to their own a foreign country, France or Italy or Spain. For me that country is America. It has not always been popular in England to be as profoundly pro-American as I am. I have had it said to me, impatiently, 'If you think the place so wonderful, why don't you become a citizen?'

254

It is a problem for all those who feel as the years pass a growing kinship with the ideals and people of the United States, and who spend for personal and professional reasons much of their time there. Each man has to solve it for himself. For most of us who still travel on blue passports the final deterrent is, I believe, allegiance to the Crown; a far stronger bond than any of us suspect until the time comes to question its validity. It is not easy for an Englishman who has been bred on Shakespeare, who knows he would be nothing without Shakespeare, standing in a bare bleak room with a polyglot group of Balts and Poles and Latins, to say with raised hand, 'I renounce Elizabeth of England.'

§

In the train between San Francisco and Chicago, as I wrote a long letter to Ruth, I reflected ruefully on the disadvantages of being 'the one who goes away'. He can mail back letters at each stage upon his journey, but he is moving as fast as, if not faster than the letters that will follow him. London was ten days away. At the earliest, I could not expect to hear from Ruth for at least two weeks. I had counted, however, without the existence of air mail in America and the American habit of using cablegrams for their correspondence. In my cabin on the *Aquitania*, I found a light yellow Western Union envelope and a heavy envelope that had been air mailed from Monterey three days before.

It was a long, closely written, four-page letter. It is tempting to quote from it. It might explain the nature of the spell it laid on me. But sentences read by different eyes, in different moods, strike different chords. Better to let it lie locked in its small tin box. I have no idea how many times I read it. Phrases in it still ring through my mind. My eyes can see it on the page. Six months might be a long time. A great deal could happen in six months, but with that letter to re-read, nothing that would not seem trivial.

§

I did not announce my return. I wanted to savour the drama of an unheralded arrival, but to make sure that I should not be an inconvenience I sent my mother a telegram, signed with the name of my brother's Oxford contemporary, Terence Greenidge. 'Dear dear Mrs. Waugh please can I spend the night at Underhill.' Terence often paid unceremonious visits. Once, when he was out of favour with my father, he contrived, by arriving after my father had gone to bed and not appearing in the morning until my father had left for Henrietta Street, to spend five days without my father being aware of his presence. My telegram would ensure that a bed would be prepared and an extra place set for dinner.

I taxi'd out to Underhill by way of Peters's office in the Strand. Peters's friends recognize that he conceals a warm and affectionate heart beneath a marmoreal exterior. We never expect effusion from him, but I had imagined that on this occasion he would have been disconcerted by the appearance in the Strand of one whom he had believed to be in mid-Pacific. But he was as Buddha-like as ever.

'I've been expecting you,' he said, and handed me a cablegram. It was signed 'Ruth'. 'San Francisco is desolate without you.'

'I had to open it,' he said. 'It might have been important.'

'It is important,' I informed him. He permitted himself a wintry smile. 'Otherwise, how are things?' I inquired.

'They're rather good.'

My English royalties on *Kept* had gone for ever, but my American ones had been unfrozen. There was *Guard of Honour* and a number of smaller items, from English editors. I clearly would not have to worry about money for several months. Indeed, from that point on, I should not have had to worry about money again, had I not been the kind of person who only settles his tailor's bill for one suit because he wants to place an order for two more.

On the way out to Underhill, I stopped at a post office. On an overseas cable form I wrote, 'Arrived tonight in a London that might as well be empty.'

V

The Settling of Accounts

It was on a Friday I returned—board-meeting day at Henrietta Street. After dinner my father said, 'My dear boy, I can't tell you how glad I am to have you back. At the board meeting today, I was wondering how I could go on. It will be all so different now.'

I knew what he meant. In January 1926 W. L. George had died; in May, Courtney and Truslove had resigned. He was alone now with Bale and Neale. 'They are good fellows, they are loyal. I know that, but we don't speak the same language. It will make all the difference now that you are here.'

It was not easy for me to tell him that I was not coming back, that I was resigning my directorship.

'But my dear boy, you can't. Leaving me all alone.'

I did my best to explain. It was not a question of any disagreements I might have had with the firm. I had fallen in love; I had made a rendezvous in August, in Tahiti. I told him about Ruth. He was broad-minded, he was not censorious. He took a practical common-sense point of view. 'It can't come to anything,' he said. 'How can it? She's married. She's an American. She won't want to be transplanted, nor will you. You tell me her husband's a fine fellow. He's rich, he's prominent. She won't want to break that up. In a year's time you'll have realized that, both of you.'

Give it time, he urged me. There was no need to do anything drastic. He was certain that the board would give me a further leave of absence. They appreciated what I had done for them. They would recognize that I was a special case. Give it a year.

The British spirit of compromise. Give a situation time to

heal itself. Nine times in ten it does. It was eminently sound advice. But there are times when one has to burn one's boats; and this was one of them. I never regretted my decision. But I did feel sad upon my father's count.

The next three years were to be the least happy in his life. Over sixty now, he was depressed by the approach of age, by the sense of waning powers. He had put on weight and the English winters fed his asthma. During the war, for reasons of economy, he had taken to returning to Underhill for lunch. He left the house every morning at 8.20, reaching Henrietta Street at nine. By leaving his office at 12.20 he could be back at Underhill by one o'clock. He left at 1.45. It was a bad arrangement. The long pull up from the station strained his heart. He had no time to relax. Lunch did not give him the pause and the refreshment that a hard-worked man needs. And then, when he was warm from his walk down the hill and his pores were open, he would be exposed on the open platforms of Golders Green to the bleak northern winds. But he was a man of habit, and he did not want, in his restricted circumstances, to abandon an economy.

Nor were they easy years at Henrietta Street. The financial situation did not improve, and it became increasingly clear that it could only be saved by a merger with another house which would cut down overhead expenses; but none of the directors were prepared to admit this, yet. They were anxious to retain their independence. In consequence, there was an atmosphere of anxiety at the board meetings and my father, who disliked discussions, felt that every question was a personal reproof. He dreaded the board meetings, he felt that he was on trial in the witness-box. He had, in fact, the loyalty of every member of the staff, particularly of Bale, but he had been a benign autocrat for twenty years. He was irked by the new climate. He once said to me, 'I would give anything to be able to say at the end of a meeting, "And now, gentlemen, there is one final thing. I must ask you to accept my resignation."' But he had never saved any money. He had to stay in harness, to the end.

My heart often bled for him during those years, and he looked reproachfully at me sometimes, when he talked over his troubles. He felt that he should not be facing them alone. But if I had been on the board, my own anxiety about the firm's future would have increased the tension for him. Standing above the battle, I could be of far more help to him. I could give my sympathy and encouragement far more whole-heartedly. My only regret was that my own books were still published by Chapman & Hall. I wished that I had no occasion to discuss business with my father.

§

My last act as a director of Chapman & Hall was not without its ironic quality. It underlines how strong a part chance plays in publishing. When I was in Tahiti I had met James Norman Hall. He had then collaborated with Charles Nordoff in a few collections of travel essays that had been published in America, but not in England. Nordoff was a man with some private means. But Hall, married and with two children, was in financial difficulties. He could not afford a car, and rode into Papeete on a bicycle. It occurred to me that I might help him. Why should he not make a selection of the essays that were by his own pen in the Nordoff and Hall volumes, and Chapman & Hall would issue them in a separate edition under his own name? I was authorized to enter into any agreement within reason on the firm's behalf, so I signed up Norman Hall for a book of essays to be called *On the Stream of Travel*, with an advance of £50 on account of royalties. £50 went a long way in Tahiti in 1927.

I did not expect the book to sell. I doubted if it would earn £20. I had qualms, but I felt that Chapman & Hall could afford to lose a few pounds on a good writer who had been a gallant airman. It was the one occasion during my employment with Chapman & Hall when I strained my conscience on a friend's behalf. Yet ultimately it proved to be my most profitable contribution to the firm's finances. Hall was a loyal man. He was grateful for that unexpected £50. Eventually Chapman & Hall got the *Mutiny on the Bounty* trilogy. I should not be surprised if the profits on those three books paid my salary for six and a half years.

PART 5

'His Honour Rooted in Dishonour Stood'

I

Return to Tahiti

I sailed for Tahiti in the *Louqsor*, in mid-June. It was in the eyes of the public an unimportant sailing. The ship was berthed at the far end of the docks. Her ungainly hulk looked very unimpressive among the elegant greyhound ocean liners with their gleaming superstructures. No local dignitaries had assembled to see her off. There was no crowd of visitors and friends; no clicking of Press cameras, no band. How different had been her sailing from Papeete, five months earlier, with a guard of honour to salute the departing Governor, and the sailors singing farewell to their five-day sweethearts.

At the head of the gangplank, on a small blackboard was inscribed in chalk, *Le* Louqsor *partira pour Pointe-à-Pitre à 11.30 hrs.* This was the big adventure of my life. Its lack of drama deepened its dramatic content.

On the third day out we passed the straits. On the left, high on a hill, sprawled the white city of Tangier. Three months earlier Ruth had written, 'A bad shock yesterday. Max Blake, the American consul in Tangier, cabled us to spend the summer with him there. Govie nearly said 'Yes.' Thank heavens I dissuaded him.' The house in which they would have spent that summer is now Barbara Hutton's.

Tangier looked very calm and beautiful in the morning sunlight, with its bastion walls, its minarets, its blue houses breaking every so often the monotony of white. The new town consisted then of a few scattered villas. The ideal place, it seemed, to be alone with one beloved. Later, in Tahiti, 'a house in Tangier' became a part of the dream world that Ruth and I built up for one another. One day we would be alone together in a house there, with Gibraltar across the water symbolizing the world from which we had exiled ourselves, to be together. I sometimes think life sends us warning signals, premonitions of the road that we shall take. Twenty-eight years later my road led to Tangier.

It was a long slow journey, six weeks and a day, with only three ports of call, Guadeloupe, Martinique and Panama. Each day was made the longer because we were travelling westwards, with the clock going back. We lunched at 11.30; at about 12.20, as we were finishing lunch, a bell would ring and the clock would be set back to midday; those twenty minutes to be lived through again had a symbolic malevolence. The afternoons seemed endless, particularly as the heat increased. I had not yet acquired the siesta habit. I do not believe anyone appreciates the value of a siesta till he has reached his middle forties. When I did take a siesta I would wake from it with my head heavy and my tongue coated. Instead, in a corner of the saloon, I pitted against my drowsiness my determination to write two thousand words a day. By the time I reached Tahiti I would, I vowed, have broken the back of a chronicle 'cradle-to-grave' novel. I arrived with 70,000 words completed. Very few of them found their way into print. But perhaps my time was not wasted. When my two elder children were three and four years old respectively, my son Andrew performed a series of somersaults by tucking his head under his knees and spinning forwards and over. His sister commanded me to do the same.

'I can't,' I said.

'Show me how you can't.'

I think writers learn a lot by showing themselves 'how they can't'.

After two and a half weeks we arrived late in the afternoon at Guadeloupe. A year later a hurricane swept the island, and apologists for Pointe-à-Pitre will always say, 'You should have been here in the early 'twenties,' but my few hours there in '27 left me with no urge to return. Martinique, however, was very different. We docked early in the morning. Out of a blue sky, the sun shone brightly on to a wide square flanked with mango trees; on to yellow houses, on to crowded cafés; the women were tall and handsome, with wide ankle-length skirts, with bright scarves round their necks and handkerchiefs knotted in their hair, with the points going upwards. There was an air of bustle and animation. In the centre of the savannah, set about with guardian palms, was a statue of the Empress Josephine, her head turned towards Trois Islets where she was born. Here, I thought, is another and less far Tahiti; an island in the tropics, under French rule, as far north of the line as Tahiti south of it.

I idled away the morning in a café, where I had my first experience of Martinique rum. All good rum is good, but I like best the dark Rhum St. James. A punch is made very simply. They put on your table a bottle of rum, water that has been cooled in an earthen pitcher, a slice of lime, and either sugar or a small bottle of sugar essence. One of sour, two of sweet, three of strong and four of weak, is the classic formula for a rum punch. Two such punches, sipped slowly in the shade, with the heat about you, constitute an admirable introduction to a lunch; they make you think the lunch better than it is. I am sure that the conventional French-style meal that I ate in the Hôtel de France was no better than the one I would have had on the *Louqsor*, but after those two punches I was convinced it was. And punches are not like dry Martinis. They subside gently, slowly, harmlessly . . . provided you drink only two.

The ship was due to sail at four o'clock, but the *Louqsor* never sailed punctually from Martinique, so the first officer assured me; and next day it sailed at half-steam. Martinique was the crew's favourite port of call; the sailors ordered *vin du pays* and because the local rum cost five francs a bottle they could not realize that it was three times as strong as claret. From two o'clock onwards, the gendarmes were busy, collecting stragglers. The last hour was hilarious; with one reveller after another being brought in in custody, laughing, singing, shouting, struggling; as often as not with a girl beside him, while the crowd applauded, clapping their hands, waving their arms, gesticulating to one another. They looked very gay, with their dark faces and their bright clothes. Yes, I thought, I must come back here one day.

§

There were not more than twenty first-class passengers on board. Our boredom mounted after we had passed Panama. We had nothing new to say to one another. Conversation would lapse at meals. The *Louqsor* was rated as an intermediate-class ship. The food became monotonous. It was impossible to arrange any entertainments other than bridge, chess and draughts. There was no band, no dancing. There was a piano but nobody could play it. The only diversion was the slaughter of a bullock once a week; I could not bring myself to watch it, but the performance was attended by the greater part of the ship's company; the butcher pretended to be a matador and strutted about with an imitation cape. He gave himself as many airs as a real bull-fighter.

Twenty-two days without a sight of land. But each day was bringing me nearer to the morning when I would stand on the quayside, watching the *Tahiti* berth.

§

It was an impossible situation. I had known it would be, but I had not known in what way it would be. I had to find that out. There is a point in a love affair when it is possible to back out; once that point has been passed there is no retreat. I had reached that point during the long, slow morning in the smoking-room of the *Manganui*. I had passed it that evening when Ruth and I had sat together on the settee outside the bar.

In a novel called *So Lovers Dream*, that I wrote four years later, I tried to show in what ways it was impossible. I took a parallel situation. I set the story in the south of France. The hero, a young novelist, was staying in Villefranche, at the Welcome Hotel. The American woman with whom he was in love was with her husband, in a rented villa on Cap Ferrat. The husband was a stock character, a Wall Street financier, noisy, aggressive, hospitable, always picking up the check; dominating every conversation. He would insist on the young Englishman being his guest. When the Englishman tried to return his hospitality, he would arrive at Villefranche with a group of

266

friends and say, 'I'm sorry about all this. You must forgive me, but these characters suddenly arrived. I have to cope with them. But I can't inflict them upon you. You must let me this once be your host instead.'

Govie was not in the least like that, but he was older than I was, a man of substance, a more effective personality, with a wider acquaintance, familiar with a more large way of life. I could not meet him upon equal terms. I was always at a disadvantage, humiliated in my own esteem. My only defence was to refuse his invitations wherever possible. The situation had resemblances. In my story I made my Englishman say to the heroine, 'I am not coming over to Cap Ferrat. I will stay here in Villefranche. When you have a minute to spare, drive across and see me.'

That was how it was in Tahiti. Ruth and Govie were living in a furnished bungalow some twenty miles out of Papeete. I was staying in a hotel half-way between. She would have many occasions to go into town. My hotel had a central building where guests took their meals. There were a number of cabins along the beach. In one of these was staying a Californian friend of Ruth, whose husband was on a pearl-buying expedition in the Paumotus. Ruth had every excuse for visiting her friend. Govie had as his house-guest a man friend, a painter. Ruth had no qualms about leaving him alone. Every so often she would stay the night. She did not like driving back alone at night, she said.

The husband in my novel was not in the least like Govie; nor was my heroine in the least like Ruth. My heroine was elusive, indefinite, accepting situations not creating them. She had none of Ruth's vitality, rebelliousness, sweetness or quick temper. I was desperately anxious that none of Ruth's friends reading the book should take it for a portrait. From the point of view of the book's interest, I suspect that I succeeded far too well.

In my novel I made my hero feel himself a prisoner tied to the waterfront in Villefranche, waiting for a grey-green Chevrolet to swing down into the market-place. That was how I felt in Tahiti, sitting before my cabin on the beach, trying to write, wondering whether she would come that day or not. There was no means of communication. The telephone was on a party-line; when her plans were changed at any moment, she had no means of warning me. I had no alternative but to sit and wait. I told her once that I was in the position of an Edwardian mistress, tucked away in a small house in Acacia Road to be visited when a busy man could find the time for her. I said it laughingly and she laughed. But it was true.

§

I do not know how convincing I made my account of my hero's predicament; perhaps not very. The novel suffered from the fatal defect of having a novelist as the hero. It seemed a playboy's predicament, but I could think of no other profession which would expose its practitioner to that particular predicament. Moreover, the predicament itself was unsympathetic; a furtive intrigue, two people cheating behind his back someone who had trusted them. 'They should never have got themselves into such a mess.' That would be the conventional criticism. There is only one reply. They got into such a mess because the attraction was overpowering.

Is it surprising that our few stolen moments should have been so unutterably rich? They had been purchased at so high a price. For three days, four days, once for as long as a week, I had no sight of her, only an occasional letter sent by the hand of her Californian friend, and then at the end of a long and lonely day, when I had swum and walked along the beach and tried to write, I would hear the hooting of a car horn, an aged black Ford would swing into the drive, and a voice would call, 'Is anyone at home? I've come for dinner.'

We quoted Dowson's poem that held the phrase 'the little grace of an hour'. For us that 'little grace' was mercifully set against the magic of Tahitian nights, with the Southern Cross low on the horizon, with the moon throwing its alternating shadows across the mountains and valleys of Moorea; with the torches of the fishermen gleaming red in the lagoon; with the scent of the *tiare* in the air, and the sound of waves washing on the reef.

'My honour rooted in dishonour stood' and yet it was during those weeks that I learnt what Robert Keable had meant when he talked of a recovery of faith. On the morning after our second night together, after she had driven back, I walked along the beach alone in a hush of spirit. I felt that I had been vouchsafed a vision, a revelation of the wonder and mystery of life, and of the ultimate purpose that lay behind all living. Life was not, after all, the pouring of so much water through a sieve. There was a meaning to existence; a goal unperceived but apprehended; not knowledge but intuition; a basic certainty of soul.

The memory of that hour has never left me. It has coloured everything that has happened to me since. I dedicated myself that morning. I must stay worthy of that vision. And even though I may have failed, I have never been unconscious of that troth. Through the crowded 'thirties, though Ruth and I had gone out of each other's lives, I was always aware of her, there on the Pacific coast. I had one standard, one criterion, and it was this, a resolve that she should never hear of something I had done, or read something I had written, with a sense of shame, with the thought—'How could I have?' I vowed that she should stay proud of me.

I learnt of her death on an April morning in 1940, when I was back in the army, stationed in Dorchester. I read it, in a letter from California, as I was hurrying down the High Street, to my company's parade ground. The news in the morning papers could not have been worse. 'She should have died hereafter,' that was my first thought; then came a tightening of that old resolve. I had to stand upon my own feet now, in the memory of that distant summer.

§

In *So Lovers Dream* the husband, because of the stock market crisis (the story was dated in 1930), was forced to return to New York earlier than he had planned. He left his wife behind him on the coast. She moved across the bay to Villefranche. There was a parallel situation in Tahiti. Govie and the painter went over to Moorea for nine days. If I had not had those nine days, my life would have been half lived.

Happiness has no history, and I cannot describe the passing of those days. We swam, we hunted for shells on the reef, we watched the antics of a small purple crab that had made its home among the coral. We picnicked down the coast. We read poetry to each other. We talked, talked endlessly, like Russian lovers in a pre-war novel, talked of 'our white house in Tangier', of the day when we would be at last together there. She was always certain that we would be married one day. She told me about Alex Moore and Lilian Russell. Does Lilian Russell, that sumptuous beauty of the Edwardian stage, linger in any memories today? Not many, I suppose. Alex Moore was her fourth husband. After her death, he went to Madrid as United States ambassador. Ruth became a great friend of his. There is an oblique sly reference to her in *The Sun Also Rises*. He had waited for twenty years for Lilian, Ruth told me. They would become engaged, then she would run off and marry someone else. She did that twice. But he knew that he would get her in the end. They had nine years together. Nine years that settled amply the score of twenty.

To wait for twenty years; was Ruth, I wondered, holding up Alex Moore as an example to me, promising me that one day she would be free? Twenty years; I could not look twenty months ahead. The Statue and the Bust indeed. I was insisting that we must cut and run, that there was no alternative. When I left England in June, I had no definite plans. Everything depended upon what happened here. In London that spring I had made friends with the Rajah and Ranee of Sarawak. They had invited me to stay with them. Even though Maugham had gleaned the Malayan harvest, it was a tempting invitation, but I no longer had the time to spare. I must get back to England, reorganize my finances, put myself in a position to start a new life with Ruth. I had booked myself back by the October sailing. I was conscious of the dangers of delay; a great deal could happen in three months. Strike while the iron's hot.

If we had been anywhere but in Tahiti, we should have run away then, during Govie's absence, presenting him with a *fait accompli*. But you cannot run away from an island like Tahiti, or at least you could not in 1927. There were only those two monthly sailings; there were the occasional Messageries liners, but a ship was not due for several weeks. One of Tahiti's charms was its separation from the outside world; but the medal had its obverse side. No one could get at you there, but at the same time you could not get away. There were schooners to outlying islands, to the Marquesas and the Paumotus islands, but eventually one would have to come back to Papeete and how could one have had money sent there? Cutting and running was not a practicable proposition in Tahiti.

And so the Russian lovers talked and talked, each following the thread of private thoughts; Ruth refusing to believe that what her heart wanted Fate would not allow her; somehow, eventually, we should find ourselves in that white house on the hill; 'somewhere,' she once wrote, 'somewhere beyond stars and time, the answer lies'. I was more practical. My finances were relatively solvent, but an elopement needed substantial backing. I should need three months to establish my reserves. In January I would present an ultimatum. 'I will meet you when you like, where you like; I will take you anywhere you want. You're mine, I'm yours. We must take up our fate together.' So we talked and so we brooded, and all the time the measure of those nine days was running out. Ninety-six hours, seventy-two, forty-eight; *O lente, lente currite noctis equi.*

To wait twenty years; to wait till 1947, it seemed an impossibly long time to a young man of twenty-nine. In the winter of 1938, in the West Indies, I saw a film about Diamond Jim Brady in which Lilian Russell was one of the characters. I thought of Alex Moore. Twenty years did not seem such a long time now. I should have already served half my sentence; time had telescoped the years. A great deal would lie ahead of me after 1947.

§

The impossible situation. It is what in their secret thoughts most young men wish for themselves. To love desperately, to be loved in return, under the shadow of hostile fates; to feel that existence will be intolerable without the loved one; to invoke high heaven as one's witness, and yet not to be taken at one's word. Daudet wrote *Sappho* for his sons to read when they were twenty years old. He wrote it as a warning; but most young men would be delighted to have a similar experience; to be loved by the woman who was *toute la lyre* and yet be free at the end to make a comfortable bourgeois marriage. Had a gypsy told me eighteen months earlier that I should spend nine such days with someone such as Ruth, and yet remain unbound by responsibility, I would have been overjoyed. But the reality was very different from the preconceived picture of it.

I did not know on that last morning whence I would draw the courage to go on living. For the last thirty-six hours I had been sustained, as it were by ether, on a level of acute awareness of aroused perceptions that I had believed to be beyond my reach. At any moment a thread must snap and I collapse like a marionette.

Eight months earlier, lying back in a deck-chair, reading myself a lecture on my future, I had been amused by the anti-climactic nature of a sailing from Tahiti. I was tortured now by the slow drawn agony of the good-bye. When the gangplank was raised, Ruth went back to the Club. I could see her at her table on the balcony; the table where I had been sitting a quarter of an hour earlier, from which the dilatory Chinese waiter had not cleared away my glass. She was with her Californian friend. I watched them toast each other. The *Makura* slowly manœuvred herself towards the buoys that marked the wreck of the *Zélie*. Ten minutes passed; quarter of an hour; twenty minutes. We were poised to swing towards the reef. I saw Ruth rise from her table on the balcony. She came down on to the quay; she waved, then stood there, watching the ship move slowly to the gap. Her features were distinct no longer. She turned away, trailing a white parasol, and it was no good trying to be literary about it.

II

Reunion in Monterey

I have been rarely jealous. Jealousy is in the main a mean emotion, partly antediluvian, the result of self-doubt, and of possessiveness; a greedy, ignoble instinct to acquire, to retain, to hoard. But I think that the man who has not felt jealousy once in his life is only half a man. If you really love a woman, if you have given yourself to her completely, you expect, you demand reciprocity. For the most part—how well one knows it —one gives a fraction of oneself, a third, two-thirds, a fifth; and if one has worldly common sense one recognizes that a woman in her turn makes reservations, that she withholds a third, a half, three-quarters. She can only give as much as one is able to take. And one should recognize that waiting in the wings, as yet unknown to her, is the man to whom she can give more; for that is what matters to a woman, the man to whom she can give the most. The wise man is grateful for what he has and prays that that entrance from the wings may be delayed as long as possible.

But it is very different when one gives all oneself—it cannot happen often in a lifetime; it has only once happened to me since, and then I was on my guard, knowing that the return was meagre, a surrender wrung reluctantly, a weakness because of fondness, a weakness before persistence. It is very different when you are convinced that for her as well as for you, this is 'the real thing at last'.

There is another point too. When you adore a woman utterly, with heart and senses, with every vein and artery and nerve cell, you regard her body as a shrine. You do not, in the twentieth century, demand a vestal virgin as your bride, but you pray that she has been spared certain things. When Ruth, speaking of her first experience, told me that Jack London had taken her by force, I was revolted. That this should have happened to her, casually, brutally and through 'the great white knight of San Francisco'. I have never been able to open a book by Jack London since.

Of other experiences, she spoke very little; I do not think that they were numerous. She was fastidious; she was also an extrovert. She liked having crowds about her, she was at her best in crowds; she enjoyed holding court. She brought out the best in her courtiers. She was not the kind of woman whose instinct, at a large party, is to withdraw into a corner and whisper to one person. She said to me once, 'I love arriving in a new place, among strangers, finding what it's all about; making friends of strangers. That's my *métier*.' She paused, reflectively. 'I've always been happy in crowds, I've given happiness, I've taken happiness. But when it's been one person, there's always been something wrong.' She paused again. 'Govie,' she added, 'is the one exception.'

There must have been lovers in her life, before she met Govie. But she never talked of them. She did, however, talk a good deal about 'the lad', the young sailor whom she had met on the R.M.S. cargo ship between London and San Francisco. She told me, for instance, how on her return from one of her trips she had found a large pile of letters from him. She had written to him during her trip, but she had had no opportunity of posting the letter. That afternoon the telephone had rung. Govie had answered it. He had raised his eyebrows as he listened, then he had handed over the receiver. 'Western Union, for you.'

It was a long cable interspersed with 'darlings'. There was no letter from her. Was she well? Had she forgotten him? Recriminations were mixed with protestations. Ruth cut the message short. 'I'll be right down,' she said. Within five minutes, she was well aware, the story of this cable would be all round Monterey, if she did not fix it with the girl at Western Union.

'It's from a lunatic I met abroad,' she said. 'A Welshman. You know what the Welsh are like. You don't? You should;

they are an education. I can't think why he imagines that I should care whether he's in love with me or not. But that's how European men are. They've got women where they want them. They've only to lift a little finger to have the slaves flocking round.'

She had the girl laughing, and on her side; if the story were to be repeated, and no doubt it would be, Ruth's reputation would not suffer. She recounted the story as a joke. 'But it wasn't a joke at the time,' she said. 'I really thought he had more sense.' She paused. 'When I get back I'll fix up a post office box under another name where you can write to me,' she added.

I listened to her stories of 'the lad' with detached curiosity. He was out of the picture now; he was a predecessor; just as for me certain women had been predecessors. It is ridiculous to be jealous of another's past. Ruth was what she was because of what had happened to her, just as I was myself. A new life, a new joint life starts when two people meet and recognize that they are going the same way.

§

Ruth and Govie left Tahiti by the sailing after mine. As usual, they spent two or three days in San Francisco before going down to Monterey. In her second letter, she wrote, 'Who do you think turned up here? The lad! But I'm not in the market for glamour any more. Those two partings from you are as much as I can take in one year.'

Poor chap, I thought, with confident superiority. I trusted her as completely as I did myself.

I lived for her letters and her cables. I counted the days until I could get back to her. I was working extremely hard. I had promised Ruth to write a book for her. The novels that I wrote between the wars are all of them dated now. This is more dated than the others because it turned on an inequality in the divorce laws which exists no longer, but I think there is a certain poetic quality about the first chapter and the last. The book was a love letter to Ruth. I had arranged for it to be published on August 15, her birthday, and Napoleon's. The dedication would read, 'To Ruth, as a birthday present.'

§

Within a week of her return to Monterey, Ruth had cabled the suggestion that I should come out to Monterey for the polo tournament. I had accepted, but with a mental reservation. How could I possibly stay in the same house as Ruth, as Govie's guest? It was a scheme typical of Ruth's belief that she could get five self-contradictory things at the same time. I had another plan. I should start off, ostensibly for Monterey. Ruth would meet me at San Francisco. We would sail at once for Honolulu. I would present this plan to her a week or so before I sailed, so that she would not have too long to think about it. I would present it as an ultimatum.

During the summer I had taken a furnished flat in London, but this time I did not want to distract myself with city life. I wanted to concentrate upon my writing. I went straight down to the White Horse at Shenley, only returning to Underhill for week-ends. I was in a daze. I felt incomplete. Three-quarters of myself was six thousand miles away. There was always a letter from Ruth, every week; sometimes there were two. Usually there was a cable. After Christmas there was a gap. Then there came a cable—'Have been ill have not written for a week am writing now Fond love.' That meant that I could not hear from her for at least eight days, even though there was an air-mail service between California and New York. I was anxious on her account. I felt lost without her letters. I wrote the letter that perhaps I should have written earlier, urging her to run away with me.

I impatiently awaited the first letter I should receive after her illness. It took ten days to come. It was a long affectionate letter, but it shook me as few letters that I have received have done. On the first page she said, 'The lad is on his way back to England. I suppose that you will have left before he arrives; but I hope that you two meet one day. Then you will realize how much he has of glamour. His name is ——.' So she had seen 'the lad' again; again that word 'glamour'. Something must have happened. There was no reference to her illness. Had she been ill at all? In the course of the letter she twice used the word 'silly', as a form of address. 'Silly, what are you

276

worrying about?' She had never used 'silly' in that sense before. Was she using it now because she had been in the company of someone who had used it, and was echoing his accents? She never, incidentally, used the word again.

It was a letter that any impartial person could read without suspecting that there was anything amiss. A natural, normal, friendly letter. But with the second sight of love I knew that something had happened. I was tempted, strongly, to cancel all my plans, to turn eastwards and sail for Sarawak. What was the point of going to see Ruth in this new glamour-sodden mood? I read and re-read the letter. To my intuitive senses, there was a warning in every line. Yet I could not believe that anything had really happened; surely she was as committed as I was; what right had I to doubt her being ill? Had she ever lied to me? Had she lied to anyone? Did not her truthfulness constitute one of her main problems? She could not hold herself in check. She had to speak out what was in her mind. Why should I doubt her? I had read, hadn't I, innumerable novels about lovers' misunderstandings, lovers' suspicions of each other. Seeing 'the lad' again had no doubt worried her. How could it not have done? But that did not mean that anything had happened. On the contrary, she might need me more than ever now. Govie was too old for her, a father rather than a husband; she needed a man of her own age. In ten years' time, when Govie was over sixty, she would be at the mercy of creatures like 'the lad'; she with her need for youth. I could not desert her now.

In my answering letter I made no reference to 'the lad'. I repeated my earlier arguments. If the situation had been impossible in Tahiti, how would it be in Monterey? She must meet me in San Francisco and take the first ship sailing westwards, Honolulu, Japan, Australia; it did not matter which. If she did not meet me in San Francisco, then I would go on alone.

I left London late in January in the *Berengaria*. I had had no answer to my letters. I had not expected one. She would be there or she would not be there.

It was a rough crossing for the first two days; then the sea abated. P. T. Eckersley, captain of the Lancashire XI, was on board. So was Tony de Bosdari. He figures in Tallulah Bankhead's autobiography. We sat at the same table, with Gordon Beccles, the journalist. Tony had been in the Winchester XI; he was an effective salesman; by the time we docked he had been invited to play for Lancashire. We were late in docking. A fog descended on the Hudson; we were held up for two days within New York's territorial waters. Prohibition was in operation, and the bar was closed. Eckersley was bound for the West Indies, with an M.C.C. cricket tour. He had crossed by a Cunarder to save time. The delay meant that he would be late for the first match. G. V. Weigall was the tour manager. 'There'll be Gerry Weigall buckling on his pads,' he said. In the fog the boat that he should have caught for Jamaica bumped against the *Berengaria*. Eckersley could have thrown his cricket bag over the side and jumped after it. I kept thinking, 'Two days late at least. Will Ruth know about this?'

My one night in New York I stayed for the first time in the Algonquin—my future home—and marvelled at the smallness of the baths. I cabled Ruth that I would arrive on St. Valentine's day and make for the St. Francis. During that long four days' journey—it was the third time I had made that journey in twelve months—I wondered what fate awaited me; I quoted Hamlet, 'But it sufficeth that the day will end, and then the end be known.'

I arrived at 9 a.m. I drove straight round to the St. Francis. No, there was no message. I inquired about Ruth. No, they told me at the reception-desk, she had not been in town for several days. I rang up Monterey. It was the first time I had heard her voice upon the telephone. It sounded very far away. Marcella Gump would call for me at noon, she said, and bring me down by the afternoon train. So that, then, was my answer.

It was 9.30. I was dirty after the long train journey. Was there a Turkish bath in the St. Francis? Yes, there was. I relaxed to the heavy heat. I had my answer. Ruth was not coming to Honolulu. She was resolved to try to have the thing both ways. And I had planned how to deal with that; to go on alone. The mantle of heat folded round me. I was very tired. Had I the right to take the law into my own hands? Did I not owe it to Ruth to hear what she had to say? She had far more at stake than I had. Govie looked after her mother and her step-father. She owed a debt to them. Ruth might have thought things out, have an alternative plan. Oughtn't I to hear it? I was still wavering when I came up into the main entrance hall. 'Has Miss Gump asked for Mr. Waugh?' I asked. Yes, I was told. She is over there. She was seated, negligently, smoking. I am not at all sure, even now, how I should have acted had she been less attractive. But she was, as she is, exceedingly. After an interval of thirty years, I met her recently in Tangier. She has changed very little, except that her hair is white; perhaps through her own devices. She was very dark-haired then, short, a little plump, white-skinned, with long-lashed lustrous eyes, and an amusing birdlike way of putting her head on to one side and looking up and smiling. I introduced myself.

'Are you going to give me a drink?' she asked.

'How do I do that here?'

'Call this number.'

Ten minutes later, standing on the steps of the St. Francis, I bought my first bottle of bootleg liquor. It was handed me in a brown-paper parcel by a smart young salesman. It called itself gin. It cost ten dollars.

'Where do we drink it?' I asked Marcella.

'I'll show you.'

She took me to a coffee-bar that had a curtain across an inner room. 'Order two set-ups,' she said.

The gin was strong. Marcella was lively and amusing. She brought me many messages and commissions. There were a couple of gramophone records that Ruth needed. There was also a list of books. Everything was fine at Monterey. Polo in the afternoon; parties every night. The best players in the world were there. Eric Pedley and the Partagos. I let myself be persuaded. I had come all this way. I had to find out what was in the air, what Ruth had in mind. I owed it to her, didn't I?

Usually, at points of crisis, even if I may not have known exactly what I wanted, I have known what I did not want. But I was always weak with Ruth.

We caught the afternoon train down the coast. It was dark by the time that we arrived. Ruth's house was on a hill, above the town. It was an old, one-storied rambling house; the main room was long and narrow, with a curved arched roof. It had been built in the colonial era. It was in this room that in the Mexican war the Spanish general had signed the treaty of surrender. It had a black-and-white-squared carpet. It was lined with books to the ceiling. It had an open fireplace. The walls were bright with blue Chinese porcelain and the colouring of old Spanish maps. The dining-room and Govie's study opened off it.

We sat, the four of us, over gin and ginger ales. Dinner was an interlude between highballs. Ruth played over the records I had bought in San Francisco. I began to feel sleepy. 'I'm sorry,' I said, 'but four days in the train with the clock going back throws one off one's balance.'

I was staying in a self-contained annexe across the courtyard. Ruth came to see that I had everything. It was the first time that we had been alone. We faced each other. There was a silence. Then, 'I've seen "the lad" again.' She blurted it out, excitedly, as though it were a hot piece of news.

'I know,' I said. I glared. 'Are you having an affair with him?' I asked.

'You haven't any right to ask me that.'

We began to quarrel. We went on quarrelling.

My three weeks at Monterey should have been three of the best weeks of my life. The sun shone ceaselessly, but not oppressively; the nights were cool. The coastline between Pebble Beach and Del Monte wore regally its beauty of pines and rocks and long Pacific breakers. There were the Carmel Mission bells and the seventeen-mile drive. Monterey was in a festive mood. There was polo to watch, and championship golf to gallery. A number of well-known figures had gathered in a holiday mood. There was something new every day. I was in the open air, felt aboundingly well. I was being intro-duced to American life under the best conditions; privileged in a way few Europeans are. For most Europeans, America is New York and Hollywood. I was seeing the American equival-ent of English country-house life. I was an integrated part of a way of life that was completely new for me. It was a wonderful experience for a novelist. Yet for me those were three of my worst weeks.

My irritation, my indignation against Ruth poisoned every moment. We conducted a long, serial argument. There were people in the house all the time; or else we were going to other people's houses; a constant party. We were hardly ever alone, and when we were, it was unexpectedly. There would be a momentary pause in the ebb and flow of guests. We would come into the long, low living-room by different doors, hesitate at the sight of one another, then move across to the black Chesterfield by the fireplace and resume our quarrel. We never got anywhere with that quarrel, any more than we had got anywhere in Tahiti with our talk of the white house in Tangier. We were still Russian lovers, only now we were at outs, and the gold was in her voice no longer. 'You ought to be sorry for me,' she once said. I thought, I still think, that was about as outrageous a complaint as a woman could make.

I was mad at her. Yet I was as much in love with her as ever. In some ways more in love because, seeing her in her own home, I could appreciate more fully how unique she was. Her vitality was boundless. She was now among very much more sophisticated and worldly-prominent men and women than she had been in the *Manganui* and in Tahiti. She was moving in a higher League. Yet she held her own as easily, with as little effort, as a guest and as a hostess; she had seen so much, travelled so much, been a part of so much. No matter what subject was under discussion, she could make her contribution. She was the most many-sided woman I have seen. She was inexhaustible. She was always ready to 'go on somewhere else', yet she was always the first at the breakfast-table. She was the centre of every party, yet she never dominated the scene. Other women liked her. She was interested in everyone, wanting to know what each new acquaintance was about.

Her restlessness had its defects. During Prohibition nearly everyone in America drank too much; and a great deal of what one drank was poor. In California it was very poor. Gin all the time, the taste of which was concealed with ginger ale; a combination that soon destroyed one's power to appreciate food. After two weeks my tongue felt as though it had been covered with absorbent fur. Nearly everyone drank too much. Ruth drank much too much. Arguments became quarrels and she made scenes. Every other day there would be a scene of some kind, invariably with Govie as its butt, no matter how it started. Perhaps these frequent rows kept their relationship alive, but it imposed a strain upon their friends. No one really minded, though. 'She doesn't mean it,' people said. Everyone knew that a party went better when she was there.

Watching her with angry eyes, I realized in how many ways Tahiti must have starved her zest for novelty. Once I said, as a retort in self-defence, 'Anyhow, we were happy *there*.'

She shrugged. 'Happy? We were good lovers, but I loathed the place.'

Loathed it because there was so little variety, because there were so few people there and those few, with a very few exceptions like Norman Hall, Nordoff and Robert Keable, were dull and nondescript. It was only, I recognized it now, because there were so few competing interests that she had concentrated so strongly upon me, that she had seemed to be giving herself to me so completely. Love could only be a side-show for her when she was leading the full life which her many-sided nature imperiously demanded.

'I see how it is,' she said. 'I love Govie. I'm in love with you. I'm fascinated by "the lad".' I am still astonished that she should have expected me to be reassured by this acute self-diagnosis.

She said that to me on the evening before I sailed. I had stayed three weeks in Monterey arguing, quarrelling all the time. I could have left earlier, perhaps I should have left earlier, but vanity restrained me. I do not set much store by appearances, but I did not want to look ridiculous to Ruth's friends and I should have looked ridiculous if, after travelling six thousand miles, I had taken my leave after a five-day stay. I decided that three weeks was the correct length for a visit, and accordingly in terms of that resolve booked myself on a coastal steamer running via the Central American ports to Panama. There I could take my bearings. Why not the West Indies on my journey home?

For three weeks we had growled and snarled at one another, but at the very last we were vouchsafed again 'the little grace of an hour'. The gold came back into her voice and because it had,

I could listen, as at Monterey during our disputes I could not have, to all she had to tell me.

'I've got to tell you everything,' she insisted. So it was all poured out, the whole story of 'the lad' from the point where she had met him on shipboard at Tilbury on a bleak December day, and he had been rude to her because she had asked him for cigarettes, as though he were a steward not an officer. A romance that had begun, in fact, in the classic manner with a quarrel; a long saga culminating a few weeks ago when he had stormed into her suite in the St. Francis demanding to know what she had been doing in Tahiti 'with Alec Waugh'.

'You broke my heart,' he said. 'I went away believing that you would be a real wife to Govie, in loyalty to me, to us, and then I hear that you are playing fast and loose, again.'

'He has such glamour,' she said, 'and such a wicked wit. And his voice . . . if he had been a singer.' On and on it went, a constantly interrupted story, through a long, long night. Do men, I wonder, inflict such confessions upon women? I would not know. I never have myself. There is no surer way to lose a lover. He had touched, I saw it now, a side of her I never had. That happens usually in love, but I had thought those Tahitian weeks, because I had been Ruth's without reserve, to be the one exception. They hadn't been, for her, and that was that.

To hold her in my arms again after the long separation, after the weeks of discord, was a peace, an ecstasy that life has not twice for giving. I adored her utterly; but never again, I vowed never, never again.

III

A Flat in Chelsea

I had booked myself on a passenger ship that did not cater for the tourist trade, that pottered down the Central American coast, delivering and taking on cargo at ports like Manzanille, Acapulco, La Libertad, La Union. She was scheduled to take four weeks to reach the Canal. She flew a Panamanian flag, so I should be able to get a legal drink on board. I had a small, neat cabin. It promised to be restful journey. It was not. The owners had decided to scale the paint during the trip. From dawn to dusk there was the sound of hammering. The assurance that I should have the cabin to myself was not in writing. Within a week, I had had to accommodate two extra passengers. We loitered for three days in Acapulco, under a grey, humid sky. I had hoped to work upon the cradle-to-grave novel I had started in the *Louqsor*. But the heat, combined with the noise of the hammering, tore my nerves to shreds. I had no escape from my thoughts and they were dark thoughts.

I read *Othello* with new eyes. 'O curse of marriage, that we can call these delicate creatures ours, and not their appetites.' I was helpless, impotent in face of the knowledge that there was a side of Ruth which I had never touched, which I could never touch; that lay outside my scope. I could understand a woman throwing vitriol in a rival's face. 'This face,' she thinks, 'has come between me and my happiness. But for that face, I would have retained my happiness. Well, this can deal with that.' What had 'the lad' that I hadn't got? A few physical attributes, the stretching of skin on bones, the pitch of vocal chords. Vitriol could settle that score.

Why had she had to tell me? I could have still been happy if

I had not known. What had Othello said? The general camp pioneers and all could have enjoyed Desdemona, so had he nothing known. And yet, what did I know? Ruth had talked of five days in San Francisco after Christmas, when Govie had sent her down to see about some garage fitment. 'The lad's' ship was in port. She had stayed on. 'I was dazed, I was wretched, I felt lost. I drank because I felt so lost.' This was when she said she had been ill. She had talked to me of those five days, but what had happened? Had they been lovers? I did not know. I tried to persaude myself that they had not. Had they or hadn't they? I assured myself that either way it did not matter. This was the twentieth century, not renaissance Venice. But jealousy has its own black logic. It did matter; it mattered desperately. So my doubts, speculations, intuitions pursued one another through the jungle of my jealousy. And all the time there was the incessant din of hammers upon iron, with the sweltering heat of a mosquito-ridden port as the sole alternative.

I took a train into the interior, motoring through Salvador and Guatemala, picking up the boat at La Libertad. The avenues of Guatemala city were strewn with the pale mauve petals of the jacaranda. In Salvador I learnt that I had to be vaccinated before I could pass the frontier. It was a Saturday afternoon. It was not easy to find a doctor. The heat increased as we moved farther south. The hammering continued. In the harbour at La Union, I found a French cargo boat, bound for the canal. I made friends with her first officer, in a bar. I described my plight. Would he let me come aboard? I didn't need a cabin; I could sleep in the saloon. He didn't see why I shouldn't.

In the ship was an official of a Norwegian line; he was young and lively. He was joining one of his company's ships in Panama. He was bound for London. We made friends during the four days' sail. Why did I not come with him? It was a cargo boat. It carried no passengers. I should have to sign on as a deckhand, at a nominal wage of a daily shilling. I could contribute a pound a day to the ship's expenses. It seemed to be an admirable idea.

It took us three and a half weeks to reach London. They were among the healthiest days of my existence. Apart from a glass of Schnapps at the beginning of each meal, there was no alcohol on board. I paced the deck, I read, I wrote a little, I breathed the fresh clean air, and once again, in a deck-chair, beneath a funnel, on my way back to England, I read myself a lecture.

Never again, I vowed, never, never again. I had had my lesson. I would reorganize my life. I should be thirty in July. It was high time that I made better sense. I would get myself a flat, at once.

§

I did, in Chelsea, in the Royal Hospital Road. It was a new building christened No. 35 Cheyne Place, because Cheyne sounded a good address and could command a higher rent.[1] It consisted of a large sitting-room, a bedroom, two small rooms, one of which I furnished as a spare bedroom, one as a dining-room. It had a kitchen. It was not a service flat and it had no central heating. It was a pleasant enough flat for anyone but a novelist, who works at home and who needs quiet. For me it was an injudicious choice. It flanked the Royal Hospital Road. There was a great deal of traffic, and a bus service—No. 39—that seemed in constant operation except when I was waiting for it at Leicester Square tube station. I should have recognized this, but I was impatient to get settled quick, quick, quick. I looked at less than half a dozen flats before I made up my mind. The rent was £250 a year. I suggested £225 for a seven-year lease. I did not stipulate an option to break after three years, so anxious was I to get myself pegged firmly down. How I was to curse my improvidence two years later!

I moved into the flat at the end of June. The sitting-room looked very bright and fresh, with pale primrose walls, with green bookshelves running to the ceiling on either side of the fireplace; with the sofa and armchairs and windows covered with green silk; with rugs on a polished floor and the Roger Fry screen before the door. I went to the Tooth Galleries to acquire a good modern painting to hang above the mantelpiece. I hesitated between a flower painting by Matthew Smith and a

---

[1] It exists no longer. It received a direct hit from a bomb in 1940.

Cedric Morris landscape. Each cost fifty pounds. I decided on the Cedric Morris.

The bedroom was sumptuous; a wide, low, walnut bedstead, draped with a pale pink canopy; a black pile carpet; blue blankets, yellow sheets; a yellow French dressing-table, and a long hanging mirror over it. The dining-room was narrow and austere; white walls, and black-framed woodcuts by Nevinson and Wadsworth.

I looked round my home with satisfaction. I installed a housekeeper. I engaged a secretary. I was established, I told myself, as an independent author.

And 1928 was a good year to be just that. There was no equivalent in England for the stock-market boom in America, just as there was no equivalent three years later for the American depression, but even so there was a high level of prosperity. There were a great many fiction magazines upon the market, and a short story had to be very poor not to find a purchaser, or a great deal better than anything I could produce. There was a general air of optimism. The collapse of the General Strike in 1926 had reassured the established order's faith in its own permanence. The radius of my own life had lengthened. I had no longer to spend two days a week in Henrietta Street. I had more time to know more people. Lord Hastings, now the Earl of Huntingdon, owned then a property in Moorea, the sister island to Tahiti. He had invited me across for a visit, during the three weeks when I was awaiting Ruth's arrival. He and his wife travelled back in the same ship as I, so that their child— now Lady Moorea Wyatt—might be born in England. A very real friendship started then and through Hastings and his family I mixed intermittently in a larger world. I learnt the difference between a house in the country and a country house.

My brother also enlarged my life. *Decline and Fall* was published in the autumn of 1928. Through him I met a number of men, four or five years younger than myself, who were beginning to make their mark in public life, men and women who were grouped under the label of 'Bright Young People'. Nineteen-twenty-eight was a good year for claret; it was a good year too for cricket. The sun shone, wickets were fast and games were finished. I was under no tramnels. I was free for the first time to enjoy London and England fully. I had returned resolved to enjoy it. I had written for the *Sunday Times* an article entitled 'East West, Home's Best'. But before October was through, my flat was in the house agent's hands, and early in December I was waving good-bye to England from the deck of the *Pélérin de Latouche*, bound for the Caribbean.

One can say, 'Never again, never, never again,' but you cannot, with one jerk of the wrist, dislodge a plant that has put down deep roots. I busied myself with the furnishing of my flat. I arranged lunch-parties. I accepted invitations. Now that I had a secretary, I made the experiment of dictation. I increased my output; by the early autumn, I promised myself, I would have pulled that cradle-to-grave novel into shape. But though my body was in London, my heart was in California.

I was in a fog, whose density I had not appreciated till I began to write this chapter. I am writing it in Nice, away from my diaries and records; and I am astonished to find that I can remember very little of what happened then. In respect of dates I can claim to have an exceptional memory. I can usually remember what I was doing in any given month in any year; I can often, if given time to think, get the week and day of the week. But 1928 is inextricably confused for me with 1929, the other summer of my bondage. I know, for instance, that in 1928, after a three years' interval, I went on Clifford Bax's Old Broughtonian cricket tour to Bath. I had wanted to refer to it a couple of pages back when I was writing about the cricket of that year, but I found I could not remember a single match or incident. I must have made a few runs, or my repeated failures would have been embedded in my memory; I cannot have made very many long scores; those too I would have remembered; my mediocrity smudged the camera. All that summer I was thinking of something else; my real self was somewhere else. 'As a dream fades at the opening day,' the fun, the parties, the work, the games of what is now known as the high summer of the 'roaring 'twenties' missed my consciousness. A flat in Chelsea was not the answer to my problem. I remembered Martinique.

IV

Hot Countries

I sailed from Plymouth on December 5. I was away five and a half months; I saw most of the smaller islands, the Windwards and the Leewards; I also visited Barbados, Trinidad, Jamaica, Haiti. The tourist boom in the Caribbean had not yet begun. Travelling first-class, without exercising undue economy, I spent under £500. I travelled with Eldred Curwen—one of the last eccentrics; the product of a way of life that exists no longer. He was three or four years younger than myself. He came of a north-country family, of which a gossip columnist once remarked that it was old enough to make the Plantagenets seem parvenus. The family seat was at Workington. His mother died when he was eleven. His brother was killed in the First War. His father never recovered from his loss, and became a recluse, living in a hunting-lodge on the lake. No one bothered about Eldred's education. He was superannuated from Shrewsbury and at the age of sixteen he was allowed to wander about Europe, on a monthly allowance of £30. He was never expected to earn a living. On his coming of age his allowance was raised to £900 a year. At the age of twenty-seven he broke the entail on Workington, in return for an annuity of £2,000. In 1930 he inherited from an aunt a charming Victorian villa in Antibes, which became his base.

He was uneducated in the sense that he had no systematized information; his spelling was atrocious and he did not know how sentences were constructed; he would, for example, spell 'didn't' 'dident' because he did not recognize it as a contraction of 'did' and 'not'. But he had sound common sense. He spoke fluently and ungrammatically French, German, Spanish and Italian; and it should be remembered that many medieval monarchs never learnt to read and write, regarding that as a menial, a clerk's occupation. He handled his finances shrewdly and never got into debt. His concern was not how to earn an income but how to spend one, in such a way that he derived the maximum amusement from his money. He led a selfish life— he rarely did anything he did not want—but he was always considerate of other people's feelings and wishes.

He was short, sturdy, well-built, red-haired; he looked a little like the Prince of Wales, for whom he cherished an under-graduate hero-worship. He had a gay, friendly face. He enjoyed considerable success with women. He was noisy and irresponsible, playing the clown in public. But he had an instinctive appreciation of what was the seemly thing to do in any crisis.

I had not known him very well when we started upon our trip, and he told me afterwards that he had had qualms before he started out, but we made an excellent team. He organized the staffwork of the expedition, booked passages, kept accounts, watched our social diary, ordered meals in Martinique where we rented a villa for a month. I am an early riser and was usually at work by half-past six. He was a late riser and a pensive dresser. He would not be hurried. He progressed through his shaving and hair-brushing at the pace of a slow-motion film. By the time that I had finished my daily stint of writing, he was ready for his morning swim. We never got in each other's way; and it was a great advantage to me to be with someone who made friends quickly. Many invitations came my way because I was with him. He is the only travelling companion that I have had. I have believed that I see more when I am alone, that I can be more easily fitted into parties when I am a solitary male. There is always room for the extra man. But on this trip I know that I not only had more fun, but saw more of the countries that I was visiting, through having Eldred with me.

We always meant to take another trip together, but we never did. Perhaps it is as well we did not. It might have been an anticlimax. But we remained the closest of friends until he died of cancer in September 1955. He was one of those who should not grow old. He would have loathed being seventy. He depended so much on physical self-expression, skiing, tennis, love-making. One should not have wished him a longer life, but for me the world is a different place without him.

§

People talk of getting over a love affair, but 'getting over' are the wrong words to use; one 'comes through' a love affair, and that is very different. A regiment goes into battle; it comes out mauled, part of its equipment lost, a third of its personnel written off as casualties. It refits at the base; its ranks are filled, its losses are made good; it returns to the line under the same name, flying the same standard, but it is not the same regiment. By the time I returned to England in early May, I had come half-way through. I was armoured now with impersonal interests. My trip to the West Indies had been completely different from my trip round the world, my second trip to Tahiti and my journey down the Central American coastline. Those trips had been taken to solve a personal problem, but I crossed the Atlantic this time to see what Martinique was like and I found in the Caribbean the fresh material I needed. Apart from Haiti, which had recently inspired John Vandercock's *Black Majesty* and Seabrook's *The Magic Isle*, the West Indies had scarcely been in the news since the emancipation of the slaves. For nearly a century they had smouldered away there in the sun, with the white planters spending their compensation money in Europe instead of on their estates, drawing away the profits that should have been ploughed back into their plantations. Houses were abandoned, warehouses collapsed, docks rotted. In 1888 J. A. Froude, paying his first visit to the area, was horrified by what he found. His account of what he saw—*The British in the West Indies*—is still essential reading for anyone who wants to understand the Caribbean.

The tide had begun to turn by now, and the educated West Indian was nearly ready to take over. I was excited by the dramatic history of the area, I was moved by its beauty, I was fascinated by the West Indians themselves. They were so friendly, so willing, so fierce and so intractable. They were capable of the wildest frenzies of delight and rage. They were unpredictable. Here were the stories I was looking for. I pictured myself returning a dozen times and always finding something new.

I had begun, too, during this trip to discover the technique of travel, the arrival with letters of introduction, the signing of the book at Government House; the sorting out of the various groups, so that I should have a pipeline on to the various social sections. I learnt, too, that a writer is very lucky in that, having no axe to grind, he is likely to be accepted on his appearance and behaviour. So many travellers have some end in view; they are out to sell something or to promote themselves, or they represent a mission. They are consequently graded by the importance of their mission, by the status of the group to whom they are reporting back. I.P. treatment for the I.P.s, V.I.P. treatment for the V.I.P.s. The writer needs no status symbol. He may get no treatment at all. But the officials who do receive him are able to relax. They do not have to be on their guard. No report is going back to Whitehall. Their only cause for alarm is the novelist's tendency to make copy out of his acquaintances. I had begun, in fact, to enjoy travel for its own sake; to see it as a way of living. This time I returned to England with no plans for permanence. I was on the wing.

Marcella Gump was in Paris then, recovering from a quick, range-finding marriage. I thought it would be amusing to cross the Channel for a quiet Whitsun. I was caught up into a group of bright young people and found myself in the Normandie in Deauville. There was some talk of marriage after that. I phrased in imagination the cable that I would send to Monterey. 'Marcella and I are going to be married Please wish us luck.' And Evelyn, in one of his Basil Seal moods, actually announced our engagement to the Press. A few months ago in Tangier, a friend of mine asked Marcella if it was true that we had once been engaged. She replied obliquely, 'He was too much on the rebound.' I expect that she was right. Dreams have often given me clues as to how I should feel should certain situations arise. More than once during that summer I dreamt that I was married and each time I thought with dismay, 'But this cuts me off from Ruth.' It was a great relief to realize when I awoke that a frail thread still held me to Monterey.

I was still in the fog, but the fog was thinning. 1929 is a far

clearer year than 1928. I came up this year as a candidate for
M.C.C. and played half of my probationary matches. The pace
of life was quickening. This was the 'bright young people' period
of which Evelyn wrote in *Vile Bodies*. I was only on the fringe of
that group, but I attended the Tropical party in the *Friendship*,
a river restaurant-boat that was moored against Charing Cross
pier. Vyvyan Holland was one of the hosts. We went attired as
dervishes and hula girls; it was strange looking up from the
cushioned bows of the boat to buses swaying across Westminster
Bridge and decorous citizens hurrying to catch their last tube
home to Wimbledon.

I had brought two manuscripts back with me from the
Caribbean, the cradle-to-grave novel and a travelogue about
the South Seas, the Far East and the West Indies. I entitled
the travelogue *The Coloured Countries*—a play on the word
'coloured' and a twist on Housman's 'Coloured Counties'. I was
hopeful about this book. I tried to think it was different from
other travel books. Most travel books described a single journey
or a single place. Mine was a discursive narrative, moving from
one place to another, one subject to another; the outcome of
three years' travelling.

My novels were published in America by Doubleday-Doran,
and *The Coloured Countries* was offered to them. At that time,
however, Doran's ex-son-in-law Stanley Rinehart and John
Farrar, one of Doran's chief editors and my particular friend in
the office, were starting a business on their own, and taking a few
Doubleday-Doran books along with them. Mine was one of
them. This was a great piece of luck for me. They had a small
list and had to concentrate upon it. They changed the title of
my book to *Hot Countries*, and illustrated it with woodcuts by
Lynd Ward, making it a very handsome volume.

During that summer I worked on a light contemporary novel
about the modern girl, but I no longer had a secretary; I could
not work in London. I went away to write, just as I had five
years earlier when I had gone down to Shenley every Monday
night; only now that I was no longer bound to Henrietta
Street, I went farther afield and for longer periods. I would
take away with me a definite stint of work and not return till I
had finished it. I went to Rambouillet, where my parents were

taking their summer holiday; at the end of the cricket I joined Berta Ruck and her family in Villefranche and thus began my long association with the Welcome Hotel that has been my refuge and home on more occasions than I can recall; in the winter I went to Margate to the Grand Hotel where G. B. Stern was working a refractory play into shape. I was discovering, in fact, the peace that lies for a writer in the small hotel bedroom. The novelist's problem, it cannot be insisted on too often, is to find the material for his stories, the peace of mind in which to write them, and to accommodate within that settlement those others whose lives are personally and emotionally bound up with his. There is no satisfactory solution to the problem. Every writer finds his own design for living. For very many of us the hotel bedroom is a most potent aid. It has the austerity of a monk's cell; it assists concentration; it absolves you from the cares of livelihood. Meals come without your giving thought to them. My kind of novelist is at his best, writes best, has most peace of spirit when he is in love, when he is divided from his love by miles or money, when he takes with him to a 'café restaurant in the sun' the manuscript whose proceeds will restore him to her. He writes all day, her 'constant image' in his heart, thinking at each day's close, 'I am fifteen hundred words nearer to her.'

I was not exactly in that position in September 1929 as I sat in my small room at the Welcome, looking out over the little harbour with the fishing-boats awash against their moorings, finishing my modern girl novel, but I was partially. I was a captive revolving around Ruth in a circle whose radius was, I hoped, diminishing. Until I had seen her again—this I knew very well—I could not get my life restarted. But I had to see her under the right conditions. In Monterey I had been taken off my guard. My forces must be organized next time.

I had relived, how many times, those three weeks in Monterey. I had speculated on the impression I had made upon Ruth's friends. Those speculations had not ministered to my self-conceit. I am not, as I have already said, an extrovert. I am not an effective public personality. But usually without unduly exerting myself I can hold my own. At Monterey, however, caged in the private hell of my own discomfiture, I must have seemed pitiably inadequate. I cannot have raised myself in Ruth's opinion. I was anxious, desperately anxious, to re-establish myself in her eyes and in her world's, my particular irritation lying in the fact that I had been enchanted by the warmth, gaiety, vitality, many-sided friendliness of that world. One does not mind if people whom one despises think poorly of one, but it is galling to fail to earn the respect of those whom one admires. During those months in small hotel rooms, crouched over my manuscript, my pipe-dreams built for me the day when I would redeem my lost estate. How it would come, when, where and in what guise, I could not guess; but it would come, it must come. I felt confident of that.

§

The fateful October day that shook the fabric of American life passed unnoticed by me and by those whom I frequented. There must have been a certain number of Englishmen who were badly hit by the Wall Street crash, but I did not know them. For most of us Christmas 1929 was little different from any other Christmas. At Underhill it was, in fact, a particularly happy one, for my father had been at last persuaded that his chest would not stand the strain of daily journeys to Henrietta Street, and he had resigned the managing directorship of the firm, retaining his chairmanship and taking on the position of adviser and consultant with a loss of salary so small that it could be adjusted through the extra time he had for his own writing.

It was a great relief for us all. It had been pathetic at times to see him on winter evenings. He would go out from the book-room into the cold draughty passage; he would return coughing and choking. He would stand beside the fireplace, fighting for breath, his face scarlet, his stocky frame shrunken within itself. His asthma would be with him all his life, but now it would not be aggravated by that long pull up the hill and by the cutting winds that swept that exposed station. Moreover, he would no longer be responsible so directly for the uncertain fortunes of the firm. His role was now that of the elder statesman; a central cause of anxiety was removed.

For me, it was a release as well as a relief. As long as my father had sat in the managerial chair, I had had out of loyalty to publish my books through Chapman & Hall. I was under no such compunction now, with Bale in control. I need never again have to talk business with my father; there need never again be a point at issue between us and there never was. It is surprising that my father and I should have found it impossible to work harmoniously together, for I do not think that publishers, editors and agents have on the whole found me an awkward man to work with. Evelyn, on the other hand, who is not invariably easy, and who in early days by no means saw eye to eye with his father, always conducted his business affairs with Chapman & Hall with the greatest cordiality and has never wavered in his allegiance.

My father appeared to be distressed when I told him that I should ask Peters to find me another publisher. But he only did, I think, because he was nervous lest his co-directors should hold him to blame for my defection. I am sure that at heart he was relieved that the harmony of my visits to Underhill would no longer be disturbed by 'shop talk'. I know my mother was. The 1930s were, I think, the happiest decade of my father's life.

It was a quiet Christmas; just Evelyn and myself at Underhill; the last such Christmas that there was to be for us. *Vile Bodies* was in the press. It was then that I first read, in proof, the novel with which Evelyn's name, journalistically, is primarily linked, as a 'sign of the times'. *Decline and Fall* had been a success, but *Vile Bodies* set the seal on his reputation. Had he any prescience then of the high destiny that awaited him a few weeks off? He had at the moment private sorrows, he may have been too absorbed by them to be over-concerned about his novel's fate. But surely he must have sensed the future? I have often thought about that Christmas since, wishing I could relive it, so that I could recognize the signals that I missed.

I was finishing at that time a serial for the *Daily Mirror*. I was booked to sail for East Africa in early February. I went down to Margate to polish off my serial. I read there the reviews of *The Coloured Countries*. I was disappointed. Its reception was friendly, but unenthusiastic. No one seemed to see anything especial in it. I presumed that I had mistakenly set high store by it because it was personal to myself.

My trip to East Africa was unambitious. A Messageries Maritimes liner from Marseilles to Mombasa. I planned to spend two weeks there, partly in Nairobi, and then return to Villefranche. I was going for the sake of the sea trip. I was tired and wanted to think out my future writing. I had usually found plots came to me at sea. It was a quiet eighteen days' journey. French colonial ships did not encourage sports committees to organize elaborate entertainments. I had brought several books on board, one of them *The Idiot*. I had already read it, in Mainz. It had seemed to me fantastic and unreal. I had since heard it praised so highly that I thought I should give it a second chance. I am glad I did. My first failure to appreciate it was possibly determined by the circumstances under which I read it. Lying on a bed in a prisoner-of-war camp, overhearing as I read desultory conversations about food and sport and women, I could feel no connexion between my fellow prisoners and the verbose, erratic, ecstatic Russians of Dostoevsky's novel, but *The Idiot*, read alone on deck, under the stars, in the warmth and silence of a tropic night, had an intense white-hot reality that I had never before encountered on the printed page. *The Idiot* was for me the big event of that pleasantly idle trip, during which I walked many miles along the deck, ate much good food, drank much sound wine, and waited hopefully for plots to come. None did. Perhaps I was overtired, I reassured myself. I might be in a different mood on the journey back.

I was; in a more different mood than in my wildest fancies I had dared to hope. At Mombasa I was brought a cable from Peters's office telling me that *Hot Countries* was the Literary Guild selection for May.

I have had in all four cables and one telephone call, announcing good news from America which have involved a reorientation of my life. This was the second; in many ways it was the most exciting, because of the corollaries attached. I did not know what was involved moneywise, but I knew that by my modest standards I would be on the receiving end of a substantial sum of money. One thing I knew and knew for certain; it would open the gateway to America and that meant seeing Ruth again.

There was no air-mail service to East Africa in 1930. London was three weeks distant. I could not expect to hear from Peters until I reached Marseilles and that was five weeks away. It was tantalizing, but intriguing too, to continue with my plans as though nothing extraordinary had happened. I had planned to return to Europe as a third-class passenger, partly as an economy partly in search of copy, to see what it was like. I did not change my plans. I would savour the dramatic irony between the actual and apparent state of my finances. I saved £40 by this device. But I obtained no copy. Poor people are not necessarily more interesting than those who are in comfortable circumstances—not in themselves, that is to say. The conditions of their lives are interesting, but one does not see those on shipboard.

I arrived in Marseilles in early April. A large mail awaited me. A long enthusiastic letter from John Farrar urged me to come over for publication day; a short congratulatory, less enthusiastic letter from Peters set out the financial details of the deal. The Literary Guild, he said, would pay ten thousand dollars for the right to issue their own edition. Of that ten thousand, Farrar & Rinehart would take half. The book, however, might have a substantial sale in view of the publicity that it would receive through the Literary Guild. 'Farrar and Rinehart,' he went on, 'are very anxious that you should go across for publication day. I cannot recommend this. They will entertain you royally; but New York is very expensive. They will defray none of your basic costs. You will, if I know you, spend £500. You have to sell a great many copies to wipe that out. Stay at home and give a celebration party at the Savile.'

He was dead right. I could expect to be £300 or £400 out of pocket, but that did not disconcert me. Magic doors were opening. I cabled John Farrar that I would come, and went down the coast to Villefranche.

I spent three weeks there. It was a happy time. Nothing is better than to be held within a contented present knowing that high drama is on its way to meet one. Every second or third day I would find in my pigeon-hole at the Welcome the green envelope of a telegram. I never now pass the old world post office in Villefranche with its rambling garden without grateful memories of the excitement with which I wrote out

there my answers to those cables. Towards the end of my stay
Evelyn came down to join me. The sun shone and we took long
walks into the hills.

§

Most solid professional English writers once in their lives hit
the jackpot in the U.S.A. It is a heady experience. I had planned
to cross the Atlantic in one of the eight-day French boats, but
Farrar & Rinehart did not consider that such a modest arrival
would be good publicity, so they transferred me—at my cost—
to the *Bremen*, where I was awarded a bridal suite at minimum
rates. A horde of reporters met me at quarantine. From the
docks I was transferred to the Chatham Hotel. Benjamin
Sonnenberg then ran its publicity and under his auspices a
sumptuous suite had been prepared for me, where I could stay
for four days without charge. A diary of my engagements was
handed me. I was to be interviewed here, speak on the radio
there; on the eve of publication a large tea was to be given in
my honour. In Prohibition New York 'tea' meant cocktails.
There were dinners here and lunches there; for three weeks
clearly I was not to be allowed to think that the many-peopled
island of Manhattan had any concern except my presence on it.
Publicity for the Literary Guild was run then by the elegant
and witty Selma Robinson, who turned into picnics what might
have been exhausting chores. Katherine Brush, whose *Young
Man of Manhattan* was a bestseller of the hour, was one of
Farrar & Rinehart's authors. We were fêted together and a
friendship began that deepened year by year until her death.
Leslie Howard was starring in *Berkeley Square* and Carl
Brandt arranged a supper-party where I could meet him. I also
met Carol Hill, who within a year was to marry Carl. There
were dinner-parties at the Harvard Club and Jack and Charlie's.
I met Elinor Sherwin, who was to become one of my closest
friends, and who was later to marry Wolcott Gibbs. Through
her I met Rollin Kirby's daughter, Janet, another of my dearest
friends. I signed contracts with Farrar & Rinehart for two new
books. Selma Robinson introduced me to Colston Leigh and I
arranged to lecture after Christmas. I had brought over several
letters of introduction; one of them was to Mrs. Franklin

x

Roosevelt. Newman Flower, the head of Cassell's was at the 'tea' given in my honour. He said, 'Peters tells me you're looking for a publisher. I hope you'll come to us.'

'I've been hoping that you'd ask me that,' I said.

Newman Flower's son Desmond was over too. Desmond is a few years younger than I; he was just down from Cambridge and was joining Cassell's in the autumn. We played a certain amount of squash together and laid the basis for a friendship that has greatly enhanced the harmony of my relations with his firm. I recognized right away that I had found through Desmond and his father the solution to my publishing problems. I would have behind me an established firm, amply capitalized, that had handled so many profitable literary properties that I would never need to worry again as to whether the best was being done for me. I could concentrate upon the writing of my books and leave the selling side to Cassell's. For over thirty years I have been deeply grateful to Peters for having introduced me to *La Belle Sauvage*.

Those three weeks in New York were as good as any I have known. I was spoilt, and loved being spoilt. But the spice that added the real savour to the dish was the knowledge that at the end of it Monterey was waiting. On my arrival in New York, I had found a cable from Ruth, welcoming me back to America, asking when I was coming out. They were all making the June sailing to Tahiti. Why did I not join them?

§

I flew out to California at the end of May. I use the word 'flew' because that was the designation given to the operation by the tourist agency. Long-distance air travel had barely started then. One of the innovations on the *Bremen* was a catapulted aircraft on the last morning of the crossing that got mail into New York ten hours ahead of schedule. Transcontinental passengers flew by day and spent the night in sleeping-cars. At least they were supposed to. I struck presumably an unlucky flight. I entrained at the Pennsylvania station at 4.30 p.m. At 6 a.m. next morning, at Columbus, I was to take a plane; but at 5.30, as I was getting up, the conductor told me I could go back to bed. Flying conditions were unsuitable.

'What happens now?' I asked.

'You'll be told in good time.'

I was not. Every few hours fresh orders were issued and then contradicted. Slowly I crossed the Middle West, changing trains twice, to arrive eventually at dusk in St. Louis, where I was instructed to detrain and was conducted to a hotel for the night as the guest of the company. Next morning I should receive fresh instructions. I did. At half-past five I learnt that a train would be starting for Kansas at 6.15. I cannot remember how many hours I spent in the air. Very few, as far as I can recall, except during the last day when I took off at dawn from Albuquerque; and those few were painful. The machines were small; they flew low and rocked. I had with me a small motion picture camera; at one point I handed it to a man across the aisle and asked him to take anything that seemed amusing. I was going to try to sleep, I told him. I emerged from my coma to find him photographing me. 'Your misery is the funniest thing I've seen so far,' he said.

I had left New York on a Sunday; I reached Los Angeles on a Thursday evening, with my nerves jangled and my digestive processes no longer functioning. The movement of an elevator made me queasy. I vowed I would come back by train.

I spent the day in Hollywood, catching a night train to Monterey.

§

I had made no plans. I had not written my script ahead of time. I never did with Ruth. I let the hour and the situation determine their own tactics. Govie, I had been told, was away in a country club working on a novelette. His two daughters, Bay and Patsy, were staying in the house. I, therefore, should be in a hotel in the village, a mile away. I had already met Bay in New York, and we had come to like each other. I was glad to have an ally on the scene.

It was twenty-seven months since Ruth and I had met. We had been in constant correspondence, in confidential letters; but twenty-seven months is a long time. I had gone twenty-seven months in one direction, she had gone twenty-seven months in another. Fifty-four months divided us. We would be different people; I did not know in what way we would be different.

She was waiting for me at the station. It was early; her red hair glinted in the sun. She looked fresh and vivid. It did not seem twenty-seven hours since she had waved me good-bye from the steps of the St. Francis. We began to talk as easily, as friendlily as we had done before that disastrous winter visit. We dropped my luggage at the hotel; then drove up to the house. Patsy and Bay were having breakfast. I joined them in a cup of coffee. They had plans to play tennis in the morning. In the evening there was a cocktail party with a family I had met on that earlier visit. They hoped I was not going to find it dull in my host's absence. Govie would be away a week. They would try to ensure that I had enough to do.

I had. There was something on every day. Tennis, a picnic, a drive out to a rodeo. In one way it was exactly as it had been two years ago, except that we were now in May instead of in March. The same people were doing the same things. But I was different. It was not only, it was not mainly, the change in my personal position; although that had to be taken into account. In California in 1928 I was a visiting English writer of whose books scarcely anyone had heard; I was now the author of *Hot Countries*. The book was very far from being a bestseller. It lacked feminine interest, and feminine reader-identification; but the publicity attached to a Literary Guild selection was even then considerable. Eighty thousand hard-covered copies were in circulation. I had become someone whom people were interested to meet. One of Balzac's favourite themes is the return from Paris of the young adventurer who has been previously looked down upon in the small country town where he was born. There was a comparison between Rubempré and myself. But that was only a minor difference. The main difference lay inside myself.

I have in recent years described myself to interviewers as 'a scattered person'. By that I have meant someone who lives simultaneously in half a dozen separate places, conducting half a dozen separate lives. That is what I am today. I had begun to become that by 1930. In addition to my life in London, I had one in the West Indies, another in Villefranche, and now yet another in New York. In 1928 I had been complete, subject to Ruth's whim, dependent on her moods, as the 'I' of J. C. Squire's poem beginning—

You are my sun, beneath your circling kindness
My meadows all take in the light and grow.

Now I was armoured by my impersonal interests, by the pattern of divided life that my separation from Ruth had forced on me. Now, while I drove beside her round the seventeen-mile drive and she tried to persuade me to come down with her to Tahiti, I was thinking intermittently of the week-end visit I should pay to Hyde Park on my return to New York, of the date I hoped to make with Elinor Sherwin, of my winter lecture-tour, of the M.C.C. cricket tour in July when I should play my final proba-tionary matches, of the history of West Indian piracy that I had contracted to write for Farrar & Rinehart; of my late August visit to Villefranche. Animals acquire a protective colouring. I had my armour now. Yet the fact that I was not defenceless did not mean that my feelings had basically changed. Ruth had still the same glamour, the same appeal. She was unique. I was enchanted by her still. Indeed those three weeks in Monterey were an enchanted period, a time of suspended animation, with the hour of decision round the corner.

We were never alone, never really alone, Ruth and I. But during our drives to this picnic and to that, in the intervals of tennis, during an occasional quarter of an hour before lunch or dinner, we were finding our way back to our old harmony with one another. We could exchange confidences. Jealousy, to my delighted surprise, had died. I think it often does when one sees again after a long time the object of one's jealousy. Yes, she said, she had seen 'the lad' again, two years earlier, before she had sailed for Tahiti. It had been confused and unsatisfactory. She had not seen him since. She had been ill a few months back, and he had rung up from New York. His voice had done nothing to her. She was cured of that, she said. She could wonder now whether she had been wise or foolish not to have joined me in San Francisco and taken that ship to Honolulu. We were still like Russian lovers, but we talked of the past now, not the future. 'But you are coming down with us to Tahiti, aren't you?' she insisted.

I shook my head. I had too many other things on hand. I produced innumerable reasons, but she knew, as I knew, that none of them were valid. I could go if I wanted.

Govie returned from his retreat at the country club; he confirmed what Ruth had already suspected, that he would not be able to make the June sailing. Alterations were being made to the house and he had to be on hand to supervise them. He would come down by a later boat.

'Then Alec's got to come with us, hasn't he?' Ruth announced triumphantly. 'He can't let three females go down there on their own.'

'He'd be very unchivalrous if he did,' said Govie.

Govie was very adroit. He had always, Ruth told me, unarmed her admirers by inviting them up to the house, entertaining them, doing for them the small, thoughtful things that are more valued than expensive gifts.

'Half the trouble with "the lad",' Ruth said, 'was that Govie loathed him, wouldn't have him to the house, made an enemy of him, so that I had to see him surreptitiously.'

I could now hear Ruth say such things with unjangled nerves. It was not that I loved her less, but that I loved her differently. There was no other woman in my life, but there were other things. There were other interests. There was life itself.

Ruth was convinced that I would go down with them. Was not this what we had always longed for, a month on our own, without supervision? I was equally convinced that I would not go down. What would I do down there? Find myself a bungalow on the beach, and wait, trying to concentrate upon a manuscript, till Ruth had time to spare for me. Three years ago I had stumbled into that situation. But now I was on my guard. That was no life for me. And the hour had passed for an elopement.

So the days went by and the sun shone; there were the preparations for departure; the bon-voyage parties, before whose close usually Ruth and Govie were embroiled in some kind of quarrel. Two years earlier I had wondered whether there was any point in two people who quarrelled so much staying together. But now I felt that those quarrels kept their relationship alive. And in the intervals of all this bustle, Ruth and I continued our *colloque sentimental.*

'You are coming down, aren't you?' she insisted.

'No, no, I can't.'

And we would start talking of the past again. We were very close during that twilit period.

Finally Ruth realized that I meant what I said, that I did not intend to come down to Tahiti. We were moving, the whole party, down to San Francisco two days before the *Tahiti* sailed. The problem of luggage was being discussed. I travelled lightly, for those days, but I had a cabin trunk. Ruth remembered this. 'Alec'll have to go to the station independently. We can't get that crate on our car,' she said.

'That'll be all right. I've checked it back to New York,' I told her.

'You have!' There was an expression of utter dismay upon her face. She had been so sure of me. From that point the entire atmosphere of our relations changed. The *colloque sentimental* was at an end. On Wednesday the *Tahiti* sailed. It was Friday now. Ruth desperately endeavoured to persuade me during those last three days at Monterey to change my plans. Why did I need my heavy luggage in Tahiti? A suitcase was sufficient. She exerted all her wiles. I had been so utterly her slave. She could not believe I had eluded her. I think she was more in love with me then than at any point in our relations. Maybe, even in Tahiti, I had bored her with my subservience, my dependence. I have read in the glossy women's magazines that what every woman needs is to be loved whole-heartedly. I am not sure that that is true. I think that women need to love, to give themselves in love, and that they choose the man to whom they can give the most. They are irritated by an abject excess of masculine devotion.

On the Monday we took the morning train to San Francisco. Ruth and Govie had a suite at the St. Francis; there was the case of bootleg gin under the sideboard, the ice and the ginger ale; room-service sent up hamburgers, then we scattered for the afternoon on our separate chores. I forget what I bought for Ruth as a bon-voyage present, but I cherish still the box she gave me. She wrote upon the card, 'Will this very old Chinese box, do you think, be a good repository for modern love letters?'

By six o'clock we were all back in the suite and the crowd of visitors had started. No chance of privacy, or quiet talk.

'Well, and has Alec decided to abandon us or not?' asked Ruth.

'He's booked himself on a train on Wednesday afternoon,' I said.

'I knew he would, that silly cricket. Every Englishman you meet is a caricature of Englishmen.'

She made a joke of it, as I did too; but in that moment we both recognized that we had reached a turning-point. Our fourth parting. Was this to be our last? Was it all over then? After forty months. I could not believe it was.

The last day had a tragic quality that made it even more intense than the other partings. We had never been closer to one another. We had a prescience that we would remember these last hours all our lives. There was so much to say, so little time in which to say it. She planned, she said, to stay on in Tahiti until Christmas. The reconstruction of the house would last until the winter. I went to the Messageries office and looked up their sailings from Marseilles. There was one in late September. I could reach Tahiti by mid-November, spend a month there, then catch the December sailing, in time for my American lecture tour. I really believed I would.

On the last evening we sat up very late, after Govie and the girls had gone to bed. Once again we were Russian lovers, watching our pipe-dreams form.

§

The ship sailed in the early afternoon; during the morning we pottered round the shops of Union Square, making last-minute purchases. We talked easily, effortlessly, avoiding last-minute things. We were so close that it was impossible not to believe that we would be picking up the threads in a week, a month, a year. As I waved good-bye to her from the quay, no inner voice warned me that I was seeing her for the last time. Two hours later, once again, there was the long slow wail of an

American train setting out across a continent. In a way it was the worst parting of the four, and yet . . . and yet . . .

One does not recognize the pattern of one's life while one is living it; which is why novels written in the first person are never satisfactory unless they are told in retrospect or with the 'I' acting as an observer, a recorder. I did not, as the train rocked eastwards, realize how fully I was armoured by the design for living that the last thirty months had imposed on me, how easily as a scattered person I could slip back into one or other of my different lives. I did not realize that I had reached a watershed. I should have been astonished could I have been told that when, in thirty years' time, I came to relive my youth on paper, I should close the story here.

I was not this time taking the direct, Union Pacific route across America. I wanted to see New Orleans and planned to spend a night there. I was to have five days in the train. A long train journey can be very restful. It was the first time I had had to think, to take stock of myself, since I had landed three months earlier in Marseilles; I could now take an estimate of my good luck. I had every cause for optimism. I was a part of the American scene. A new market had been opened. My income would at least be doubled. But it was not only in terms of money that my future was about to be enlarged. America itself would add a dimension to my existence. In three weeks, staying in a hotel, I had only been able to glimpse the excitement and variety of New York life. In the winter, for a four months' visit, I would take a flat; I would live as New Yorkers did; as I myself did in London. Then there would be London in the summer, the parties and the cricket. In the spring and autumn Ville-franche, the little café restaurant in the sun where I would do my writing; and then once a year there would be a long trip to somewhere off the map, that would provide the material for a successor, for a series of successors to *Hot Countries*; and every so often, I assured myself, my path and Ruth's would cross. I saw my life taking shape. It was four years since I had begun to travel; four experimental years when I had not known what I wanted, what I was looking for. Now I knew and saw.

How would it have all turned out, I wondered, if that cable had not reached me in Tahiti, if I had never met Ruth, if the restlessness contingent upon knowing Ruth had not sent me back to Tahiti, had not pulled up my London roots, had not set my course westward to the Caribbean? If that cable had not arrived in time, if it had contained different news, would I have really settled down in London, or would Providence have intervened with some equivalent deterrent? I shrugged. It was no use wondering about that; the cable had arrived on time, and I had met Ruth, and the meeting of her had set me on this road, a road that climbed and wound, that was always turning a corner on to some fresh countryside. I would not have it any different.

So I brooded, as the train rocked southwards to the Crescent City; the ache in my heart diminished, and the chunking of the wheels beneath me cradled contented thoughts.

I had left San Francisco on a Wednesday evening; early on the Tuesday morning I saw through my carriage window the tall towers of Manhattan glinting in the early sunlight. This was to be my city soon.

Index

309